Barbecuing Around Texas

Richard K. Troxell

Republic of Texas Press

Library of Congress Cataloging-in-Publication Data

Troxell, Richard K.
  Barbecuing around Texas / Richard K. Troxell.
      p. cm.
  ISBN 1-55622-697-7 (pb)
  1. Barbecue cookery—Texas—Guidebooks. 2. Restaurants—Texas
  —Guidebooks. I. Title.
  TX840.B3 T76 1999
  641.5'784'09764—dc21   99-046395
                                                           CIP

Republic of Texas Press is an imprint of Wordware Publishing, Inc.
No part of this book may be reproduced in any form or by
any means without permission in writing from
Wordware Publishing, Inc.

Printed in the United States of America

ISBN 1-55622-697-7
10 9 8 7 6 5 4 3 2 1
9909

All inquiries for volume purchases of this book should be addressed to
Wordware Publishing, Inc., at 2320 Los Rios Boulevard, Plano, Texas 75074.
Telephone inquiries may be made by calling:

(972) 423-0090

Contents

Contents

Contents

Part One

Introduction

When you mention barbecue in Texas, various opinions sally forth as to what constitutes real barbecue and where you can find a good barbecue place. Everyone has a favorite barbecue stop, and more than likely the one proffered by someone else is not your favorite.

So where is the best barbecue place in Texas? How would I determine that?

First, I read every book or article I could find about barbecue. Arguments persisted. Gas cookers or wood? Which wood? Hickory, oak, pecan, fruit, or mesquite? Smoke brisket 6 hours or 72? Cook at 170, 190, 240, or 450 degrees? Indirect heat (with fire off to one side) or direct heat? Pit or rotisserie? Chewy or tender meat? Sauce or no sauce? Sweet or vinegary sauce? Thick or thin sauce? Rub or no rub? What rub ingredients?

I hoped the answers would come as I traveled the state and talked to the experts and to the people who owned barbecue places. A friend said, "Most of them don't even know how to spell barbecue." True.

I decided my first job was to get a list of barbecue restaurants. The Internet disclosed over 2,000 barbecue places in Texas. And those places had telephones. Probably another 2,000 existed without telephones. *Zounds. It might take me five years to visit all of them. I am seventy and may not have five years.* I realized I had to be selective. I would visit only recommended establishments. I determined that if a place only opened for weekends or some schedule that made using them only an option for neighbors, they were out. I began to poll as many people as possible. I telephoned or personally interviewed hundreds of Texans, purposely omitting newspapers and chambers of commerce (I felt they would recommend their clients).

Next, I needed a way to organize my work. I adopted the *Texas Highways* "Regional Divisions for Travel and Tourism Planning" map. The map is very controversial and receives the most mail at the magazine. For example, how in heaven's name could Palestine not be in the Piney Woods?

While polling, someone would answer my telephone call, and I would say, "I'm Richard Troxell from Fredericksburg. I'm writing a book on the best barbecue places in Texas, and I'm headed your way. Have you a good barbecue place in your neck of the woods?"

At this point, the person answering the telephone might go into deep thought or ask others. Whether it was in a golf club locker room, an office, a shop, or a service station, an argument ensued and answers came fast that were often surprising.

I read. Many other writers surveyed the field and came up with different answers. For example, a statewide publication (owned by people in New York City) announced "The Big Three" of Texas barbecue joints. Oddly, the folks I interviewed seldom mentioned even one of "The Big Three." The published article also named "The 50 Best Barbecue Joints in Texas." Naturally, I checked out their findings. Those writers, like others, had a bias for old and almost unkempt buildings near Austin (near where they worked). Many of those 50 Best failed to impress.

Granted that atmosphere is important, and if that is all you are interested in, you should love my selections. Atmosphere abounds.

But I did not search for atmosphere. I wanted to find the best barbecue.

A Texas barbecue book listed some places I would not visit more than once and some places that did not even barbecue. I gave thumbs down to a number of recommended places for reasons I will elaborate on later.

So it went with everything I read. That brings up another big point about barbecue: Everybody is entitled to his or her own opinion. If your favorite place is not listed in this book, it may be that I rejected them because of my tests. My daughter Laura thinks I'm wrong not to include Underwood's in Brownwood. Underwood's is not my idea of barbecue. They boil beef. Underwood's has great food like any other cafeteria, but I do not recommend them for barbecue. Others failed to make this book because they have no pit.

If you think you know a place that should be in this book, drop me a letter. Maybe I can get it in the next edition ... if it passes the tests.

Armed with knowledge, laptop, and hunger, I started my survey in counties around my hometown, Fredericksburg, and branched out with one-day excursions.

I gained ten pounds the first month. I drove 11,802 miles. I never knew where I would be by day's end, and I stayed in a few flea traps, not by choice.

Extending my horizons, I made a week's junket to the Rio Grande Valley. I visited up to seven barbecue places in a day and wrote with my laptop at night in a motel with electricity. (I had to leave a motel that did not have a plug that worked.)

Seldom did I find a Houston, Dallas, or Fort Worth owner in his restaurant.

Eating became a challenge. I went into barbecue places and ordered two bites of everything. Most refused to give me such small portions, although I thoroughly explained that to serve more than two bites was a waste of food because that was all I was going to eat.

My Rating System

It did not take long to develop a method to determine the quality of barbecue. I set up a rating system of 1 up to 10. First came the inspection of the brisket. I measured the pink ribbon of the brisket from the outer edge.

The ribbon forms from oxygen, according to a manufacturer's studies. The more a wrangler opens the lid of the pit to check the meat, the more oxygen and the more pink ribbon. Also, the same manufacturer found that oxygen carries the smoke flavor into the meat. Conversely, fat dissipates and takes smoke with it.

The next inspection step involved aroma. I sniffed the brisket (a wonderful aroma did wonders for my judging). Next came the shear test. I pressed the edge of the plastic fork against the slice of brisket. If it fell apart with just a touch, it had the makings of a 10 for tenderness. If I had to put some effort into the first press, it fell to a 9. If I had to slice it, it went down to an 8. Two slices received a 7. And so on. If it took a knife to cut it, the barbecue probably did not make it into this book. I say "probably" because flavor and fat content of barbecued meat also had something to do with my evaluations.

I tested for flavor by slowly grinding a bite with my teeth and sucking at the same time. It worked well for me. Maurice Mikeska of Mikeska's in El Campo taught me to take a bite of pickle in between samplings of meat. "It clears the taste buds," Maurice said. I followed his advice until I realized that coleslaw did a better job for me. Visual inspection determined the fat content, except for sausage. Usually, the outside of the sausage swam in grease, making it hard to judge the fat. I became adept at squeezing a two-inch piece of sausage and counting the drops of fat. If the server sliced the sausage, I had to press the tines of my fork against it and judge the fat content. No drops meant it was lean, two drops meant a little fat content, and a puddle of fat gave the sausage the gong. Visual inspection and tasting revealed if fillers diluted the sausage. Some sausages lacked expressive seasoning. Many tasted like bologna.

Each write-up of a barbecue place explains how I arrived at my ratings of meat.

I also gave each restaurant an **overall rating**, which can be found to the right of the restaurant name. This rating leaned heavily on the ratings of brisket and ribs, the true test of barbecue in my books. Sausage usually failed to impress in my overall ratings. The skin of sausage does not absorb smoke flavor very well. Restaurants get away with grilling or baking sausage and calling it barbecued sausage. I considered chicken, turkey, and ham of less import. Atmosphere, cleanliness, and service influenced me.

If you total all the numbers and divide by the number of meats, you will not come up with my overall rating.

I suspect that after you read this book, you will develop a rating system of your own. If you wish, send me your ratings, and I will consider them for the next go 'round.

The rotisserie usually rates a 7. I'm talking about a rotisserie pit. You put the meat in and punch *on*. The meat goes round and round and usually ends up tough, above average flavor, and little fat. Doctors love them. The rotisserie pit has a Ferris wheel inside. Instead of seats, it has grates. It goes up and down and this action makes the juices of the meat drop on top of each other, which is supposed to make them more tender. (This I have yet to see. I find rotisserie meat on the tough side.) These machines have all the latest gadgets. A wrangler sets the time and temperature, throws in some logs, starts the fire, and pushes the *on* button. He walks away from it until the buzzer sounds. The rotisserie pit provides the owner two great advantages: it keeps employees from burning the meat and assures the owner of above average barbecue. That's good. Big operations cannot do without rotisserie pits. But rotisserie barbecue will never be the best. That's sad.

As far as pits go, I found that the best barbecue comes from the old-fashioned brick or metal pit, firebox on one end and smokestack on the other.

Barbecuers blow a lot of smoke. I don't know if I believe some of them when they tell me how many hours they smoke a brisket and at what temperature. Not all the equations add up. You have Kreuz Market 'cuing brisket six hours and Clark's Outpost 'cuing fifty-two hours. One wrangler barbecued at 170 degrees and another at 300.

A word to neophytes: A rub is a mixture of spices put on meat usually before barbecuing begins. It could be salt and pepper. Normally, a rub has more ingredients. Most rub recipes are deep, dark secrets. A sop or mop also has secret ingredients, and they apply it sometimes during the smoking cycle and always at the end of the cycle. Although they make much ado over secrets, most wranglers use their barbecue sauce as a sop.

I discuss in the book the various styles of barbecuing: Texas, Memphis, Kansas City, and the Southeast. Basically, Texas barbecue features beef and is not as sweet as the others, and the Texas method calls for meat to cook from the heat of the smoke and not from direct heat. A number of places in Central Texas, the Panhandle, and West Texas cook over coals (direct heat) the way the out-of-state guys do. They claim that cooking over coals is the true Texas way, pioneered by the cowboys. The great majority of wranglers say that's grilling. Why have a pit?

The barbecue battle goes on.

As you near Mexico, the barbecue sauce becomes spicier. As you go north, sweeter. Bee, my wife, likes spicy barbecue sauce and wants it poured over her meat. Some servers do this without asking. If you prefer sauce on the side like I do, speak up.

A nice feature about barbecue is that it competes with fast food joints. One place offered a brisket plate to Seniors for $2.90. Some offer a brisket plate to everyone for less than $4. Unlike fast food places, the plate comes with your choice of vegetables. (Who can resist and not come back for more carrot soufflé at Willie Ray's in Beaumont?) Because barbecue is smoked, it requires less salt. Most places trim the fat. If they do not trim the fat, hand it back and ask them to do so. If your approach is right, barbecue can be a very wholesome and healthy food to devour.

I entered information about vegetables and desserts, but I did not set out to rate them.

If you have diabetes or wish to avoid sugar, order sauce on the side. Some restaurants have a bad habit of adding sugar to vegetables. Many sops I tasted had sugar. Caveat Emptor.

Nutritionists point out that heartburn comes from the fat that drops on the coals in grilling. The burnt tallow smoke clings to the meat and, when digested, causes heartburn. A few barbecuers wrap their meat in foil (aluminum is not good for you, too) to avoid smoke. My answer to that is why barbecue? Why not do it the way Ohioans do, roast the meat and add barbecue sauce.

A number of paragraphs in this book address the origination of the word *barbecue*. Someone from the Southeast will claim it came from Indians in the Indies or from the Spanish word *barbacoa*.

Remember, Spain owned Florida and West Indies islands.

I looked up *barbacoa* in an authentic Spanish dictionary (not one designed for Anglos). It read,

Barbacoa, -cua (voz indigena del Caribe) *f. Amer.* Parilla (an earthen jar with two handles –Ed.) usada para asar al aire libre carne or pescado.

Earthen jar?

Any way you try to explain the beginning of barbecue falters. The word *barbacoa* could have easily been anglicized to "barbecue." Look what our ancestors did with Mexia (Ma hay ah) or Refugio (Ray feeur ee oh). Smoky Hale, of Southeast perspective, stated flatly that "Barbecue, whatever the origin of its name, means slow cooking in the dry heat of wood coals." Most of the wranglers I talked with would react to that statement with, "Easterner." Smoky believes that the word comes from the Taino, members of the Arawak tribe, native to the Caribbean. These people preceded the Spanish. The Taino word *barabicoa* means "the sticks with four legs and many sticks of wood on top to place the cooking meat." Chief Peter Guanikeyu, a real Taino, came up with this translation: *Ba* from *baba* (father), *ra* from *yara* (fire), *bi* from *bibi* (beginning), and *cu* from *guacu* (the sacred fire). He said, *"barabicu* means sacred fire pit."

The French word for a wooden rack for cooking is *boucan.* The word buccaneer came from that word. Evidently, the pirates enjoyed barbecue. A pirate trying to muscle into line might be told *"boucan queue (tail)."* French for "from beard and tail" is *de barbe et queue* (pronounced barb ay cue). That has its possibilities. The Tex-Mex barbecuers in the Valley *barbacoa* everything from snout to tail.

Then you have the possibility that *barbacoa* evolved from another language like the English word barbecue.

If Eve had not eaten the apple, maybe she would still be around to tell us how she invented barbecue.

As my work progressed, I found that real estate people gave the best recommendations. Clerks at service stations kept me from wandering aimlessly and not finding my destinations. I want to thank all the people who assisted me.

I need to mention a humorous happening without mentioning the barbecue place. The sign over the main entrance said, "Gateway to the Best BBQ." Near the handle, a small sign read, "Please use the other door."

After reading this book, I sincerely hope that you will never want for a good barbecue place again. Also, I urge you to add another dimension to your life—begin testing barbecue.

Part Two

Big Bend Country

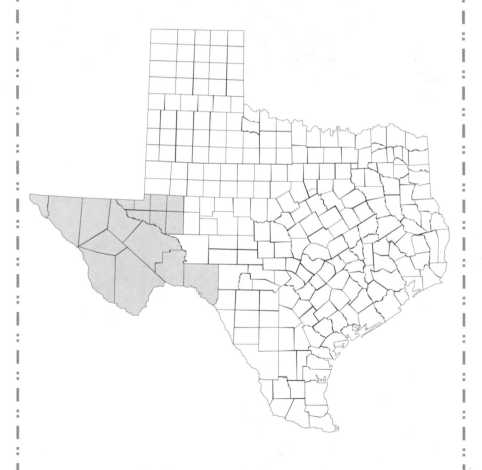

Del Rio

The Feed Store

Rating: 8

1001 E. Ogden Street,
Del Rio, Texas 78840-5665
Phone 830-775-2998

Dine (sort of), dine out (sort of), counter order, take-out, catering. Beer served. Brisket $6.95 a pound (no plate).

Open 11 A.M. to 6:30 P.M. Open for take-out from 6:30 A.M. to 7 P.M. Closed Sunday. Accepts checks.

Terry Bowen, owner of The Feed Store, entertains customers and bulls. As "T" Texas Terry, he entertains rodeo crowds as a bullfighter/barrel man clown and sells feed for livestock. As for customers, he feeds them some good barbecue when they line up at The Feed Store. His hat reads, "PEOPLE FEED, ANIMAL FEED."

The animal feed store occupies the left side of the building, and the people feed store has the right.

The Feed Store is hard to find. Ogden Street runs under the 7th Street railroad overpass. Seventh is the street that leads to downtown Del Rio. Keep asking the locals and you will find it.

When I pulled up on the yard (hard to call it a parking lot), I noticed people eating beneath an open-sided barn-like structure on the north side of the driveway. Signs directed me to a smaller ranch-styled building on the south side. I opened the door and almost walked into a counter (it was about four feet from the door). A raven-haired and mustachioed cowboy asked me what I wanted. I ordered my usual small slice of brisket. He wore a self-effacing smile. "Is that all you want?"

I tried some cowboy talk. "Yep."

A slim sidekick left the building without saying a word and returned with a small piece of brisket on a piece of butcher paper.

I took a plastic fork and looked around for a place to sit. The cowboy nodded toward the open barn across the way. I was only going to take a bite out of it. *Why walk all the way across the yard to the barn? I can test it right now.*

I observed the meat, and mustache and slim observed me.

"Now that's a great pink ribbon. Must be 5/16 of an inch," I said. Their smiles did not change a wrinkle. I pressed lightly on the meat, and it did not part. That got the attention of the two men. I pushed harder and the meat separated. The cowboy stretched his eyes. I sniffed it. "Good aroma. Mesquite?"

"Yep."

I took a bite. "Good flavor." It was a little tough, but the brisket was good meat. With their eyes following my every move, I could not write a number down without their notice. I said, "How about one rib and a two-inch cut of sausage?"

The sidekick left and came back with the order.

I picked up the rib and looked it over. The rib had some fat and some hard crust from sop. Their eyes followed my every move. I made a desultory remark: "I think the best bite is underneath, near the top. What do you think?" They nodded. I took a bite. It was tender inside and crunchy outside. "Good flavor." They smiled. I squeezed the sausage. Eyes bulged as four drops hit the paper. I chewed it. *Mild. Polish.* "You make this?"

"No. We get it from Opa's in Fredericksburg," said the cowboy.

The sides were traditional—the way most folks like them. No dessert.

It turned out that the mustachioed man was Terry Bowen, and I told him what I was up to. He showed me his two oddball pits. He made one from a propane tank and the other from a water tank. "The barrel can do fifteen briskets and the water tank can do forty. We only use the big one when we have a catering job."

I asked him how long he smoked his brisket. "One hour per pound, depending on the brisket. It isn't done until the fork slides out easily. And we use nothing but mesquite."

He went on to tell me that he rubs all his meat. After much cajoling, he gave me his secret rub recipe. Here it is:

6 ounces paprika
3 ounces garlic
3 ounces coarse ground black pepper

1 ounce fajita spice
Mix and rub onto the meat.

I felt lucky to get that much out of this hombre.

He told me that he also sops with vinegar and oil. "You want a jalapeño?"

I hesitated. He said, "If you do..." he nodded at a vegetable garden, "you pick your own. I grow jalapeños and chili cerranos, and customers help themselves."

Bowen's a one-of-a-kind cowboy and knows his barbecue. You would have to drive an awfully long way to find better barbecue.

Back in my car, I gave the brisket and the rib an 8 on the strength of their flavor, the sausage a 6 because of its little-above-average flavor.

Hot Pit B-B-Q

I arrived at a bad time, 3 o'clock (I can't be everywhere at 12 noon). Three other couples sat, devouring barbecue. The lady in charge had to quit doing menu work to come to the cafeteria counter to help me. I ordered a small slice of brisket. Cost 81 cents. I took my plate to a table and gave the brisket the fork test. It took some real shoving to break the meat. The meat had a 1/8-inch pink ribbon. *That's bad. Probably a rotisserie.* The aroma wouldn't come out of hiding. I ate a bite. It had average flavor. I gave it a 6. Since a 6 puts a barbecue place in my book, I went back to the counter for more ribs, sausage, and anything else I could test.

If you like ribs, don't eat here. They don't have ribs. Stunned, I ordered a two-inch cut of sausage. It was Polish and yielded two drops of fat from the squeeze test. The flavor was mild, and I gave it a 7.

The owner had gone shopping or something else, so I did not get to talk shop. The lady in charge showed me the rotisserie smoker in back. It varied from the standard as it had a horizontal circular movement—like a merry-go-round. She said they 'cued the brisket for fourteen hours and did not use a rub or a sop.

Hot Pit started in 1968 and thrives. Del Rio folks love it. Give it a try.

Rating: 6

309 Avenue F, U.S. Hwy. 90 North and U.S. Hwy. 377 North, Del Rio, Texas 78840-4659
Phone 830-775-3883

Cafeteria style, take-out, catering. No beer. Brisket plate $5.15.

Open 11 A.M. to 7 P.M. Closed Sunday. Accepts checks.

El Paso

Bill Parks Bar-B-Q

Bill Parks got up there in years and decided to sell out to Filemon Fuentes. Today, Fuentes holds the reins, and Parks handles the pit.

The change of ownership surprised me. Many a publication featured this place and said nothing of Fuentes.

I had a hard time finding Bill Parks Bar-B-Q. I-10 runs through El Paso. West of the U.S. Hwy. 54 interchange, called the "Spaghetti Bowl" by El Pasoans, I took the Copia exit and U-turned.

The frontage road on the north side of the I-10 bears the name Gateway Boulevard West, and the frontage road on the south side bears the name Gateway Boulevard East. Bill Parks is on Gateway Boulevard East. Clear?

In 1850, fourteen years after Texas won its independence from Mexico, El Pasoans voted to be a part of Texas and not a part of New Mexico. Good thing, because El Paso is the last bastion of good barbecue going west.

Entering Bill Parks Bar-B-Q, the red Naugahyde booths and tablecloths contrasted sharply with the Interstate concrete and West Texas desert sand. I ordered one of everything and began my inspection. The brisket had a 5/16-inch pink ribbon and showed little fat. In the shear test, the meat parted with the second slice of the fork. The aroma beckoned. The flavor was above average. I gave the brisket a 7. The pork rib was very tender, had some fat, and effused good flavor. I gave it an 8.

Parks had sold out of sausage. I had to take his word that his half pork, half beef smoked sausage deserved acclaim.

The barbecue sauce seemed to have some paprika for one-alarm fire, vinegar, ketchup, and Worcestershire sauce.

Rating: 7.5

3130 Gateway Boulevard East, El Paso, Texas 79905-1015

Phone 915-542-0960

Menu order, take-out, catering, banquet or meeting room. Beer sometimes. Brisket plate $5.75, Senior Citizen $3.50.

Open 7 A.M. to 11 P.M. Closed Sunday and Monday. Accepts credit cards.

11

Parks had a large selection of sides: potato salad, pinto beans, collard greens, rice and gravy, black-eyed peas, and fried okra with tomatoes.

The dessert list had peach and apple cobbler, pecan pie, banana pudding, and a mysterious sweet potato pie.

Filemon had to go to the bank, so he left his nephew Steve Fuentes to talk shop with me. It seemed that Bill Parks wants out of the business, so he is training Steve to handle the barbecuing. Steve showed me their two brick pits. He said they marinate the brisket with a secret blend of spices and then smoke the brisket for eight hours using mesquite wood. *Ummm.*

Hope you make the right move off of Interstate 10.

Johnny's Pit Barbecue

Gilbert Estrada started to work at Johnny's washing dishes. One day Johnny Gonzalez sold the business to his daughter. The daughter did not want the business. She wanted Gilbert to buy it. Gilbert went to the bank, borrowed enough money, and is now the successful owner of Johnny's.

In America, anything can happen.

To get to Johnny's, I took the Sunland Park Drive exit off Interstate10, turned left and then took a right at Doniphan. The street honors Col. Alexander Doniphan who, along with his Missouri Farm Boys, conquered the disputed area for the United States.

I found Johnny's in a small, unobtrusive yellow building. The interior yawned white, white, white. The only touch of color was the mustard-colored plastic stack chairs.

I walked up to the counter and asked for small pieces of barbecue meat. I took my order to a table and dug in. The brisket almost shocked me. *What was this? A half-inch ribbon? In West Texas?* Yes. It had a small amount of fat. I sniffed it, and the aroma sparkled. I put the fork edge to it, and it took a good push to break through the brisket. In my mouth, it made beautiful music. I gave the brisket an 8.

Johnny did not have pork ribs, but he did have pork shoulder. It had above average tenderness, too much fat, and little flavor. I gave it a 6. The sausage

Rating: 7

3716 Doniphan Drive, El Paso, Texas 79922-1406
Phone 915-833-2828

Counter order, take-out, catering. No beer. Brisket plate $4.55.

Open from 11 A.M. to 6 P.M. Monday through Saturday. Accepts checks.

came from El Paso market. Gilbert calls it a hot link. The coloring blared red. Two drops of fat fell from the squeeze test. The seasoning was average and produced one-alarm fire. I cannot really recommend it. *Something about that red casing*. A slice of ham had more fat than I normally see on a slice of ham. It was tender and the flavor was above average. I gave the ham a 7.

Delighted with the brisket, I wanted to see how Gilbert barbecued it. He showed me his homemade barbecue pit. It had a firebox on one side with a giant vertical smoke box on the right. He said he used pecan wood. He put the brisket in to smoke at 4 P.M. and took it off at 10 A.M. Little wonder the brisket tasted so good.

The sauce had the usual ingredients. The biscuits were fluffy and melted in my mouth.

Johhny's potato salad had dill instead of sweet pickle. *A nice change*. He added pineapple to his coleslaw. The macaroni salad had celery, eggs, olives, and purple onion, and, of course, macaroni. The pinto beans had chili powder.

For dessert, I had a choice of Mexican favorites, flan or flan cake.

Gilbert bought this business in 1990.

It is only a matter of time until El Paso folks catch on and jam the place.

I recommend you go there, order the brisket, biscuits, any of the side orders, and the flan.

Smitty's Pit Bar-B-Que

Smitty's is on the way to the airport. Treat your taxi cab driver to a barbecue lunch, and maybe he won't keep the meter running.

I stepped into Smitty's and stepped back into the fifties. It looked like a diner. Neon lights, ceiling fans, and a long counter that served sit-down bar-stool diners and stand-up drinkers.

The brisket had a wide, promising ribbon on it. The aroma lured me on. In the shear test, the meat parted with the second slice of my fork. I found the flavor sensational and the fat too evident. I rated the brisket an 8. A pork rib showed no sign of sop, was very tender, and displayed too much fat. I gave it a 7. The all-beef sausage came from Eckridge Farms. Two drops of fat fell from the squeeze test, but its flavor inspired. I gave the sausage a 7.5. Then came the crème de la crème: honey glazed, barbecued

Rating: 7.5

6219 Airport Road, El Paso, Texas 79925-2027

Phone 915-772-5876

Menu order, take-out, catering, meeting and banquet facilities. Beer and wine served. Brisket plate $7.75.

Open 10:30 A.M. to 9 P.M. Monday through Saturday. Closed Sunday. Accepts checks and credit cards.

ham. I crowned it with a 10…perfect in every way.

The barbecue sauce contained secret ingredients, but I knew that paprika, vinegar, and Worcestershire sauce swam around in it.

Side orders loomed big at Smitty's. Everything was homemade. The potatoes in the potato salad were not overcooked, pineapple sweetened the coleslaw, they smoked the pinto beans, the chili beans had red chili and jalapeño, and then came the special treat: German fries. Here's the recipe:

4 medium size potatoes (new potatoes fall apart and are too soft)
Vegetable oil for frying
Salt to taste
Peel and cut potatoes into quarters, lengthwise. Boil the pieces about 10 minutes, but do not cook until done (by 15 or 20 minutes the potatoes will be tender enough to pierce with a fork—that's too well cooked). Remove potatoes from hot water, drain thoroughly on paper towels, then pat dry, taking care to keep each quarter in one piece. Heat oil in a deep skillet or deep fryer to 375 degrees. Fry potatoes in hot oil, doing only a few at a time. Keep potatoes far apart, not crowded in the oil. Fry until dark golden brown, about 7-8 minutes. Remove potatoes from oil and drain on paper towels. Salt to taste and serve immediately.

I had to choose between brownies and chocolate cake for dessert.

Heriberto Payan Jr., Smitty's owner, knows barbecue. He showed me his large firebrick pit. He likes fruitwood when he can get. Said it made the best flavor of all. Other than that and the German potato recipe, everything else is a secret.

Smokey's Pit Stop & Saloon

Driving along Lee Trevino Drive, I spotted Smokey's in a strip shopping center. Cars packed the parking lot. I lucked out. A pickup pulled out near Smokey's entrance, and I took the spot. When I went through the front door, I was relieved to find most of the crowd in the saloon to the left and only three people ahead of me in the barbecue serving line. The man behind the counter cut deftly and exactly the barbecue pieces I wanted. I added potato salad, pinto beans, and coleslaw to my order, paid, and took a seat.

I looked around. The décor said half western, half New York deli. One might say it had a neighborhood look. My brisket slice had a familiar 1/4-inch pink

Rating: 7

1346 Lee Trevino Drive,
El Paso, Texas 79936
Phone 915-593-6332

9100 Viscount Boulevard,
El Paso, Texas 79925
Phone 915-592-3141

Cafeteria style, take-out, catering. Full bar. Brisket plate $5.95.

ribbon. *Another rotisserie.* The meat parted on the second slice of my fork. The flavor mumbled. It had little fat. I rated it a 6. The pork rib had great flavor and tenderness but a little too much fat. I gave it an 8. Hillshire supplies the all-pork sausage. I squeezed a piece and a small puddle of fat formed on my plate. The flavor lacked seasoning. I gave it a 5. A slice of turkey had above average flavor and one-alarm fire. I gave it a 7.5.

Opens 10:30 A.M. Closes 10 P.M. Sunday through Thursday and 11 P.M. Friday and Saturday. Accepts checks and credit cards.

The potato salad seemed normal. The coleslaw had pineapple. The beans stole the sideshow. They had barbecue trimmings and jalapeños.

Unfortunately, Smokey's had no desserts, unless I ordered a Mud Slide or a Pina Colada, or a B-52, or whatever from their bar.

Bill Armstrong and Ed Nations own Smokey's. Armstrong had taken off. I talked to Ed, who reminded me of singer Phil Harris. Ed confessed that they used a rotisserie and bought *oak* wood from *Mesquite*, Texas. *Hmmm.*

I asked Ed if anything unusual happened here.

"Well, we used to feed guys who rode up here on horses. Another time we fed 11,500 people in one day." He told me how an amusement park hired them for a special one-day promotion. Ed and Bill rented a refrigerated trailer and began ordering supplies and meat and barbecuing one week in advance. "On the day of the promotion, we heated 800 pounds of barbecue at a time. We served five tons of barbecue."

Bet no one can top that.

State Line Barbeque

I parked in Texas, walked through a gateway into a verdant patio, over a small garden bridge, entered the restaurant, sat down, and ate in New Mexico.

County Line owns this establishment, and the fare is the same as in all their other restaurants.

State Line has a roadhouse forties look, according to general manager Mike Shahan. Old copies of *Life Magazine* fill slots between booths, and background music features swing bands of the forties.

I asked Mike, "Which state gets the sales tax?"

He smiled. "Our address is in Texas, but New Mexico gets their cut."

For more information on food, see "County Line," San Antonio, Texas (page 292).

Rating: 9

1222 Sunland Park Drive, El Paso, Texas 79922-2408
Phone 915-581-3371
Fax 915-833-4843

Menu, take-out, catering, banquet facilities. Full bar. Brisket plate $10.95.

Open 11 A.M. to 2:30 P.M. for lunch; open 5 P.M. to 9:30 P.M. Monday through Thursday, 5 P.M. to 10 P.M. Friday and Saturday, and 4 P.M. to 9 P.M. Sunday. Accepts credit cards.

Fort Stockton

Camphouse Pit BBQ

Fort Stockton shimmers like a mirage in the West Texas desert until you get close. Then you see the greenery of an oasis. The original source of Fort Stockton's magic emanated from Commanche Springs, the effusion of an aquifer. Two wells pumped the aquifer dry, but other underground reservoirs brought new wealth: the world's largest gas and oil wells.

Today, another kind of wealth draws folks to Fort Stockton: Camphouse Pit BBQ, my only recommended barbecue place on Interstate 10 between Kerrville and El Paso, a 484-mile stretch.

Camphouse owners Garry Zesch and James Ledford knew each other in Brady, Texas. Garry owned Old Time Pit Barbecue in San Angelo and wanted to open another. He heard that his friend James had quit as chief of police in Brady and moved to Fort Stockton. He called James and asked him

Rating: 7

1216 North Hwy. 285, Fort Stockton, Texas 79735-4408
Phone 915-336-8714

Counter order at the pit, take-out, catering. Beer served. Brisket plate $5.99.

Opens 10 A.M. Closes 9:30 P.M. Sunday through Thursday and 10 P.M. Friday and Saturday. Accepts checks and credit cards.

if he would like to be part owner and run a new barbecue place in Fort Stockton. Five months later they were off and running.

A real estate lady told me about Camphouse. She said it was brand new, and it was. The building resembled a large ranch house. I went through the screen door into an outside porch area and—déjà vu—where had I seen this set-up before? Cooper's, in Llano. The man serving the barbecue stood aside one of four large metal pits. He asked me what I wanted. I told him. He opened the pit lid, took out the necessary pieces of meat, and cut me off small portions of each. Unfortunately, he sold his last rib before I arrived. He weighed the meat, put it on a plate, and pointed to a door. Through the door I found myself at a cafeteria-style serving line where all the condiments, sides, and desserts resided. I ordered a little of each and took a seat at one of dozens of wooden tables and benches.

The interior looked part ranch, part national park. The walls and ceiling had natural finished pine paneling that matched the tables and benches. Someone placed ranch collectibles, including some stuffed deer heads, in appropriate spots on the walls. Although the room was large, it felt friendly and cozy.

The man at the pit cut my brisket incorrectly. He sliced off a corner that contained enough fat to take care of my cholesterol allowance for the next five years. In the shear test, the meat parted with the second slice of my fork. The aroma was barely detectable. The brisket had above average flavor. I rated it a 7. I squeezed a two-inch piece of Polish all beef sausage and it oozed three drops of fat. The flavor was superior, and I gave the sausage a 7. A piece of chicken had above average tenderness, little fat, and superior flavor. I tagged it with an 8.

Turkey and hams move fast during the holidays. Camphouse smokes them in steam and sells them by the pound.

The potato salad potatoes were not overcooked. The coleslaw and pinto beans were from traditional recipes.

The dessert line-up: apple, cherry, and peach cobblers and banana pudding.

When in Fort Stockton, be sure to take a photo of yourself with "Paisano Pete," an eleven-foot-high statue of a roadrunner.

Midland

KD's Bar-B-Q

You have two good reasons to slow down on Interstate 20 when you near Midland: KD's Bar-B-Q and State Highway Patrolmen. KD's has brisket with a half-inch pink ribbon and a robust flavor. The patrolmen like KD's barbecue. Get the picture?

KD's looks like a revamped icehouse.

When I walked through the side screen door, a man stood beside a big metal pit. A sign read, "Pick Yer Meat from the Pit." The man opened the lid and asked me what I wanted. *Déjà vu Coopers.* He carved small pieces of barbecued meat, placed it on butcher paper atop a tray, and marked the cost on the paper. He motioned toward another screen door. I went through and found myself in a cafeteria line of side dishes, desserts, and drinks. I paid the cashier at the end of the line and headed for a large island bar that had three barbecue sauces, condiments, and a tub of beans. I took a seat and stared at the beautiful half-inch pink ribbon on my brisket. *Promising. This couldn't be a rotisserie.* I gave it the fork test. I had to push my fork to separate the meat but cut it with the first slice. I sniffed it, and the brisket had gangbusters aroma. Very little fat. I ate it, and it made my most wanted list. If the brisket had been more tender I would have given it a 10. I gave it a 9.

I arrived at one o'clock, and KD's was sold out of ribs.

I looked at three sausages. The German oozed three drops of fat from the squeeze test and had a little above average flavor. The jalapeño gave up two drops of fat from the squeeze test and had way above average flavor and three-alarm fire. The hot link yielded three drops of fat and scored above average with two-alarm fire. I gave the German sausage a 6, the jalapeño a 9, and the hot link a 7. A slice of ham fell apart when I touched it with my fork. It had very

Rating: 8

3109 Garden City Hwy.
(Business 158 West just off Interstate 20), Midland,
Texas 79701
Phone 915-683-5013
Fax 915-687-0648

Cafeteria style, take-out, meeting room, catering. Beer and wine served. Brisket $7.50 per pound.

Opens 11 A.M. Closes 2:30 P.M. Monday through Wednesday, and 8 P.M. Thursday through Saturday. Summer hours: Same for Monday through Wednesday, but 11 A.M. to 9:30 P.M. Thursday through Saturday. Closed Sunday. Accepts checks and credit cards.

18

little fat, excellent flavor, and I gave it an 8. A slice of turkey was very moist and tender, had above average flavor, and had very little fat. I labeled it with a 9.

Their three barbecue sauces excelled. The regular sauce had tomato, black pepper, and possibly some cayenne among other things. More vinegar made the vinegary sauce. More sweetener made the sweet sauce. *Was it brown sugar?*

The pinto beans were normal. The potato salad had a mustard base and tasted flat. The coleslaw had fine chopped pieces including carrots.

Peach and cherry cobbler made up the dessert list.

KD's had lots of space. It seated 300 people. I called its interior "warehouse modern." Farm and ranch collectibles hung on corrugated metal walls. In one dining room, KD's had a large number of mounted trophy deer and antelope heads. I thought I knew all about deer, but these had unusual markings, color, and antlers. I suspected a taxidermist got drunk and swapped antlers and heads.

Barbecue eaters sat at picnic tables with galvanized tops. A tree grew in the middle of the main dining room and out the roof.

In the summer, on Saturday evenings, they have country western bands and, on occasion, rock bands. The activity takes place in back on a huge covered patio. Dancers sit at Carta Blanca tables and toss drinks and horseshoes.

When I left I went five miles an hour under the speed limit. A highway patrolman loomed ahead of me and one fell in behind me. Such nice guys to do all that just to protect me.

Price's Barbeque

Run down to a run-down place in a run-down part of town for barbecue renowned. It's Price's, one of Midland's best kept secrets.

You have to know someone who knows about Price's to find it. They do not advertise. My junior and senior high school friend Charlie Tighe told me about it. Charlie was an All-Conference guard on the Rice Institute basketball team, got a law degree from the University of Texas, and started his practice in Midland about the same time Mosetta Price started practicing barbecue at Price's . . . in the early fifties.

Rating: 7

700 East Texas Avenue,
South side of Interstate 20,
Lamesa exit, Midland, Texas
79701-5358
Phone 915-684-9453

Counter or menu order,
take-out. Beer served. Brisket plate $4.

Mosetta served me samples of her barbecue, and I got down to business. The brisket had a disappointing 1/16-inch pink ribbon. In the shear test, the meat parted with the second slice of my fork. It lacked flavor and had too much fat. I gave it a 6. The pork rib had little fat, superior flavor and tenderness. I gave it an 8. The beef sausage had some filler, yielded two drops of fat from the squeeze test, yipped one-alarm fire, and possessed above average flavor. I gave it a 7.

Open 11 A.M. to 3 P.M. Tuesday through Friday. Closed Sunday and Monday. Accepts company checks.

I had two choices for the rest of my meal: potato salad and pinto beans. Both delicious. Not much to choose from but better than no-choice-at-all-Kreuz Market.

Mosetta began her career working at her family's barbecue place in Corsicana. "I know nothing but eating," she said. I asked her about how she barbecues. She smiled. "Everything's a secret." I checked in back after my visit. I found a long pit working and a lot of stacked mesquite.

Price's is the place where downtown Midlanders go for lunch. Lawyers love it. If you can't find a lawyer, eat barbecue at Price's and take your pick.

Sam's Barbeque

No blues music, no wine and mixed drinks, but the same barbecue as Sam's in Odessa. See Odessa listing for Sam's Bar-B-Q and Blues Alley on page 22.

Rating: 7.5

11113 East Scharbauer, Midland, Texas 79705-7741

Phone 915-570-1082

Menu order, take-out, catering. Beer served. Brisket plate $6.50.

Open 11 A.M. to 9 P.M. Monday through Saturday and 12 noon to 7 P.M. Sunday. Accepts credit cards.

Odessa

Rockin' Q

Miss Texas, Tatum Hubbard, eats at the Rockin' Q all the time. You have no guarantee that you will look as pretty as she if you do likewise. But it's good to know in these days of keeping slim and healthy that you can do it eating barbecue.

Other than keeping in shape, Tatum eats here because her father, Maurice, is the general manager. Maybe you should eat here?

I ate here. The brisket had that rotisserie quarter-inch pink ribbon. In the shear test, the meat parted after two hard slices. It had superior tenderness, little fat, and third-runner-up flavor. I gave it my usual rotisserie 7. The pork ribs fared better. The rib I tasted had some fat, superior tenderness, and Miss Texas flavor. I tagged it with an 8. The jalapeño pork sausage hailed from East Texas. It had two-alarm fire, two drops of fat from the squeeze test, and better than average flavor but missed being Miss Texas sausage. I rated it a 7. A slice of turkey was moist and tender but lacked flavor. I gave it an 8.

They kept the sauce recipe in a safe, but I detected cayenne or paprika, vinegar, ketchup, and maybe a small amount of Worcestershire sauce in it.

Their potato salad and coleslaw were traditional, but the pinto beans excelled with chunks of brisket and added secret sauce.

Picking dessert was easy. I ate what Miss Texas ate, peach cobbler, their only dessert.

The décor is modern western. Huge hand-painted Texana murals cover the walls and the tables have red-and-white checkered cloths.

Maurice confirmed my rotisserie suspicion. He said they put a dry rub on the brisket and then 'cued with oak wood smoke for twelve hours.

Bob Barns owns the Rockin'Q but was out to lunch the day I paid my visit.

Rating: 7.5

3812 Penbrook (behind the H.E.B. on Grandview)
Odessa, Texas 79762
Phone 915-552-7105
Fax 915-363-9467

Counter order, drive thru, take-out, catering. Beer served. Brisket plate $5.99.

Opens 11 A.M. Closes 9 P.M. Sunday through Thursday and 10 P.M. Friday and Saturday. Accepts credit cards.

Sam's Bar-B-Q and Blues Alley

Blues and barbecue go together at Sam's. Blues men like Jimmy Rogers, Greg Piccolo, Sonny Rhodes, and Larry Garner pour their souls out playing weekends at Sam's while Lee Hammond, owner of Sam's, serves soul-satisfying barbecue all week long.

I ordered samples of the barbecue and gave them the test. The brisket had a 3/16-inch pink ribbon. The aroma sang the blues. It took a sturdy push with the edge of my fork to part the brisket. It had some fat, and the flavor had a catchy melody. I gave it a 7. The pork ribs made the blues hit parade. Louie Armstrong soloed the flavor. I could barely hear the fat. And the rib was as tender as Peggy Lee. I gave it an 8. The sausage was homemade, 85% beef. I pushed the middle valve down, and two drops of fat came 'round. The flavor got me humming, and I scored the sausage with an 8.

I detected cayenne, paprika, mustard, ketchup, and Worcestershire sauce in the barbecue sauce. It had one-alarm fire.

Sam's serves the regular sides of potato salad, coleslaw, and pinto beans.

I had a choice of peach or cherry cobbler for dessert.

Finished with my meal, I studied the dining room. An oversized wagon wheel chandelier hung from a high cathedral ceiling. Ceiling fans moved as fast as the beginning of "St. James Infirmary." A large wood-burning fireplace filled the end wall. Red tablecloths complimented a polished brick floor. An adjacent room had the bar, bandstand, and dance floor.

Lee Hammond showed me his steel barbecue pits mounted on stands. He likes smoking with mesquite coals. He rubs the brisket with salt, pepper, garlic powder, cayenne, and black pepper and 'cues it about five hours.

Rating: 7.5

220 North Grandview Avenue, Odessa, Texas 79761-4937

Phone 915-334-6112

Menu order, take-out, catering, banquet facilities. Full bar. Brisket plate $6.50.

Open 11 A.M. to 9 P.M. Closed Sunday. Accepts credit cards.

Lee served in the Army 21 years. His uncle in Sherman, Texas, taught him the art of making sausage.

Sam's is worth a visit.

Pecos

Leroy's Bar-B-Que

A sign in Leroy's Bar-B-Que reads, "Sometimes we ain't here at all or lately we've been here just about all the time except when we're someplace else."

Don't worry. If you are concerned about whether or not Leroy's is open, just ask anyone in Pecos. They all know except Leroy.

The building and everything in Leroy's are a throwback to the thirties. It's clean, friendly, and small. Sound bounces off its hard walls. While waiting for my order, I couldn't help but hear everybody's conversation. The talk that caught my ear came from a gray-haired gent talking to another sexagenarian (that doesn't mean what you think it means). "He sure got some bad-lookin' country out there," said Charlie.

"That right?" said Bob.

"Got a few Black Angus. Don't see how he makes it."

You hear conversation like that and you know you are in the desert or very close to it.

The brisket had a 1/16-inch ribbon. *Bad news.* The meat severed with the second push of my fork. It had little fat, but the flavor was as poor as the land where the Black Angus roamed. I gave it a 7. They sold out of baby-back pork ribs, so I settled for some sausage. It was not barbecue, so I did not rate it.

The potato salad had some mustard and tasted bland. The pinto beans had bits of ham to pep up the flavor. Other sides were chef salad, soup, French fries, onion rings, and chili verde.

Rating: 7

900 West Third Street, Pecos, Texas 79772-2919

Phone 915-445-5110

Menu order, take-out, catering. No beer. Brisket plate $5.95.

Opens around 9 to 10, sometimes as early as 7 or as late as noon. Closes about 5:30 to 6, but sometimes 4:30 or 5 or maybe 11 A.M. or noon. Cash only.

For dessert, they offered pudding, pie, cobbler, and ice cream.

Laura and Herbert Esteve own this barbecue oasis. They have two metal barrel pits in back. They are very unconventional in their barbecuing. First they wrap the brisket up with a gallon of sauce and cook it all day. Then they smok it with hickory for six to seven hours.

Live and learn.

Pecos is known for its cantaloupe. Just when I thought this was a sleepy little town, I found out that they cover the land with black polyethylene and transplant seedlings to produce their crop.

My father, long ago deceased, was a geologist. He ate only Pecos melons. "The Pecos River valley is a confluence of the earth's richest minerals. You cannot find a better cantaloupe."

But what about the barbecue? Had he heard of Leroy's?

San Angelo

Jodie's

Jodie's does a big take-out business, especially with hams and turkeys. I ordered a small piece of each barbecue meat and sat at a solitary table, the only table in the restaurant. The décor was white and more white.

Rating: 8.5

1816 West Avenue North, San Angelo, Texas 76901

Phone and fax 915-949-5044

Dine in (one table), cafeteria style, take-out, catering. No beer. Brisket plate $4.20.

Open 10 A.M. to 3 P.M. Tuesday through Saturday. Closed Sunday and Monday. Accepts checks.

The brisket had an eighth-inch ribbon on it, and, when I pressed lightly against it with my fork, it parted. The flavor was superior and had very little fat. I gave the brisket an 8.5. Jodie's does not barbecue ribs, but they have sausage once in a while. Partner John Robbins makes the sausage when he's up to it. I did get pieces of ham and turkey. The ham was very tender, had above average flavor, and contained almost a zero amount of fat, and I gave it a 9. The turkey was extremely tender, had little fat, and had a very good flavor. I gave it a 9.

I could see why so many people bought their holiday and un-holiday hams and turkeys from Jodie's.

The potato salad recipe came from the mother of the original owner, Jodie. It has a tad of pickle juice in it and a speck of mustard for color. It was delicious. The pinto beans had chili powder, salt, garlic, and Season Supreme.

Dessert was completely different from other barbecue places. Jodie's offers only Mississippi Mud cake. No cobbler. No pecan pie. No banana pudding. Wife Valerie's mother, Pat Snow, makes this lovely concoction fresh every day Jodie's is open. The bottom layer is a cross between fudge brownie and cake. The next layer is a marshmallow crème. The top layer is rich, chocolate fudge. I gobbled it down. Some people come into Jodie's just for the cake.

Jodie's goes back to the sixties. Doc Scott owned it then and sold it to Jodie in 1970. John and Valerie Robbins became the owners in 1998. Doc Scott died a few years back. This brings up an eerie story. Sometimes the front door opens mysteriously for no apparent reason. When it does, employees whisper, "It's Doc Scott."

The door opened, and I hurried out. Driving away, the thought of sending all my favorites a Jodie's Mississippi Mud cake for Christmas crossed my mind. *Maybe send a turkey to the "turkeys" and a ham to the "hams."*

Mule Creek Bar-B-Q

Rating: 8.75

1207 West Beauregard Street, San Angelo, Texas 76901
Phone 915-658-2740

Counter order, take-out, catering. No beer. Brisket plate $5.95.

Opens 11 A.M. Closes 8 P.M. Monday through Saturday and 3 P.M. on Sunday. Accepts credit cards.

Mule Creek barbecue is one of the best in West Texas.

Born in Texas, computer expert R. H. "Skipper" Gaston ended up in Kentucky. He decided to go into the barbecue business up there. He opened three places. One succeeded. He pined to return to Texas. He subscribed to the *San Angelo Standard-Times* newspaper and read that Mule Creek Bar-B-Q needed a new owner. He sold out in Kentucky, came home, and bought it.

I ordered at the counter, took my barbecue to the dining room, and began my tests. The brisket had a large pink ribbon. *Encouraging.* In the shear test, the meat parted with one slice of my fork. Mesquite smoke twitched my nose. It had very little fat. I rated it an 8. The beef rib impressed me. It was extremely tender, had very little fat, and the pink went all the way to the bone—as did the flavor. I gave the beef rib a 9. The pork rib also impressed. It had almost zero fat, superior flavor, was very tender, and I gave it a 9. I dug into a slice of boneless pork loin. It had superior flavor, above average tenderness, but had too much fat, and I tagged it with a 7. Polish sausage yielded a puddle of fat when I squeezed it. The flavor mumbled. Some people may like mild sausage. I like sausage with seasoning that makes sausage sausage and not bologna. I rated this sausage a 5. The chicken had above average tenderness, lacked flavor, and had some fat. I gave it a 7.

Three squeeze bottles of barbecue sauce graced the table. In the mild version, I detected ketchup, Worcestershire sauce, onion, and liquid smoke. The smoky sauce had more liquid smoke. The hot sauce clanged three-alarm. Watch out for this sauce. Have plenty of bread on hand to put out the fire.

Skipper told me that they have an old J&R rotisserie. He used mesquite wood and smoked the brisket for ten hours during daytime and maybe fifteen hours during nighttime. Up until this moment, I did not think a rotisserie could produce superior barbecue. But this old rotisserie allowed enough manual-control to provide the quality barbecuing of a long pit.

Side orders included pinto beans, potato salad, coleslaw, macaroni salad, green beans, baked beans, cut corn, and Spanish rice.

I had to choose from Mexican spice cake, pecan pie, and cobblers for dessert.

I looked around and thought the interior décor to be Tex Mex. Framed Windberg prints, old photographs, and other printed art brightened the walls. Antique farm implements vied for space. Ceiling fans sent zephyrs of air toward the brown brick Mexican tiles. Windows had Mexican arches. Hanging baskets held abundant ivy.

A Mule Creek specialty was longhorn stew. It had a thin tomato base, some chili powder, and chunks of lean barbecue.

When you go to Mule Creek barbecue, be sure to ask for some homemade corn bread.

Old Time Pit Bar-B-Que

At first glance, it looked like a mosquito fogger loomed ahead. Smoke poured out onto the street. Then I realized the smoke came from a charcoal furnace at Old Time Pit Bar-B-Que. All that mesquite smoke going up into the heavens without touching a piece of meat. *Another disciple of charcoal grilling.*

I found a parking spot among all the pickups and sports utility vehicles. The building had a front porch and looked like a setting for an oater movie. I entered an area screened in on three sides. A man stood at a serving pit, and three cooking pits hunkered behind him. I ordered my cuts of barbecue, went through the usual door into the main dining room, and selected sides and dessert from a serving line. Raw wood walls and ceiling, ceiling fans, and a concrete floor fashioned the interior.

The brisket showed a small pink ribbon. The aroma beckoned. The meat parted with slight pressure from my fork. Very little fat showed. The flavor warbled a love song. I bestowed an 8 upon it. A beef rib had little fat, superior flavor, and tenderness beneath the crust. I gave it an 8. A super surprise came with a bite of a pork rib. I found it very tender, had little fat and great flavor, and packed one-alarm fire. I gave it a 9. The sausage yielded three drops of fat and had above average flavor. I gave it a 7.

The potato salad, pinto beans, and coleslaw were typical. If I had room, I would have tried corn on the cob, green beans, and new potatoes. They looked good in the serving line.

Texas regulars made the dessert list: apple, cherry, and peach cobblers and banana pudding.

The manager verified that Old Time Pit did use coals to barbecue.

Whatever, Old Time Pit's barbecue sure hit the spot with me.

Rating: 8.5

1805 South Bryant Boulevard, U.S. Hwy. 87 and U.S. Hwy 277, San Angelo, Texas 76903-8707

Phone 915-655-2771

Cafeteria style, take-out, catering. Beer served. Brisket plate $5.49 per pound.

Opens 10:30 A.M. Closes 9 P.M. Sunday through Thursday and 10 P.M. Friday and Saturday. Closed Sunday. Accepts credit cards.

Smokehouse BBQ

"You better hurry up and finish. Burt is coming."

I looked up. "Oh yeah?"

"Burt's in charge of the barbecuing, and he's been known to set the place on fire."

I asked Burt if that was true. He said he could not deny it. "Let me tell you about the biggest fire I had. One day it seemed like everybody knew we were running out of brisket. People lined up, and I had to hurry up the barbecuing. I threw on some more logs and got the heat up pretty high. I looked inside the pit and flames started rolling. Something told me that I'd better get out of the way, so I jumped back. Flames shot up 20 feet. The Fire Department came. Fire trucks were everywhere. They roped the place off. A crowd gathered, and the Fire Department finally got the fire out."

As I pondered that, I became thankful that today's business was slow and that Burt might keep away from the pit.

"One thing that fire did real good was to clean the pit. All the buildup in that pit just crumbled off."

"What about the meat?"

"Ashes at the bottom."

When Sue and Burt Whitaker came to San Angelo, Sue could not find a job. Sue's brother had a barbecue business in Salado and encouraged her to buy the Smokehouse. Sue and Burt became fast learners.

I went through the line, took my tray of small portions of meat to a table, and began my analysis. The brisket had a quarter-inch pink ribbon. *Another rotisserie.* The fork test parted the meat with a little shove. The aroma and flavor scored above average, and it was lean. I rated the brisket a 7. The pork rib delighted my palate. The rib had some fat, above average tenderness, and flavor that zinged. I gave the pork rib an 8. The Polish sausage had a lot of fat and little flavor, and I gave it a 5.

Rating: 7.5

3302 West Beauregard, San Angelo, Texas 76901
Phone 915-942-0868

Cafeteria style, take-out, catering, drive thru. No beer. Brisket plate $5.95.

Open 11 A.M. to 7 P.M. Monday through Saturday. Closed Sunday. Accepts checks.

Smokehouse prided itself on its potato salad. The recipe came from Al Bagley, who has a barbecue place in Big Springs and is renowned for potato salad. I found the base creamy, the potatoes firm, and relish thin. I liked it. The coleslaw, pinto beans, and macaroni salad had traditional recipes.

For dessert, I had a choice of cherry or peach cobbler.

Finished with the meal, I surveyed the interior and tagged it country.

Burt took me out back and showed me the pit. It was a very old rotisserie. *Ah, ha. I knew it.* They burned mesquite and barbecued the brisket twelve or more hours depending on the temperature outside. "On a cold day," Burt said, "in San Angelo it may take eighteen hours before that fork might slip out."

Smokehouse had three sauces: mild, smoky, and hot. In the mild sauce, I detected maybe lemon, honey, black pepper, vinegar, ketchup, and some Worcestershire. The mild sauce apparently made the base for the other two. The amount of liquid smoke and hot sauce made the difference in the other two sauces. The hot sauce bonged two alarms, and the Smokehouse sauce had three-fire heat.

If you want to try them out, you had better hurry. No telling when Burt may start another inferno.

Part Three

Gulf Coast

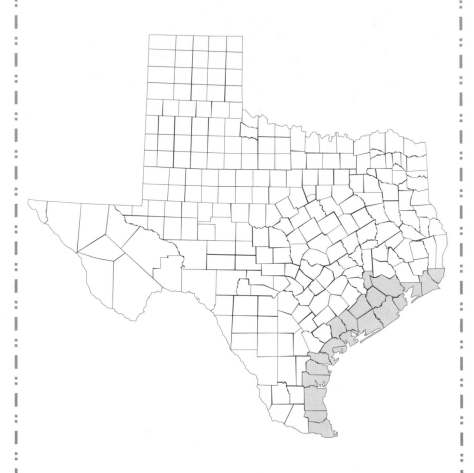

Alvin

Joe's Barbeque Company

Rating: 8.5

1400 East Hwy. 6, Alvin,
Texas 77511
Phone 281-331-9626
Fax 281-331-5016
E-mail joesbbq@flash.net
Web site www.joesbbq.com

Menu order, take-out, catering, banquet facilities. Beer served. Brisket plate $6.95.

Opens 11 A.M. every day, closes 10 P.M. Sunday through Thursday and 11 P.M. Friday and Saturday. Checks and credit cards accepted.

The Houston Chronicle picked Joe's Barbeque (that is the way he spells it) as one of the top five restaurants in the Houston area. Inspired by that fact, I headed for Alvin. I almost missed Joe's because the building was so huge. Joe's building looked big enough to be a gymnasium. I parked beside a windmill and entered a large room three plus stories tall. Shooting straight up to the ceiling in the middle of the room was a 6x9 stone chimney. Exposed wooden trusses supported an expansive cathedral ceiling. Fans spun from long pipes attached to the ceiling. I decided to stop looking like a gawking tourist and moved to the counter at the back of the area. I ordered one small slice of brisket. The server, who happened to be the manager, gave me that you-have-to-be-kidding look. He complied with my request and, maybe because I am elderly, gave me the brisket free of charge. Thanking him, I switched my role to one of adversary. I knew the meat could not be very good, because the New York

City owned monthly magazine of Texas did not mention it in the top 50 barbecue places in Texas.

Observing the brisket, I noticed a bit too much fat. I lightly pressed my plastic fork edge against it. It did not give. *I knew it.* I pressed a little more. The meat fell apart. I eagerly sniffed it. Good aroma. I carefully chewed this delicacy. The flavor was very good. I did what my conscience told me: I gave it a 9. I hurried back to the order counter. I asked for a two-inch slice of sausage and a pork rib. The manager smiled and said, "This time it's going to cost you." I nodded. $2.06.

Back at the table, I picked up the rib and saw a little bit too much fat on it. I took a bite. *Delicious and tender.* I gave the rib an 8. The sausage came from Eckermann's of New Ulm, Texas. It was made with Joe's recipe and contained half beef and half pork. It had good seasoning. I squeezed it and two drops of fat came out. I gave it an 8.

Then I met owner Joe Saladino, an affable guy, who lives with a smile on his face. I gave him my card, and he was pleased to know I was from Fredericksburg. It turned out that he owned a beautiful piece of land, a few miles north of Fredericksburg, overlooking Enchanted Rock. We talked barbecue. He showed me his barbecue pits, located in another building behind the restaurant. He had four 4'x15' half-inch steel pipe pits for smoking his brisket and three Southern Pride rotisserie pits for cooking the sausage. He stated flatly that the rotisseries would never replace the pits for smoking brisket and ribs. He contended that the rotisseries cooked too fast and made the beef tough. He revealed that he begins 'cueing brisket at 3 A.M.

First they take all meat in the pits out and begin new batches. They rub the new brisket with his secret ingredients. He 'cues at a low heat and uses nothing but post oak from Goldthwaite, Texas. The beef is Iowa Beef Packer U.S. Choice or better.

I told him I was amazed at the huge barbecuing pit complex. He explained he needed that much to feed from 850 to 1,000 people a day plus 150 to 200 catering jobs a month. He caters for NASA, Lockheed, Monsanto, and Amoco just to name a few of his 1,000 plus clients.

Joe's grandfather introduced him to barbecue. Grandfather had the Winkler Drive-In in Houston. When Joe got old enough, he started a four-table barbecue place in Manville (further up the road from Alvin toward Sugar Land). At the same time, he worked for Hendrix Food. Hendrix sold out to SYSCO, and the first edict from the new owner to all employees was to wear a coat and tie. That did it. Joe resigned and went to work full time at his Manville place. The rest marked success. Today, he has sixty-three loyal employees and sales of $3.5 million.

Side orders abound at Joe's. He presents a large buffet as well as the usual orders of potato salad, pinto beans, and coleslaw. He said they make everything from scratch including fabulous blackberry, peach, and cherry cobblers. The only exception is Blue Bell ice cream. Get this: You can eat all the dessert you want.

Nolan Ryan spends a lot of time eating here as does Bum Phillips, George Strait (this man gets around), Rudy Tomjanovich, and Warren Moon. Maybe you ought to add your name to the list.

Angleton

Bo's Barbecue House

Angleton neighbors the Brazoria National Wildlife Refuge, the nesting area for mottled ducks and home to many marsh and waterfowl. The highest number of species of birds in the U.S. concentrates here including roseate spoonbills, great blue herons, and sandhill cranes.

I found another large concentration of creatures, barbacoa carnivores, at Bo's Barbecue House. Most are locals, but "birders" also attend. Birders can be detected. Look for longer necks and noses.

I went through the cafeteria line, and the server cut me small samples of barbecue. I sat down next to a man who had the peculiar habit of jutting his lower jaw. Perhaps it helped him swallow. *Strange. Pelican like.*

The brisket had a familiar quarter-inch pink ribbon. *Another rotisserie?* In the shear test, the meat parted with the second slice of the fork. It had little fat, above average flavor and leanness. I gave it my usual rotisserie 7. The pork rib had too much fat but above average flavor. It was fall-apart tender. I gave it a 7. The Polish sausage surrendered a puddle of fat from the squeeze test. The flavor was like bologna. It came from J Bar B in Houston. I hammered it with a 4.

I identified onion (maybe), vinegar, ketchup, and Worcestershire sauce in the secret barbecue sauce.

Rating: 7

2024 East Highway 35,
Angleton, Texas 77515-3923
Phone 409-849-0781
Fax 409-849-0011

Cafeteria style, take-out, catering. Beer served. Brisket plate $6.25.

Opens 11 A.M. Closes 8 P.M. Sunday through Thursday and 9 P.M. Friday and Saturday. Accepts credit cards.

Potato salad, pinto beans, and coleslaw had traditional ingredients. A popular dish was barbecue stuffed baked potato. I had three choices for dessert: brownie fudge cake, cheesecake, and pecan pie.

Chasing my food with a sip of water, I studied the interior. I dubbed it ranch style. It had a cathedral ceiling with steel beams, dark walnut paneling, picnic tables with plywood tops and benches, and wagon wheel chandeliers. Ceiling fans twirled and ESPN clattered on the TV.

Owner Tom Tilton and I talked barbecue. He confirmed my suspicion about the rotisserie. He said they rubbed the brisket with pepper and garlic powder and then smoked it for eighteen hours.

His parents, Bo and Alice, started the business in 1971. They sold it to Tom in 1975. "We have the best barbecue in the state," Tom said. "We sell a ton of barbecue. We do it right and treat our people right."

The Wildlife Refuge holds "Open Houses" twice a month, the Brazosport Birders host on the first weekend of the month, and the Friends of the Brazoria National Wildlife Refuge host the third weekend of the month. Visitors can take an auto tour, walk bird-watching trails, fish from a pier, hunt waterfowl in season, and peck at barbecue at Bo's Barbecue House.

Aransas Pass

Mac's Pit Barbecue

See **Gregory,** Texas, (pg. 48) for more information.

Rating: 7.5

1933 West Wheeler, Business Hwy. 35, Aransas Pass, Texas 78336

Phone 512-758-0641

Menu order, drive thru, catering. No beer. Beef plate $5.50.

Opens 11 A.M. Closes 9 P.M. Monday through Saturday and 8 P.M. Sunday.

Bay City

A & A Bar-B-Que & Catering

Allen Korenek, the owner of A & A, is the son-in-law of Rosemary and W. C. Hinze, owners of Hinze's Bar-B-Que & Catering in Wharton, Texas. Unlike his in-laws, he located in a hard-to-find place in Bay City.

Now Bay City is not on the way to anywhere, unless you fish, hunt, or like to look at nuclear power plants. The South Texas Project Electric Generating Station lies south of Bay City. It is one of the largest and most advanced nuclear power plants in the world. The plant attracts protestors, and the cooling pond of the plant has more than fifty alligators that like tourists.

I was attracted to A & A by a realtor who claimed it to be the best in the state. It took me a while to find it, but once I realized the streets ran alphabetically, it presented no problem. I arrived late, and the main lunch crowd had dispersed. Three cars sat in a huge asphalt parking lot.

I viewed a tan building with a metal roof and two unadorned picture windows. The sign and a huge stack of pecan logs provided the only color.

I strolled in, went up to the counter, and ordered a small slice of brisket. I received that beyond-belief look. "Is that all? How about some bread?"

"Thanks. And some sauce on the side."

"Would you like it on a silver tray?" He laughed. I laughed.

I reposed on what might be called an American ladder-back chair. I thought of the room as country Spartan. Three long rows of uncovered fluorescent ceiling lights contributed to the bleakness. I placed my tray on the wooden table and dropped my napkin on a light muddy-colored tile floor. I picked it up knowing it was clean, because the place was spotless. The walls had imitation wood paneling, but the

Rating: 8

1601 Avenue H, Bay City, Texas 77414

Phone 409-244-5186

Counter order, take-out, catering. Serves beer. Brisket plate $4.75.

Opens 10:30 A.M. Closes 4 P.M. Sunday and 9 P.M. Monday through Saturday. Accepts checks and credit cards.

wall behind the counter was genuine vertical beaded board. Continuous mirrors ran above the beaded board. I suppose the mirrors hung there to make the room seem larger, although the room was big enough to seat eighty.

Looking at the brisket, I found the mark of the rotisserie smoker: a quarter-inch ribbon. *Whoever sells these rotisseries must be a very good salesperson. They are popping up everywhere. What happened to good, old-fashioned pits?* I pushed on the slice of meat with my fork. With the extra effort it always takes to fork slice a rotisserie smoked brisket, the meat parted. The aroma sang. *Hmm.* I could not see any fat. I champed on it. It inspired me. I came up with a slogan for the rotisserie people: "Tough but superior flavor!" I gave the brisket an 8.

Since a rating of 6 can get a barbecue place in my book, I headed back to the counter for more 'cue. I bought one pork rib, two inches of sausage, and a slice of Boston butt pork. I think the man behind the counter enjoyed my tightwad approach.

At the table again, I sampled the rib. It had very good flavor, was tender, and had a little fat. I gave it an 8. I squeezed the sausage and too much fat dripped out. The flavor was mild. I gave it a 6. The slice of Boston butt pork had a light seasoning, which I enjoyed. It had above average tenderness and little fat. I rated it an 8.

I bought a slice of chicken and a slice of ham. They were both tender and had mild flavor. I gave each an 8.

Since this was the sixth place I had been to that day, I asked for small samples of side orders. The guy must have felt sorry for me, he gave them to me free of charge. The potato salad, pinto beans, and coleslaw tasted normal, the way most folks like them.

A big seller here—and it seems almost everywhere in Texas these days—was the barbecue meat stuffed baked potato.

Dessert consisted of pecan pie and cobblers.

Allen Korenek had taken his boy to baseball practice but hurried back to talk with me. He related that he did indeed have a rotisserie smoker. He said he smoked brisket for eighteen hours. I told him that most rotisserie owners smoke in less time. He agreed and said the extra time adds to the flavor.

Checking my notes on other places, I found that my mark for his brisket flavor was one mark higher than most.

I asked Allen if anything unusual happened here. "Houston Oilers used to eat here all the time. One thing big here is the Bay City Rodeo Barbecue Cook-off in March. The winner goes to the Houston Rodeo and Livestock Show Barbecue Cook-off. Other than that, not much has happened around here since the Oilers left."

I complemented him on his food and I was gone.

Next time you head this way to go fishing or hunting or to see a giant alligator, stop for lunch at A & A Bar-B-Que. You will be a happy gourmand.

Beaumont

Luther's Bar-B-Q

See **Houston** listing of Luther's Bar-B-Q on page 60 for further information.

Rating: 7.5

5860 Eastex Freeway, Beaumont, Texas 77708-4824
Phone 409-899-2485

Counter order, take-out, catering. Beer served. Brisket plate $7.59.

Opens 11 A.M. Closes 10 P.M. Sunday through Thursday and 11 P.M. Friday and Saturday. Accepts credit cards.

Willy Ray's Bar-B-Q & Grill

Rating: 10

145 Interstate 10 North, Beaumont, Texas 77707
Phone 409-832-7770
Fax 409-832-4371

Cafeteria style, take-out, catering. Serves beer. Brisket plate $6.50.

Opens 11 A.M. Closes 9 P.M. Sunday through Thursday and 10 P.M. Friday and Saturday. Accepts credit cards.

Come hungry 'cause Willy Ray's may be the best 'cue in Texas. Get set for some lip-smackin' homemade sausage—arguably the best ever made. I bestowed a 10 on the sausage.

Of course, this whole thing started with my

testing brisket. The brisket fell apart when I touched the meat with my fork. The aroma awakened my senses. The brisket melted in my mouth. *That's grand championship brisket.* I gave it a 10. *What's going on here? Two tens?* Folks who like their ribs on the sweet side will give the ribs a 10. They were tender but had a little too much fat. I gave the ribs an 8. The ham got a 10 and the turkey a 6 (slightly on the dry side and lacking flavor).

Side dishes change daily, but I'm told by others that the carrot soufflé is always there. I don't rate side dishes, but this deserved a rave. I think the soufflé had a gingersnap topping. I gave it an 11. The boiled cabbage also deserved a rave. It had a dash of cilantro.

I started to give Willie Ray's an all around rating of 9 until I saw Stewart's Sodas in an ice barrel. Willy Ray's is a first-class act.

The décor is definitely saloon style. A large crystal chandelier and numerous ceiling fans hang from a pressed metal ceiling over a bare concrete floor. A classic longhorn head oversees eleven booths, fourteen tables, and many smiles.

Owner Mike Dougay says he slow cooks the meat up to sixteen hours using only wood. I checked out back and found oak and hickory.

Willy Ray's is the real thing, and it's Bee's (my wife's) favorite place.

Bellaire

Hickory Pit Bar-B-Que

Hickory Pit began in 1959. I found two big reasons why some places stay on the scene: children who continue the business and great barbecue.

Costas Kondylopoulus is a second-generation owner of this place. It has not been easy. In 1996 the City of Bellaire widened Bissonnet Road, and Costas lost half his of his already limited parking space. Despite the inconvenience, customers park a block away and walk to their favorite barbecue spot.

The building is old but well maintained. The interior is not the Waldorf Astoria but it's neat and clean. Old pictures of Houston and Bellaire hang on the walls, and a small TV softly broadcasts ESPN. Costas personally greets his customers, most by their first name. This is a small town restaurant in a big city.

Rating: 8

6601 South Rice Avenue at Bissonnet, Bellaire, Texas 77401

Phone 713-666-0661

Cafeteria style, take-out, custom cooking. Serves beer. Brisket plate $6.24.

Open 11 A.M. to 8:30 P.M. Monday through Saturday. Closed Sunday. Accepts credit cards.

A slice of barbecued brisket had a rotisserie-like quarter-inch pink ribbon. The brisket showed little fat, and I parted the meat with light pressure from my fork. The flavor sang "O-opah." I rated it a 9. A pork rib had a little too much fat, superior tenderness and flavor. I gave it a 7. The pork and beef sausage gave up two drops of fat from the squeeze test, and the flavor shined. I gave it an 8.

Costas peppers his chicken. My piece was moist and tender but had a little too much fat and not enough flavor. I tagged it with a 6. The ham was salty, but the smoke flavor came through. It had a little fat and was tender. I labeled it with an 8. A slice of turkey had great tenderness, superior flavor, almost zero fat. It was moist but a little salty. I gave it a 9.

Sides: pinto beans, potato salad, French fries, cheese fries, coleslaw, onion rings, and vegetable rice.

Dessert: What dessert would you expect from a Greek American owner with Tex-Mex employees in a barbecue place? Greek baklava, of course. But for all you diehard Texans like Costas, there's peach cobbler.

Costas hickory smokes his brisket for twelve hours in an old-fashioned metal pit built into the building. No rotisserie here (and no gauge or thermometer either). He puts in four or five sticks in the evening and then checks it at 8 A.M.

"When you come to Hickory Pit," said Costas, "you have the same cook, the same people working the same job. It has a family atmosphere, and we know our customers and call them by their first name."

"See ya."

"Efcharisto."

Brazoria

Kresta's B.B.Q. Restaurant & Catering Service

Rita and George Brenhem started selling barbecue from their house in 1979. A year later they moved into a restaurant that went out of business. That year they won the barbecue cook-off at the Houston Livestock Show and Rodeo (the biggest in the state). They outgrew the place in town, and when everybody else moaned from the eighties oil crunch (a depression in Texas), they built and moved into their present ranch-style building.

Rating: 7.5

From Hwy. 36 turn west onto Hwy. 521. Go 300 yards.
Brazoria, Texas 77422
Phone 409-798-9563

Counter order, take-out, catering, banquet facilities.
Brisket plate $6.25.

Pulling into the parking lot, I spied a full-size statue of a Charolais bull standing beneath the roof overhang. I knew instantly that the entrance was not that way. Entering, I sensed that the food had to be good. The décor was country. Farm implements covered the walls.

Open Monday through Friday from 10 A.M. until 3 P.M. Closed Saturday and Sunday. Catering and banquets at night. Checks accepted.

I ordered at the counter, sat down, and commenced my tests. The brisket parted with a stout push of the fork. The aroma was inviting. The ribbon measured a quarter of an inch. *Smoked too fast and too hot. Another rotisserie.* The flavor was superior and the meat lean. I rated it a 7. The pork ribs had good flavor, little fat, and were tender. I gave them an 8. The sausage was half beef and half pork. The flavor was above average, but it had too much fat. I gave the sausage a 7.

The sauce stood out. I detected onion, brown sugar, vinegar, Worcestershire sauce, and ketchup.

Side orders of potato salad, pinto beans, and coleslaw contained no surprises. Onion rings tasted good and were not greasy, and a long salad bar added to the fare.

Beneath ceiling fans suspended from a cathedral ceiling, I cooled off as I talked with partner George. He told me that everything was made fresh every day, including pies, cobblers, and cakes. The brisket was live oak and pecan smoked in a Southern Pride rotisserie from ten to twelve hours. The cook applied a secret rub. When done, the brisket landed in a cooler. Then they warmed it up before they served it.

"Folks seem to like it," George said with a smile.

Clute

Brian's Bar-B-Q

When Larry Wright, CEO of Dow North America, wants to impress associates in Midland, Michigan, he flies an order of barbecue from Brian Devine's place to Michigan via Lear Jet.

If you want some "Devine" barbecue, you could pick it up in your jet or you could have it shipped some other way or you could show up at one of Brian's two barbecue places.

Dow has a large chemical plant in Freeport, and when Larry Wright worked there, he frequented

Rating: 7.5

151 Commerce, Clute, Texas and 201 Park Ave E, Freeport, Texas 77531
Phone 409-265-1232
Fax 409-265-5757

Counter order, catering. Beer served. Brisket plate $4.75.

Brian's. He fell in love with the place and kept coming back. I understood why when I sampled Brian's
barbecue.

Open from 11 A.M. to 8 P.M.
Monday through Saturday.
Closed Sunday. Checks and
credit cards accepted.

I pulled into the parking lot and observed the
place. A sculpted, full-size bull perched *on* the over-
hang leading to the door. The exterior hiccuped steel building saloon, and the
interior mooed ranch. The head of a huge buffalo garnered my attention as I
entered. It was not just a stuffed head, it was the entire front half of a buffalo.
Surveying the room of raw wood paneling, I spotted a sailfish, a wooden
Indian, and a jackalope. Shelves packed collectibles. A sign read, "BEWARE
OF PICKPOCKETS AND LOOSE WOMEN." Bravely, I sauntered up to the
counter and ordered one small slice of brisket. You should have seen the look
I got. The server cut a slice and put it on a plate. "Bread?"

"Please, and sauce on the side."

He gave me a fixed customer-is-always-right smile.

I paid my 92 cents and sat down. In minutes, they brought me a plate with
all their barbecue and side orders. *They were on to me. The barbecue owners
had to be in cahoots. Surely another owner called and told these folks I was on
my way. Or, maybe they figured that only a snoop would order a small slice of
brisket? Why fight it?* I dug in. The brisket had the familiar quarter-inch ribbon that blared "rotisserie." The meat parted with an extra push of the fork.
It had little or no fat. The flavor was mild. I gave it a 7. The pork ribs had good
flavor, little fat, and were extremely tender. I gave them an 8. Eckermann's
Meat Market, Shelby, Texas (between Brenham and LaGrange), supplies the
half beef, half pork sausage. It oozed three drops of fat from the squeeze test.
I thought the flavor was above the norm. I rated it a 7. The chicken was
moist, tender, and low in flavor. I gave it an 8. The ham and the turkey scored
the same as the chicken.

The side orders included the regulars: pinto beans, potato salad, and coleslaw. The former two were average, and the slaw was sweet.

Barbecue stuffed baked potatoes sold rapidly. The servers piled on the
meat and other fixings.

Sweet tooth lovers chose from banana pudding, carrot cake, pecan pie,
and other cakes.

Through eating, I noticed a large black object protruding in the back banquet room. Curious, I moseyed back and found—astonishingly—the rest of
the buffalo.

Brian Devine introduced himself and we palavered. He started as a dishwasher in DJ's in 1979.

He allowed that he buys Iowa Beef Packer meat, and before he smokes the meat, he rubs it with secret ingredients. Then he sits the meat in tubs for twenty-four hours. They 'cue brisket twenty-two to twenty-six hours, and keep the temperature between 200 and 220 degrees. He uses nothing but live oak wood for his fire.

Like the buffalo, you should end up here.

DJ's BBQ

This is a story about the American Dream, a Horatio Alger thing.

Six years ago D. J. Hybner told his hard-working young employee Rory Neal that he was selling his business to him. Rory jumped on his offer, continued to toil, and now has something to show for it. Rory started as a dishwasher. Today, he wears about ten hats. His main job is to provide customer satisfaction. "I'm thirty-one, and I've been here sixteen years. If I don't know about barbecue now, I guess I never will."

From the outside, the place looked like another restaurant. Brown wood paneling concealed the steel building structure. The inside intrigued. Hybner hand built fourteen picnic tables with benches. He used large planks of wood. I had that homey feeling the moment I spotted the benches. Old farm contraptions hung on the walls. Wagon wheels were everywhere.

Entering, I strolled up to the counter and ordered a sampler of everything. Parked on one of the picnic benches, I observed the brisket. It had a familiar quarter-inch of pink ribbon. *A Southern Pride rotisserie?* The brisket parted with a second strong push of my fork. The aroma did not sing. It appeared to be on the lean side, which I like. I champed it down. It had better-than-average flavor. I rated it a 7. The pork ribs were exemplary. Although they had too much fat (meaning they were cooked too fast), the ribs had superb flavor and melted in my mouth. I gave them a 9. The sausage was Polish. If you like bologna, you would like this

Rating: 8

906 West Plantation Street,
Clute, Texas 77531
Phone 409-265-6331

Counter order, take-out, catering, banquet facilities. Serves beer. Brisket plate $5.50.

Opens 11 A.M. Closes at 3 P.M. Monday and 8 P.M. Tuesday through Saturday. Closed Sunday. Checks and credit cards accepted.

sausage. H&B in El Campo makes it. When I eat sausage, I want sausage, not bologna. I gave it a 5.

The sauce had a thick consistency, and I loved it. I detected lemon, garlic, onions, black pepper, salt, thick ketchup (maybe a paste), little sweetness, and a touch of Worcestershire sauce.

DJ's big seller was a stuffed baked potato. They piled chopped barbecue—brisket, sausage, ham, and turkey—on it along with standard fixings. It sold for $3.95.

Desserts included cookies, carrot cake, banana pudding, and mud pie.

Rory said he had two rotisserie pits. I asked him if they were Southern Pride and he affirmed it. *I knew it.* He added that he had a gigantic 48-inch by 15-foot barrel pit. He said they use live oak for wood and can cook seventy-two briskets in a day.

That is a lot of business.

Clute citizen Junior Fullen eats barbecue everywhere he goes. The best he has ever had is DJ's. "I went to DJ's the first day it opened up, and I've been going there every day since—unless if I'm sick or something. I don't know why I like it so much. That's the one food I don't get tired of eating."

Anybody hungry out there?

El Campo

Mikeska's Bar-B-Q

Rating: 8.75

218 Merchant (downtown)
and 4225 U.S. Hwy. 59 at
Bluecreek Road (exit after
city limits sign), El Campo,
Texas 77437
Phone 800-388-2552 or
409-543-8252
Fax 409-543-8296
E-mail mikbbq@wcnet.net
Web site www.mikeskabbq
.com

Welcome to the stuffed world of Mikeska's Bar-B-Q. Stuffed patrons and stuffed animals.

Dozens of each. Thrust your hand into the mouth of a twelve-foot alligator. Photo pose next to an elk or a deer or a goat or an antelope or a jackalope.

The Mikeska family got started in the meat business when papa was a member of a beef club back in the twenties, before refrigeration. Members met every Saturday, and they butchered a calf. They started at 4 A.M. so the meat would be reasonably cool. They cut the calf into hunks that would feed a family for three to four days. Members went straight home and cooked the meat. Refrigeration came along, and beef clubs died out. Then Maurice became a butcher in 1945 at the Merchant Street address. This original building had two previous owners and was probably fifty years old at that time.

Menu order, take-out, catering, banquet facilities. Drive thru at Merchant Street location. Serves beer. Brisket plate $4.95.

Opens at 8 A.M. Closes 8 P.M. Monday through Wednesday, 8:30 P.M. Thursday, Saturday, and Sunday, and 9 P.M. Friday. Checks and credit cards accepted.

The meat business declined so Maurice started barbecuing in 1952. Brothers did like Maurice, and at one time seven Mikeska barbecue places dotted the state. Age took its toll and the number is down to four: El Campo, Taylor, Columbus, and Temple.

The original place on Merchant Street is loaded with atmosphere of days gone by. The ranch-style building came together one addition at a time. You step back into the Old West when you go through the door. You order at the counter and sit down on benches that are probably older than you. The Hwy. 59 place is the opposite: new and spacious. The main dining room seats 200 and a banquet room next to it seats another 200. The pits at both places have white glazed Elgin brick and stainless steel. Pecan wood smokes brisket for twelve hours at 275 degrees. The meat is rubbed with a special seasoning the evening before it's 'cued. No sop is used.

The Mikeska brisket yielded to a firm slice with my fork, and the ensuing aroma enticed me. The ribbon measured about 5/16 of an inch. It had little fat, and the flavor murmured. I gave it an 8. The pork ribs had little fat, were chewy, and had superior flavor. I rated the ribs a 9. The sausage was homemade and tasted great. One drop of fat fell from the squeeze test. I gave it a 9 (a rare high rating from me for sausage). They make several kinds of sausage, but their best seller remains the half beef, half pork. I tried a slice of Boston butt pork. It had a very appetizing flavor. I remembered thinking I would come back another day and feast on this succulent meat. The chicken delighted. It was moist and tender, the flavor average. I gave it an 8.

Side orders are normal, the way most people like them. A mainstay is rice salad. Maurice said, "Rice farmers insist that we have it on the menu."

Desserts included banana pudding and pies: lemon, chocolate, Boston cream, apple, coconut, and the local favorite, pecan.

Maurice said that Wharton County has a barbecue cook-off in April. It has forty to fifty contestants. If you are interested, call the 800 number above.

Mikeska still has a meat market. Instead of raw meat, he offers smoked meats: barbecue and homemade beef jerky, sausages, and slabs of bacon. Turkey and ham are big holiday items. Thousands of orders inundate the place for Christmas. Better get your order in early.

Freeport

Brian's Bar-B-Q

Owner Brian Devine found this old hardware store named Toby's in Freeport. "It had to be a hundred years old," Brian said. "I had it renovated and hired Raphael Pantalone to paint murals. Just to see the murals is worth the trip."

The barbecue fared the same here as in Clute. See Brian's Bar-B-Q (page 41) under Clute, Texas.

Rating: 7.5

201 Park Avenue E, Freeport, Texas 77541

Phone 409-233-1232

Fax 409-265-5757

Counter order, catering. Beer served. Brisket plate $4.75.

Open from 11 A.M. to 8 P.M. Monday through Saturday. Closed Sunday. Checks and credit cards accepted.

Fulshear

Dozier's Grocery, Inc.

Some barbecue owners talk about how well they do in their town. Dozier's does well worldwide. President Bush loves Dozier's pecan smoked bacon. When he was president, the White House kitchen called Dozier's regularly. When the order was ready, a man always showed up and picked up the order.

When Dun Chow Ping, Prime Minister of China, visited Houston, he dined on Dozier's barbecue. Prime Minister of football, Bum Phillips, ate here,

Rating: 8

Two blocks north of FM 1093 (Westheimer Road out of Houston) on FM 359, Fulshear, Texas 77441

Phone 281-346-1411

Toll free 1-800-359-5017

as did movie actor Ben Johnson.

Then I came along, the critic, "Doctor of Doom" for some barbecue places.

Dozier's brisket fell apart when I touched it with my fork. The aroma strayed. It had little fat, and my bite produced above average flavor. I rated the brisket an 8. A pork rib had fall-off-the-bone tenderness, very good appearance, showed little fat and superior flavor. I gave it an 8. Dozier's homemade pure pork sausage gave up but one drop of fat from the squeeze test. It had a mild flavor, and I gave it a 7.5. The chicken had excellent flavor, little fat, but was a little on the dry side. I gave it an 8.

Counter order, take-out, catering. Serves beer. Brisket plate $6.40.

Open 9:30 A.M. to 6:30 P.M. Closed Sunday. Accepts checks and credit cards.

Then came the big winners, ham and turkey. Both had terrific pecan smoke flavoring. Both melted in my mouth. I gave them 10's.

Dozier's served creamy coleslaw, traditional pinto beans, and chunky and creamy potato salad.

No desserts, but if you want something sweet, the grocery store sells lots of bakery products, ice cream products, and candies.

Dozier's is a country store with a meat counter, but barbecue commands the most attention. The original Dozier's started in 1957 in a smaller building two blocks south. In 1969 owners Ed and Ug Dozier built the present store. Today's owners, brothers Smedley and Scott Evans, bought the business, including the property, in 1985.

Dozier's has an avalanche of pecan smoked turkey and ham sales during the holidays. Get your order in early.

Bee bought a pecan smoked ham to take home. That's 8 months early.

Galveston

Grand Prize Barbeque

The barbecue smoke smacked me in my face as I leaned into the Gulf wind and walked toward a joint at Winnie and 6th Streets in Galveston. Unlike the sound of Sirens, the aroma from the smoke drew me into this place, not to destroy me but to capture me and bring me back again and again. The sign said Grand Prize Barbeque.

I walked in wondering how a barbecue place could make it in seafood country. The place was

Rating: 8.5
627 Winnie, Galveston, Texas
Other locations: Texas City, Webster, Pearland, and Pasadena
Phone 409-750-9900

elbow to elbow. All the tables were high and had barstools. The music had strong vibrations, and the guests were loud. Dolls dazzled in sleek dresses and wore rocks and paint. Guys leaned over them. I found a stool and climbed on. A slinky lady in sharp threads gave me a hither look and pointed at the menu painted on the wall. This was a slick-looking place and I thought I'd get gouged, but the prices were cool. I looked into her deep blue eyes and gave her my order. She said she'd take care of me. She came back, loaded, and waited for my move. It was

E-mail
Superchop8@aol.com

Menu order, take-out, catering. Beer served. Brisket plate $6.95.

Opens at 10 A.M. Closes at 2:30 P.M. Sunday through Thursday, and 9 P.M. on Friday. Accepts credit cards.

love at first sight: a ribbon wider than a quarter inch on a good-looking slice of brisket. It split with a little extra pressure from my fork. The aroma sparked my senses. It was lean, tender, and had good to very good flavor. I gave the brisket an 8. The pork rib rocked me. Snazzy flavor. Very tender. Little fat. I gave it a 9. The link sausage had half beef, great seasoning, and some fat. I gave it an 8.

The waitress slinked up to me. I gave it to her straight. "You got what I like, doll. I'm rating you a 9."

She said she'd rather have a tip. "How about a thigh, a breast, and a leg?"

I couldn't turn her down. The chicken thigh was moist, flavorful, and had a mild flavor. I gave it an 8. The sliced breast of turkey was average. A piece of lamb's leg had too much fat but was better than most.

The place had all the regular sides plus jambalaya.

The boss, Kevin Yackley, has the reputation of a big buyer at the county fair. I suspect he can do that because Grand Prize Barbeque is a mob scene moneymaker.

I told the doll I'd come back. She said they all say that.

Gregory

Mac's Pit Barbecue, Inc.

Mac's is another family affair.

It is amazing how many barbecue places are like that.

Mother and father Mac Martinez started the business in 1974 and sold it to their three sons in 1998. Joe owns the Gregory restaurant, Jimmy the one in Aransas Pass, and Domingo the one in

Rating: 7.5

209 Hwy. 35 Gregory, Texas 78359 (a few miles north of Corpus Christi)

Rockport.

Gregory is a few miles north of Corpus Christi on the way to Aransas Pass and Rockport. The area boasts some of the best saltwater fishing and goose and duck hunting in the world, and east of Corpus lies South Padre Island and its National Seashore Park.

From the outside, Mac's looked like a taco joint, but inside it was pure country—ceiling fans spinning. I went through the cafeteria line and ordered a small slice of brisket. I got another pathetic look. "Need some bread?"

See other locations: Port Aransas and Rockport Phone 512-758-0641

Cafeteria style, take-out, catering. No beer. Brisket plate $5.50.

Opens 11 A.M. Closes 8 P.M. Monday through Wednesday, 9 P.M. Thursday through Saturday. Accepts checks and credit cards.

"Please, and sauce on the side." I paid my 83 cents and took a seat. Again I looked at a quarter-inch pink ribbon. *Another rotisserie. Half the places have them. The salesman must be rich.* I nudged the brisket with my fork. It did not budge. I pushed harder. Nothing. I had to cut it with a knife. Very little fat. I tasted it. The flavor did not sing, but it hummed. I had a tough time chewing it. I gave it my usual rotisserie-smoked-brisket rating of 7. I went back and ordered small portions of pork ribs, sausage, and chicken.

The ribs had a little too much fat but were above average in flavor and tenderness. I gave them a 7. The sausage yielded a drop of fat from the squeeze test. *Not bad.* It had very good seasonings, one-alarm-fire, and no fillers as far as I could determine. I gave the sausage an 8. The chicken scored big. It was taste bud stimulating, fat eradicating, and easy masticating. I bestowed a 9 on it. Then I noticed a slice of ham I did not order. *Was the server feeling sorry for an old homeless geezer? Or were they on to me?* The ham had mild flavor, no visible fat, and cut easy. I gave it a 7.

The barbecue sauce seemed normal—the way most people like it. I detected vinegar, ketchup, and Worcestershire sauce.

The pinto beans had chili powder, garlic powder, and some salt. The potato salad had a little bit of everything including egg and some homemade pickles. Other sides offered were whole kernel corn, green beans, and macaroni and cheese. I had some delicious oven hot bread that had bacon and onion in it.

Diners have their choice of apple or peach cobbler for dessert.

If you go fishing or hunting and wind up with nothing to show for it, stop by Mac's and take some good tasting barbecue home to the missus. You will not regret it.

Harlingen

Big John's Bar-B-Que

Six years ago this place had a produce stand and acres of cultivated land behind it. One thing led to another, and now a big barbecue restaurant that seats over a hundred people has taken over.

I strolled in and took a seat in a booth beneath a decorative roof shed. Waiting for a waitress, I took stock of the place. The décor said ranch style to me. Farm paraphernalia decorated the walls, and a large wagon stuffed with flowers sat in the middle of the room. Hundreds of displayed gimmie caps seemed to fit right in with the rural motif.

A long-eyelashed senorita-type waitress came over, and I ordered a small slice of brisket with sauce on the side. She gave me a strange look. *She probably thought "Big Spender."* When I got my order, I gave the brisket my version of a strange look. The ribbon appeared to be about a quarter inch but looked faded. It lacked strong aroma. The fork cut through with a second nudge. I spied some fat. The flavor was average and the brisket received a 7.

The waitress took my order for one pork rib and an inch of sausage. I knew what she was thinking, this guy's a lot of trouble and probably does not tip.

The plate came back with surprises. I had more than I ordered. *Somebody is onto me.* The first item on the plate was a pork rib. It had very good flavor, was tender but full of fat. I gave it a 7. *Fat lovers would give it a 10.* Next came barbecued pork loin. It had outstanding flavor and fell apart with a little nudge from my fork. Unlike most sliced pork or pork chops, it was moist. I gave it a 9. Next, I tried sausage. Polish. Average fat. Mild flavor. I gave it a 7. The meat from a second joint of chicken almost fell off the bone. It possessed good flavor. I gave it a 9. The last piece was a slice of turkey. It had good flavor, but I thought it a little dry. I gave it a 7.

Rating: 7.5

3806 West Business 83, Harlingen, Texas 78552
Phone 956-423-3240
Fax 956-423-3884

Menu order, take-out, banquet room, catering. Serves beer. Brisket plate $6.50.

Open Monday through Saturday at 11 A.M. Closed Sunday. Credit cards accepted.

The potato salad had big chunks of not-overcooked potato with skins. It had some sweetness. I detected sweetness in the coleslaw too. The pinto beans had onions and were normal in taste.

Big John's had a lot of sides. One really stood out: Texas Toothpicks. They deep fat fry dusted onion and jalapeño strips in corn oil or canola oil, which made it low in unsaturated fats.

Big John Graves of Big John's introduced himself, and we talked barbecue. Yes, he had been onto me. He wanted to know all about my book. I told him, and then he enlightened me with knowledge about his barbecue. He said he used mesquite and 'cued a little differently than others. He had a two-day process for brisket. The first day he 'cued the meat until it became medium done. Then he wrapped the meat in foil and sat it in a cooler overnight. The next day, he steamed it. *Ah ha. That is why the ribbon faded, the flavor was average, and the meats were so moist.*

He added that he sops the meat with secret seasoning, black pepper, salt, and Italian dressing. "Our meat is slow cooked to perfection, and our fixin's are prepared fresh every day right here by us."

I asked about Big John's formula for success in the barbecue business.

"We serve good food, give good service, nobody goes away hungry—we don't scrimp on food—and we're moderately priced. They come back."

I suspect another reason is that Big John's is a family affair. His wife, Sue, is active in the business, and they get a little help from Grandpa Graves, who steps aside and lets the younger generation slave away.

Houston

Baker's Ribs

Oink if you like barbecue. Beware of attack pig. Pig out at Baker's Ribs.

Enthused by such signage, I asked for a sample plate of meats, and I received beef brisket, a pork rib, hot link sausage, chicken, ham, and turkey. Three out of six were pork. Craig Biggio would accept that average. I did too.

The slice of brisket had a quarter-inch pink ribbon. I sniffed no aroma. The meat parted with a slight push from the edge of my fork. It possessed too much fat, and the flavor mumbled. I gave it a 6. Since a six gets an oink instead of a gong, I went on

Rating: 7

2223 South Voss Road, Houston, Texas 77057-3800
Phone 713-977-8725 or
281-505-1053

Cafeteria style, take-out, catering. Serves beer. Brisket plate $6.95.

Opens 11 A.M. Closes 9 P.M.
Monday through Saturday
and 7 P.M. Sunday. Accepts
checks and credit cards.

with my deliberations. A pork chop wore a pepper and savory spice rub. It had fall-apart tenderness, little fat, and superior flavor. I rated it an 8. The hot sausage hailed from Chappell Hill. It oozed four drops of fat from the squeeze test, and the flavor was above average with two-alarm fire. I tagged it with a 6. A piece of smoked chicken was extremely tender and moist. It had more fat than what I like to see, but the flavor shined. I gave it an 8. A slice of ham had salt, but the salt did not override the smoke flavor. It was very tender, had little fat, and smacked with superior flavor. I labeled the ham with a 9 and three oinks. A slice of smoked turkey breast had very good tenderness, above average flavor, and next to zero fat. I gave it an 8.

Baker's was out of pork shoulder when I arrived. *Must be popular.*

The barbecue sauce had the basic ingredients of Cattleman's Barbecue Sauce, but what was that added mysterious ingredient? Pickle juice?

Sides of potato salad, coleslaw, and pinto beans had standard recipes. Baker's also served dirty rice, marinated tomatoes made from grandmother's recipe, Texas caviar (black beans and corn salad), and a pasta salad. Like many other barbecue places, Baker's offered a stuffed baked potato with chopped barbecue beef. It went for $4.95.

Dessert came from the High Cotton Inn in Bellville, Texas. I chose from rum cake, rocky road cookies, or brownies.

The interior reminded me of a country kitchen. It had red-and-white checkered tablecloths, a raw wood exposed beam ceiling, concrete floor, and a corrugated metal serving counter. Pigs abounded.

Kelly Campbell is the owner. He was elsewhere, and an employee confided that they do in fact use hickory wood, and they smoke brisket in a handmade metal pit sixteen to twenty hours at 275 degrees.

Barbecue Inn

Frank Jungman and I went to Lamar Senior High back in the forties. On the second Tuesday of each month, us old Lamar guys get together and have lunch. Someone asked me what I was doing, and I sprung the news of my book about the best barbecue places in Texas. All other discussions ceased. I rapidly wrote their suggestions down on a pocket notepad. Finally, Frank said, "You're all wrong. The best barbecue place in Houston is the Barbecue Inn." Frank graduated number five in a class of 550. Seldom did he ever make an adamant statement. No one argued with him about his recommendation. Before leaving, Frank said to me, "Skippy and I try to get there early to avoid a long line."

Buoyed by his advice, I headed for the Barbecue Inn.

The place looked like a restaurant of the forties. *No wonder Frank liked it.* As soon as I went inside, I asked the hostess and found that they built the building in 1946.

The interior reminded me of a Frank Lloyd Wright design, especially the partitions' geometric patterns of dark-stained, one-inch boards.

My slice of brisket had a familiar quarter-inch ribbon. *Another rotisserie pit.* It had almost no fat, and the aroma beckoned me. I pressed lightly on the meat with my fork, and it fell apart. *This could not be a rotisserie.* I took a bite and discovered scintillating flavor. It was not the smoke as much as a rub that made the flavor so outstanding. I rated it a 9. A pork rib also had the seasoning rub. It had good appearance and showed little fat. A bite revealed superior tenderness and come-back-for-more flavor. I gave it a 9. A slice of pork had too much fat, but it was very tender and had exceptional taste. I tagged it with an 8. Unfortunately, I arrived after they sold out of sausage.

The beans tasted like Campbell's pork and beans

Rating: 9

116 West Crosstimbers,
Houston, Texas 77018
Phone 713-695-8112

Menu order, take-out. Serves beer. Brisket plate $6.45.

Open 10:30 A.M. to 10 P.M. Tuesday through Saturday. Closed Sunday and Monday. Accepts checks and credit cards.

with bits of green beans added. The coleslaw had a light, creamy base and bits of red bell pepper. The potato salad was like mashed potatoes with relish and egg thrown in.

Barbecue Inn offered a selection of pies and cheesecake for dessert.

I had a nice chat with part owner Wayne Skrehot. I asked him about his barbecue rub.

"No secret. It's Tex Joy."

He said they smoked their brisket in a Southern Pride rotisserie smoker.

I almost fell out of my chair. "How could this be?" I said and then explained how ninety-nine percent of rotisserie smoked meat turns out tough and with very little flavor.

"Many things. We use the rub. We buy only certified, aged longer, Black Angus beef. We use oak wood and smoke briskets twelve to fifteen hours at 220 degrees."

What the heck. It works.

Another Lamar friend, Frank Liddell, said that the Barbecue Inn was in Zagat's Top 40 and listed number one in barbecue. Frankly, who can argue with either Frank?

I asked Wayne if anything unusual happened here. He said that a man came in one evening and the hostess seated him. She asked if he would like anything to drink. He opened a magazine to a page of a pretty lady. He sat the magazine at the other end of his table and said, "This is my friend. She will be dining with me. Bring us both a cup of coffee, please." The hostess laughed, thinking it was a joke. She brought two cups of coffee and played along by setting a cup by the picture of the lady and then giving the man the other cup. The man talked to his companion and sipped his coffee. Then the waitress took his order, a specific entrée for the lady and a different entrée for the man. The man finished his meal, paid the check, folded up his magazine, took it with him, and left.

Bittersweet.

Billy Blues

The giant blue saxophone reigns over that white bread district known as Richmond Avenue. Entertainment joints fight for bucks, but the big sax magnetizes passing autos. They zip into the house of blues, Billy Blues, for barbecue and a cure for the blues.

How long can a soul suffer without them?

Rating: 7.5

6025 Richmond Avenue
(Richmond at Fountainview),
Houston, Texas 77057
Phone 713-266-9294
Fax 713-266-9296

Web site www.radiox.net/
BillyBlues

Menu order, take-out, catering, banquet facilities. Full
bar. Brisket plate $9.95.

Opens 4 P.M. Closes 12 A.M.
Monday through Thursday
and 2 A.M. Friday and Saturday. Closed Sunday. Accepts
credit cards.

Blues, the expression of a musician's soul.

Barbecue, the expression of a Texan's soul.

Artist Bob "Daddy-O" Wade created the sax. The reed is a surfboard. The bottom is an upside down Volkswagen. The hole covers are Volkswagen hoods. Odds and ends, including a beer keg, make up the rest.

I walked into an immense dining room with a full bar parked in the middle. I arrived too early to listen to a live blues band, but piped blues came through state-of-the-art speakers. I told the waiter what I wanted, and he understood. "Cool," he said and left.

When I received my plate of barbecue, the blues left me. I looked at a good-looking slice of brisket. It had a quarter-inch pink ribbon. *Another rotisserie*. The blues came back. The brisket had little fat. It took a second swipe of the fork to part the meat. The aroma said Basin Street, and the flavor sounded a couple of notes above middle C. I rated it an 8.

Baby-O bareback ribs gave my barbecue soul a lift—all the way to a 7. The score for Billy Blues sausage was a special rendition. "Fats" sang,

> *I squeezed the sausage and got two drops of fat.*
> *Oh no, no, no.*
> *I squeezed the sausage and got two drops of fat.*
> *I know, know, know.*
> *Billy Blues, now whaddaya think of that?*

The song did not help the flavor, and I gave the sausage a 6.

A piece of chicken had moisture and tenderness, little fat, and above average flavor. I hit it with an 8.

I detected lemon, onion powder, vinegar, ketchup, and Worcestershire sauce among other things in the barbecue sauce. It was thick and tangy.

Billy Blues served a medley of sides: garlic mashed potatoes, Fiesta cole-slaw, Dum Dum's potato salad, French fries, Charro beans. I had Dirty Blues rice, a Cajun dish with two-alarm red pepper, and Longneck Cornbake, a creamy, cheesy, jalapeño fire.

Margarita's pecan pie, peach cobbler, Billy's apple pie, James' brownie, and Billy's root beer float made up the dessert list.

Billy Blues uses an Oyler rotisserie smoker. *I knew it.* They smoke brisket for fourteen hours at 230 to 250 degrees—depending on temperature, the size of the meat, and the humidity. They use a secret rub on the chicken and the ribs.

If I had any blues, I left them behind at Billy Blues.

The County Line

See **San Antonio** for more information (page 292).

The County Line also has locations in Austin, El Paso, Lubbock, and San Antonio.

Rating: 9

13850 Cutten Rd., Houston, Texas 77069
Phone 218-537-2454
Fax 281-537-2757

Menu order, take-out. Brisket plate $10.95.

Open 11:30 to 2 P.M. and 5:30 to 9 Tuesday through Thursday and until 10 P.M. on Friday. Saturday and Sunday from noon until 10 P.M. and until 9 P.M. Accepts credit cards.

Drexler's Bar-B-Que

Mrs. Eunice Drexler calls the shots. Son Clyde, former Rockets basketball star and coach of the University of Houston Cougars, bounces in and out. And son James Drexler manages it. It's a great combination. Mrs. Drexler originally used the place to feed her family. Clyde brought fame to the name. And James supplied the elbow grease.

I asked James if he played basketball. "Sure did, and I taught Clyde everything he knows."

I tried the barbecue. The brisket had a 5/16-inch pink ribbon. *Encouraging.* The meat parted with a slight push of my fork, and aroma sprang out of it. It contained a little fat. I took a bite, and the flavor was a winning shot at the buzzer. I rated it a 9. A pork rib

Rating: 8

2020 Dowling Street at Gray Avenue, Houston, Texas 77003-6006
Phone 713-752-0008
Fax 713-654-0741

Counter order, take-out, catering. Serves beer. Brisket plate $6.00.

Open 10 A.M. to 6 P.M. Tuesday through Saturday. Closed Sunday. Accepts credit cards.

had game winning tenderness, too much fat, but very good flavor. I gave it a 7. Drexler's has two sausages. An outside supplier makes the regular sausage. It yielded two drops of fat from the squeeze test and revealed superior beef flavor. I gave it an 8. That's a "high five" mark from me for sausage. The homemade pork hot link gave up two drops of fat from the squeeze test. It was very lean and had three-alarm heat. I gave it 9. That rating for sausage from me was as high as Clyde the "Glide" on a ride.

I noticed onion, vinegar, ketchup, and Worcestershire sauce in the Drexler barbecue sauce. It had a good twang.

Mrs. Drexler served pinto beans, baked beans, French fries, a creamy coleslaw, and a stuffed baked potato with chopped barbecued beef for side orders. Her desserts? Lemon cake and "Sock-it-to-me" cake.

James showed me their homemade metal pit. "We use oak wood and smoke brisket for five hours." He did it manually. *Only five hours?*

Sports fans get to pour over some Clyde Drexler souvenirs. A display cabinet shows two *Sports Illustrated* covers that featured Clyde, a portrait of Clyde on the front cover of a box of Wheaties, and one shoe of Clyde's and one of Hakeem Olajuwon's. Hakeem's shoe was just a little bit longer than Clyde's.

Walter Matthau, Danny Glover, and Marvin Zindler ate here, plus the Houston Rockets, Houston Cougars, and their fans.

Mrs. Drexler ought to charge admission.

Gabby's

Rating: 8

5311 Weslayan @ Bissonnet,
Houston, Texas 77005-1047
Phone 713-666-9069

3101 North Shepherd,
Houston, Texas 77018-8333
Phone 864-5049
Catering 713-666-9069
Fax 713-666-9444

Counter order, take-out, drive thru, catering. Beer served. Brisket plate $6.99.

Gabby's looks like a saloon from frontier days. Surrounded by Houston's fashionable Montclair Shopping Center, it looks misplaced.

Open 11 A.M. to 10 P.M. Accepts credit cards.

Step inside and you will feel more at home than in one of the chic retail stores.

I moseyed up to the counter and ordered my usual plate of barbecue samples.

A slice of brisket had a quarter-inch pink ribbon. _A sign of modern times—another rotisserie._ It had very little fat, and it took one hard push with my fork to divide the meat. Little if any aroma surfaced. I took a bite and deemed it to have above average flavor. I gave it an 8, one grade above my usual rotisserie rating.

I later found the reason for the higher rating, Gabby's serves Certified Black Angus beef.

They sold out of ribs the day I dined.

The next item I tested was chicken. It had blue heaven flavor and tenderness. I awarded it a 10. A slice of ham had a slightly salty flavor mixed with smoke. It had little fat, was very tender, and teemed with flavor. I gave it a 9.

I perceived the barbecue sauce to have vinegar, ketchup, Worcestershire sauce, some onion, and for warmth a little cayenne. An employee told me that they make the sauce from scratch.

Preparing to write about Gabby's side orders, I remembered what a friend told me. The reason barbecue places call their vegetables and other fixings "sides" is because the wrangler used a sideboard on his wagon to serve them. Fortunately, for modern diners like me, Gabby's served their sides inside, and a lot of them were on a giant salad/condiment bar. Beyond the salads, I looked at potato salad, corn, fries, ranch beans, green beans, red beans and rice, coleslaw, rice, and okra.

Desserts were cobblers, banana pudding, and apple and pecan pie.

Gabby's uses Oyler rotisserie smokers. Like all other users of these units, Gabby's smokes brisket fourteen hours at 250 to 275 degrees. They use oak, no gas, and no electricity. They rub everything but brisket with their secret seasoning.

Marvin Zindler, Channel 13 Eyewitness News restaurant critic, gave Gabby's his Blue Ribbon Award for cleanliness.

Goode Co. Texas Bar-B-Q

Rating: 8.75

5109 Kirby Drive, Houston, Texas 77098-5098
Phone 713-522-2530
Fax 713-522-3873

8911 Katy Freeway, Houston, Texas 77024-1604
Phone 713-464-1901

Fax 713-464-3849
E-mail goode1@
goodecompany.com
Web site www.
goodecompany.com

Cafeteria style, take-out, catering, banquet facilities. Serves beer and Texas wine. Brisket plate $6.95.

Opens 10:30 A.M. Closes 10 P.M. Sunday through Thursday and 10:30 P.M. Friday and Saturday. Accepts credit cards.

When critics talk about Texas barbecue, they always mention Goode Co.

Visions of delicious barbecue danced in my head as I made my way through the cafeteria line. My plate of samples had appetite appeal. I hurried to sit down and began my tests. The brisket had a very familiar quarter-inch pink ribbon. *Another rotisserie.* The slice looked very lean. The aroma squeaked. It took two tough slices with my fork to part the meat. My bite revealed light flavor. I gave it a 7. A pork rib had good appearance but showed a little too much fat. It had above average tenderness and the flavor was magnifico. *Ah, this was the Goode barbecue I always heard about.* I gave it a 9.

The regular sausage relinquished four drops of fat. The flavor mumbled. I gave it a 6. The hot link gave up no fat when I squeezed it and had above average flavor. I rated it an 8.5. *Very Goode.* A piece of peppered ham was slightly salty, had some fat, but was tender and delicious. When I ate it, I wished it had more smoke flavor. I gave it an 8. Goode's white meat was exemplary. The chicken had a wonderful herb seasoning. The meat was moist, tender, and flavorful. I bestowed a 10 on the chicken. A slice of turkey also had that same tasty seasoning. It too was moist and had excellent flavor and tenderness. I crowned it with a 10.

Before I arrived, they sold out of barbecued "Sweet Water Duck." Such was life in the big city.

Side orders: jalapeño pinto beans, potato salad, coleslaw, "Jambalaya Texana," and Austin baked beans.

Desserts: pecan pie, chocolate cream pie, and pralines.

Be sure to load up on homemade jalapeño cheese bread.

Luther's Bar-B-Q

Big barbecue chains do not get big by serving average barbecue. People from all over the world flock to Luther's for the best.

I talked with a prominent businessman who said, "If I have a guest from out of town and it's time to eat, I ask them if they would like barbecue, steak, or French cuisine. Most choose barbecue. So I take them to Luther's."

"Why Luther's?"

"Atmosphere and great barbecue. It's the West. They love it."

I bought my counter order, stopped at the "fixin's" bar for pickles, onions, and beans, and took the food to a table. The brisket had an eighth of an inch pink ribbon. Through large windows, I saw three rotisseries. The rotisseries explained the small pink ribbon. The aroma must have gone downwind because I missed it. The brisket looked to be lean. It took two tough slices with my fork to sever it. The flavor sang. I rated it an 8. A pork rib had too much fat, above average tenderness, and superior flavor. I gave it a 7. The sausage surrendered four drops of fat from the squeeze test. The flavor reminded me of bologna. I gave it a 6. A slice of turkey was tender, moist, and lean. The smoke flavor floundered a bit. I put an 8 on it. The barbecue sauce had one-alarm heat from some cayenne, and in addition to the basics of ketchup,

Rating: 7.5

703 FM 1960 West
281-893-5711

1100 Smith Street
713-759-0018

3814 Little York Road
713-697-4417

8560 Gulf Freeway
713-947-9927

8777 South Main Street
713-432-1107

11311A Fondren Street
713-721-6360

9797 Westheimer Road
713-780-0081

1001 Gessner 713-465-7251

7925 FM 1960 281-890-2988

Counter order, take-out, catering (713-890-2988). Beer served. Brisket plate $7.59.

Opens 11 A.M. Closes 10 P.M. Sunday through Thursday and 11 P.M. Friday and Saturday. Accepts credit cards.

vinegar, and Worcestershire sauce, had—maybe—cola in it.

I know that's weird, but you try it and see for yourself.

Luther's offered many side orders—potato salad, dirty rice, broccoli, sweet potatoes, beans, onion-ring loaf, fries, "chop baker (stuffed potato with barbecue)," and ranch house salads.

Patrons can have unlimited side orders for $3.29.

The dessert line-up: pies, cobbler, and ice cream.

Otto's Barbeque, Inc.

Otto's **is** a Houston institution. Ask any Houstonian, and he can tell you about it. This is the favorite haunt of congressman, vice president, president, and past president George Bush. This is where bigwigs make big deals. If you are anybody, you eat here.

Rating: 7.5

5502 Memorial Drive, Houston, Texas 77007
Phone 713-864-2573
Web site www.side-walk.com/otto's

Counter order, take-out, catering, banquet facilities. Beer served. Brisket plate $6.59.

Open 11 A.M. to 9 P.M. Closed Sunday. Accepts checks and credit cards.

Otto and his wife Annie Sofka came from Shiner, Texas, and started this business in 1951 as a grocery store. They butchered meat and decided to grill hamburgers. They added barbecue, and the restaurant part of the business took over. Today, they carve one hundred briskets a day for customers.

Otto's brisket had good appearance. The pink ribbon measured a quarter inch. *Another rotisserie.* The brisket had faint aroma and a dark edge, which meant they rubbed it with a seasoning. It showed little fat. It took a hard push of my fork to part it. The flavor was above average. I rated it a 7. A pork rib had a honey crust, superior tenderness, some fat, and excellent flavor. I gave it an 8. A slice of pork roast had too much fat but above average tenderness and flavor. I tagged it with a 6. Otto's formula for sausage has never changed. It yielded three drops of fat from the squeeze test and had superior flavor. I gave it a 7.

Turkey gobbled up the honors. Although it was a little salty, I thought the flavor sang. It had melt-in-your-mouth tenderness and very little fat. I rated it a 9. A slice of ham had very good tenderness, almost no fat, and superior flavor. I rated it an 8.

The barbecue sauce smacked on the tangy side. Its recipe was a deep, dark secret.

For side orders, they served a sweet coleslaw, pinto beans, potato salad, rice, and corn on the cob.

Dessert comes from a little old lady who brings her homemade pies to Otto's every morning.

The day I visited, I talked with Michael Jenking, son-in-law and the one in charge at the time. He said they did have an old pit that they used for chicken and ribs, but most of their barbecue is smoked in rotisserie pits.

The best way to enter Otto's is from Reinicke Street, a half block north of Memorial Drive. Another parking lot is off Asbury Street on the west side of Otto's.

Pappas Bar-B-Q

In 1967 the Pappas family went into the barbecue business, a dream of Jim Pappas. He and his brothers Pete, Tom, and George opened the first Brisket House. Today, they have eighty-three restaurants, of which six are barbecue. The sixth and newest Pappas barbecue location is in Dallas.

I went through the cafeteria line and picked up a plate of barbecue samples. The brisket had a quarter-inch pink ribbon. *Another rotisserie*. In the shear test, it parted with one strong slice of my fork. The aroma was faint, and it showed some fat. It had above average flavor. I rated it a 7. A pork rib went to the head of the class. It had little fat, great tenderness, and excellent flavor. I gave it an 8.75. The sausage oozed four drops of fat and had superior flavor. I tagged it with a 7. A slice of ham was very tender and slightly salty and had little fat and superior flavor. I gave it a 9.

The barbecue sauce tasted like Cattleman's with some onion added.

Side dishes included potato salad with some mustard, macaroni salad, cucumber salad with Italian dressing and red onion, chili, pinto beans, navy beans with ham, chef salad with barbecue, and

Rating: 7.75

1217 Pierce at San Jacinto,
Houston, Texas 77002
Phone 713-659-1245
Fax 713-659-5315
Open 10:30 to 10:30 Friday and Saturday; 10:30 to 9:00 Sunday; and 10:00 to 10:00 Monday through Thursday.

7050 Gulf Freeway (I-45 South) at Woodridge,
Houston, Texas 77087
Phone 713-649-7236
Fax 713-649-0140
Open 10:30 to 10:00 Sunday through Thursday, and until 11 Friday and Saturday.

9815 Bissonnet at Centre,
Houston, Texas 77036
Phone 713-777-1661
Fax 713-541-1006
Open 11 to 11 every day.

tossed salad.

Dessert choices were strawberry cheesecake and pecan pie.

I visited the Southwest Freeway location across from Sharpstown Mall. It is a huge place with three dining areas. I called the motif modern warehouse. It had a white embossed metal ceiling, wood floor, neon beer signs, an enormous crystal chandelier, big timber rafters, a moose head, and a stone fireplace that reached to the apex of its cathedral ceiling.

Today, Eric and Chris Pappas are the owners.

I want to thank David at the I-45 store. He seemed to be the only one who could answer questions. Then again, there is no question about the quality of Pappas barbecue.

7007 Southwest Freeway (U.S. 59 South), Houston, Texas 77074 Phone 713-772-4557 Fax 713-271-8930 Open 11:00 to 11:00 Friday and Saturday and until 10:00 Sunday through Thursday.

4430 North Freeway (I-45 North), Houston, Texas 77022 Phone 713-697-9533 Fax 713-697-9570 Open 11:00 to 11:00 Friday and Saturday and until 10:00 Sunday through Thursday.

Counter order, take-out, catering, and banquet facilities. Beer served. Accepts credit cards.

Pizzatola's Bar-B-Q

In 1935 Bette Davis and Victor McLaglen won best actress and best actor in the Academy Awards; *Mutiny on the Bounty* was best picture. Detroit downed the Chicago Cubs in the World Series. SMU won the national collegiate football title. And, John Davis started Shepherd Drive Bar-B-Q.

In those days the blacks ate in the front part of the restaurant and the whites ate in back. After John and the "Jim Crow" segregation law passed away, J. B. "Jerry" Pizzatola bought the place and changed the name to Pizzatola's Bar-B-Q.

Today everyone dines in its one large dining room. Like other Houston barbecue places, many business people meet, eat, and transact deals here.

The waitress brought me a sampler of barbecue, and I began my tests. A slice of brisket had a quarter-inch pink ribbon and come-hither aroma. The flavor was exceptional. It had superior tenderness but showed a little too much fat. I gave it an 8. Another slice of brisket from the fat part of the

Rating: 8.5

1703 Shepherd Drive, two blocks south of Interstate 10 and across the street from Cadillac Bar, Houston, Texas 77007 Phone 713-227-2283 Fax 713-861-7600

Menu order, take-out, catering. Serves beer. Brisket plate $7.95.

Opens 11 A.M. Closes 8 P.M. Monday through Friday and 3 P.M. Saturday. Accepts credit cards.

brisket embodied great tenderness. It melted in my mouth. A pork rib showed promise. It had a salt and pepper rub that enhanced the flavor. It was tender and had some fat. I rated it a 9. The pork and beef sausage contained Pizzatola's specified seasonings and ingredients. The flavor was exciting but oozed a puddle of fat in the squeeze test. I gave it a 7. Pizzatola's boneless chicken breast melted in my mouth, but the flavor was light. It had very little fat, and I gave it an 8.

Mark Shayan, operations manager, said that they do not use frozen chicken. The chicken is fresh and packed in ice. I asked about the ingredients for the barbecue sauce, and he said that the recipe for the barbecue sauce originated with John Davis and is a well-kept secret. Other than basic ingredients, the sauce had a peppery taste. It was distinctive.

They served the regular sides of coleslaw, potato salad, and pinto beans, plus grilled vegetables that had one-alarm heat. They made the sides fresh every day. The potato salad potatoes were boiled. They soaked the pinto beans a full day and cooked them the next day. The only canned product Pizzatola bought was jalapeños.

I saw the pantry. No ketchup. No Worcestershire sauce. It had to be true—everything was fresh, made from scratch.

Joe's mother, Margaret Raley, made dessert—coconut cake with a pineapple filling, carrot cake, and banana pudding. A picture of Arnold Palmer holding a cup of her banana pudding graced a wall. The desserts were moist, delicious, and haunting.

Mark showed me their brick pits. The firebox burned hickory at the lower left end. The smoke traversed grates loaded with meat and exited through a smokestack in the upper right end. No thermostat. No electronics. No gas. Just man and smoker. The two pits dated back to the 1935 beginning.

Humble

Luther's Bar-B-Q

See Houston for further information (page 60).

Rating: 7.5

19713 U.S. Hwy. 59, Humble, Texas 77338

Phone 281-446-0441

Counter order, take-out, catering (713-890-2988).

Beer served. Brisket plate $7.59.

Opens 11 A.M. Closes 10 P.M. Sunday through Thursday and 11 P.M. Friday and Saturday. Accepts credit cards.

Kingsville

Mesquite Grill Restaurant

Kingsville used to be part of King's ranch. Richard King made money by selling cotton to Mexico to raise money for the Confederacy. At the end of the war, he was a wealthy man. In 1853 he bought 15,500 acres of bush country for $300. Today, the empire is a corporation and comprises eleven million acres. Some of King's descendants are the Kleberg family, and Mr. and Mrs. Tio Kleberg are regular visitors to the Mesquite Grill for barbecue.

I put on my ten gallon American beaver hat and sauntered into the joint. I saw a bunch of tough customers. *Cowboys, no doubt.* Their eyes glued to me like a cowboy on a saddle. Then they stared at my shoes. *Shoes! I did not have on boots. So much for trying to be one of the ranch hands.* I could read their minds: who is this greenhorn? He's too old to be at Texas A&M at Kingsville. He sure isn't from the Kingsville naval base. Must be a stray and not a very good one at that.

As eyes continued to probe, I decided I had better not order just one small slice of brisket. Macho problem. I ordered a platter of everything. When I did, the eyes went in other directions.

But when the waitress returned with my order, the eyes returned. The brisket had a 5/16-inch ribbon. *Promising.* I had to push hard with the fork to cut it. I began to gnaw a piece. *Tough. Good flavor.* To avoid those eyes, I draped my napkin over my questionnaire form and put down a 6. The eyes glared. I realized my mistake. Being secretive added to their suspicion. *I hope they don't think I'm from the IRS.* I tossed the napkin aside. *How would John Wayne handle this?* Boldly, I observed the pork rib. *A little too much fat.* I took a bite. *Tender. Good spices. Lemon pepper?* I rated the rib a 7.

I wrote it with flair. I looked around. The eyes

Rating: 7.5

621 West Corral Street,
Kingsville, Texas 78363
Phone 512-592-1182

Menu order, take-out, catering. Serves beer. Brisket plate $4.99.

Opens at 11 A.M. Closes Monday through Thursday and Saturday at 9 P.M. and Friday at 10 P.M. Closed Sunday. Accepts checks and Discover credit card.

were smiling. *They must think seven is tops.* The sausage shined. It had great flavor. Not one drop of fat fell when I squeezed it. And, it had a little fire. I gave it a 9. I wrote the 9 very large. I looked around. No one paid any attention. A slice of chicken breast came next. It had a mild flavor, was moist, and melted in my mouth. I gave it a 9. No one watched as I marked down another big 9.

I dug into the side dishes. The pinto beans had tomato, onion, and a disappointing mild flavor. The potato salad had mustard, mayo, and parsley. *Better than average.* The coleslaw had shredded carrots mixed in. *Slightly sweet and sour.* I liked it.

A favorite is Cowboy Potatoes with butter, onions, and parsley.

The menu listed Grandma Tootie's homemade cheesecakes, ice cream, apple and pecan pies, cobbler, and double chocolate cake for desserts.

Stuffed, I talked to Uly (you-lee) Rutkoski, the owner. Ten years ago a friend told her she should become a missionary. The Mesquite Grill ended up as her project. "Feed my sheep" kind of thing. She confided that they used a secret seasoning for their rub. They browned the brisket on both sides to keep the juice inside, marinated it in foil for four hours, and then cooked it another six hours. *How different can you get?* She said her customers differ from barbecue eaters in other parts of the state. Many locals like their brisket cut lengthwise from the end, which is stringier and has more fat. She smiled. "I gave you a nice crosscut from the front end."

She had been on to me from the start.

If you have a hankering to see the King Ranch, you can drive a twelve-mile loop that goes by its headquarters. Watch for huge, dark brown cattle—world famous King Ranch developed Santa Gertrudis cattle. Also watch for large white-tailed deer and mean little javelinas.

McAllen

Lone Star Barbecue

Some Rio Grande Valley natives call them "Snowbirds," people who come from the North to the Rio Grande Valley to escape the wrath of winter's ice and snow. It may be that they come to the Valley simply because they like the barbecue at Lone Star. I found this place off the beaten path and near the railroad tracks on Business Route Hwy. 83. The state built a new 83, an expressway, and left old 83 in

Rating: 8

315 W. Business 83, McAllen, Texas 78501

Phone 956-686-7113

Dine in—sometimes out, counter order, drive-thru, catering. Beef plate $5.75.

the dust. But that doesn't deter barbecue lovers, because they pack Lone Star. The building is unobtrusive, and you have to keep a sharp eye to find it. Here's help: It's on the south side of the street.

> Opens at 11 and closes at 8, Monday through Saturday. Closed Sunday. Checks and credit cards accepted.

I drove 142 miles from Laredo and found not one good barbecue place. Finally, a bunch of golfers recommended Lone Star in McAllen. I found it and sauntered in, not knowing what to expect. "Old" described my first impression. I went to the counter and ordered everything. Somehow, when I do that, it tips my hand. Employees seem to know immediately what I am doing.

Anyway, I took my tray into the dining room. The first thing that greeted me was a large, prominently placed orange UT flag hanging from the ceiling. The decor was very rustic country. The floor had well-worn six-inch planks. The tables had red-and-white checkered cloths. Ancient ceiling fans and light fixtures hovered. I sat down with my food, served on butcher paper on a tray.

The sliced beef brisket had about a quarter of an inch of pink ribbon. I pressed the fork edge against it. I had to push hard to cut through. I sniffed a bite and took in a deep mesquite aroma. I chewed it. Praiseworthy flavor. Very lean. I moved a slice on the butcher paper and saw no trail of grease. That says a lot to people concerned about their health. I gave the brisket an 8.5. The pork ribs had a little sweetness and good flavor. They were chewy and had some fat. *Better than most ribs I've eaten.* I gave them an 8. The sausage came from a "friend." It was half beef, half pork, had great smoke flavor, but contained a little too much fat. I gave it a 7. What I liked most was the turkey. Slices from the breast burst with mesquite smoke flavor. The meat was moist and tender. I gave it a 9. The chicken had as much flavor as the turkey, but I thought it was a smidgen drier. I gave it an 8.

The meat comes with sauce, dill pickles, and very sweet sliced onions. The sauce was thick and I discerned ketchup, vinegar, and some Worcestershire sauce in it. Of course, the recipe is a deep, dark secret.

Then I tasted the side orders. The potato salad had a little mustard mixed with the mayo and was slightly sweet. The beans had onions, meat, and other good spices. The coleslaw had fresh ingredients and smacked a little sweet. Rice had Creole seasoning of some sort. All rated high marks.

Lone Star has a family like a lot of other barbecue places—the Myska family: Ken's the dad, Virginia's the mom, and Darrell's the son. They bought the business in 1982. Darrell, a very good natured young man with orange blood in his veins from the University of Texas, ran the show when I dined. I sat at a table next to him. He was engaged in a conversation with some other folks about an orphanage in Reynosa, a city across the river in Mexico. When they ended their conversation, I introduced myself to him and he, in turn, introduced me to his friends. It turns out that when the business day is over at Lone Star, these other guests gather up all the leftover food and take it to the orphanage. Later, Darrell said a meaningful thing, "We start everyday from scratch. Everything is fresh."

I asked him how he 'cued and he said, "I use a rotisserie smoker." He saw my startled look (he knew I was expecting to hear the word "pit"). "You have to know what you're doing. Most folks don't know how to use it." He confided that he rubs the meat with black and lemon pepper and fajita seasoning and cooks the brisket slowly, all night. He checks the meat in the morning, and if it has not achieved perfection, he cooks the meat some more—until it's just right. He trims the fat when the meat comes out of the smoker (which accounted for the very lean meat on my butcher paper), and then he sops it.

In the information at the top, I wrote "sometimes" for dining out. The entire dining area has sliding windows, and when the temperature outside cools, they open the windows. Screens keep the bugs out, and you feel like you are outdoors.

Darrell confided that American Airlines did a survey of barbecue places, and Lone Star was one of only twenty they recommended—get this—nationwide. I believe it. The orphans in Reynosa are fortunate, the Myskas are fortunate, the patrons of the Lone Star are fortunate, and so was I on January 20, 1999.

Do you know what a "Winter Texan" makes for dinner? Reservations.

Orange

J.B.'s Barbeque Restaurant, Inc.

J.B. Arrington, owner of J.B.'s, had a good story about the origination of the word _barbecue_. Men chased a bear up a hickory tree. A bolt of lightning struck the tree. The burning tree and the bear fell to the ground in a pile of flames. The men were frantic because they wanted the bearskin. They yelled, "Get out of thar, B'ar! Be quick! Come B'ar, be quick!" It was to no avail because the b'ar was dead. When the fire cooled, they tried to salvage the hide, and the first thing they found was that the bear

Rating: 7

Three miles west of Orange, Texas, at the intersection of Interstate 10 and U.S. Hwy. 90. Eastbound traffic take Exit 874A (Orange Exit) and westbound take Exit 874B (Womack Road), Orange, Texas 77632

smelled delicious. When they touched the well-done bear, large chunks of delicious meat came off. Word of the disaster got back to the village, and the whole affair was dubbed, "B'ar-be-quick." As time went on, they shortened it to "B'ar-be-que." And if you believe that, you are the kind of listener this storyteller values most.

I found no b'ar in J.B.'s. I found a piece of brisket with a quarter-inch pink ribbon. *Another rotisserie.* They rubbed it with black pepper, red pepper, and salt. In the shear test, the meat parted with the second slice. The aroma was faint. It appeared to have very little fat. My bite revealed a mild flavor, and I gave it a 6. A pork sparerib had too much fat but had excellent flavor and tenderness. I rated it an 8. The sausage yielded three drops of fat from the squeeze test but had superior flavor. I rated it a 7.5.

The cafeteria line displayed sweet and creamy coleslaw, potato salad, pinto beans, dirty rice, and corn on the cob.

For dessert, I had to choose between chocolate meringue, pecan, or lemon meringue pies or blackberry cobbler.

J.B. taught agriculture and, on weekends, barbecued for Port City Stockyards in Houston. He decided he wanted to be in the barbecue business, so he stopped teaching agriculture and opened J.B.'s Barbeque.

It's a family business, and most of the jobs belong to family members.

Bum Phillips and Alex Karras ate here. Bum, by the way, grew up in Orange.

I spoke with Jay Matthews, J.B.'s son-in-law, who was in charge of the operations when I visited. He said they used an Oyler rotisserie. *I knew it.* They used oak and smoked the brisket sixteen hours at 180 to 190 degrees.

What's J.B.'s recipe for success? "I try to be consistent and be friends with all the people."

A long cafeteria line of smiling customers proved him right.

Phone 409-886-9823
Fax 409-886-5763

Cafeteria style, take-out, catering, banquet facilities. No beer. Brisket plate $6.25. Open 11 A.M. to 8 P.M. Closed Sunday and Monday. Accepts checks and credit cards.

Pasadena

Gabby's

See Houston Gabby's on page 57 for more information.

Rating: 8

4010 Spencer Highway at Burke, Pasadena, Texas 77504-1202

Phone 713-944-8424

Menu order, take-out, catering. Full bar. Brisket plate $6.99.

Open 11 A.M. to 10 P.M. Accepts credit cards.

Grand Prize Barbeque

Look for the giant Texas wagon atop a 75-foot pole. Inside, the décor is western with antiques and collectibles. Color scheme is red, white, and blue.

See Galveston for more information (page 47).

Rating: 8.5

1100 Pasadena Freeway (Hwy. 225). Pasadena, Texas 75006

Phone 713-473-3355

Menu order, counter order, take-out, catering. Dry county.

Brisket plate $6.95.

Open 6 A.M. to 7 P.M. Closed Sunday. Credit cards accepted.

Pearland

Grand Prize Barbeque

Look for a two-story building. Has lots of antiques. Big salad bar.

See Galveston for more information (page 47).

Rating: 8.5

2911 East Broadway, Pearland, Texas 77581

Phone 281-485-4999

Menu order, counter order, take-out, catering. Beer

served. Brisket plate $6.95.

Opens 11 A.M. Closes 9:30 P.M. Sunday through Thursday and 10 P.M. Friday and Saturday. Credit cards accepted.

Port Lavaca

White's Barbecue

Pioneers settled here because of the high bluff overlooking the bay and the strategic land and water setting for a port. Spain used the place to unload supplies as far back as 1815. They called it Lavaca. That meant "the cow" in Spanish. Evidently, those guys knew that Port Lavaca would eventually be more than a port; it would be the home of White's Barbecue.

Driving down the main drag in town, you might fail to see the White's Barbecue sign at the top of a long pole by the street. The dominant feature of the building is a drive-in grocery. White's Barbecue sits back and to the left of the store. You can enter one of two ways: through the store or the door around the corner. The correct outside door sports a big Coca-Cola reader board. The day I dropped in, the sign read, "RIBS ALL YOU CAN EAT MON-NIGHT STEAKS FRI NIGHT." Unfortunately, I arrived on Thursday.

Mrs. Nancy Howlett, owner of White's, and I hit it off at the start. We were senior citizens and made a good team. She served the food and I ate it. That is the kind of teamwork I like. Since she watched my every move, I could not mark down test numbers. I postponed that duty, scribbled cryptic marks, and kept smiling. She kept bringing the food.

The brisket had that recognizable quarter-inch pink ribbon on the edge. *Another rotisserie.* In the shear test, it parted with the second slice of my fork. It was very lean. The aroma was light and the flavor average. I gave it a 7. The pork ribs had good flavor, too much fat, and above average tenderness. I rated them a 6. Eddie's Packing Company of Yoakum, Texas, supplied the half beef, half pork sausage. It possessed very good flavor, born from mouth-awakening spices. One drop of fat fell from

Rating: 7

1728 West Main, Port Lavaca, Texas 77979
Phone 361-552-2235

Counter order, take-out, catering. Serves beer. Brisket plate $4.95.

Open 11 A.M. to 7:30 P.M., every day. Cash only.

my squeeze test. I bestowed an 8 on the sausage.

The sauce tasted like Cattleman's.

The potato salad had salad dressing, pickles, onions, eggs, salt, pepper, and pimento. The pinto beans had garlic and bacon. The coleslaw was sweet and creamy.

Next came dessert. Homemade goodies. I stared at a shelf with pecan, apple, coconut, chocolate, and lemon meringue pies. I devoured a piece of pecan pie.

With ceiling fans swirling above and a large cow skull staring at us, I asked Nancy how she would describe the interior. She thought it was rustic.

I asked her how she got started. She said, "My husband, Charlie, came from Taylor where barbecue is king, and he and our son, Kirk, wanted to buy this place. I told them no—too much work. We bought it anyway. It took nine months just to clean this place up. Smoke was on everything."

"How did it go?"

"We were lucky if we took in $200 a day at the start. $400 was exceptional."

"You seem to be doing all right now. Do you provide entertainment?'

"I'm about as much entertainment as you can get."

We talked barbecue. She told me that they used mesquite. They smoked I.B.P. brisket on a rotisserie from twelve to eighteen hours. *Alas. I was right again.* They used a secret rub and no sop.

I asked her if celebrities ever ate here. She could not remember. "When I forget, I tell my friends I'm having a senior moment."

You don't have to be a senior to forget, so please don't forget White's Barbecue the next time you head for the coast for fishing or hunting or just to escape the snow or hectic city living.

Richmond

The Swinging Door

This is a foot stompin,' jaw chompin' sort of place. The Swinging Door began as a weekend endeavor in 1973. The small shack sat twelve people at three tables. It burned to the ground in '74. Owners Steve and Ward Onstad built a larger place, seating seventy-five. Customers poured in. Proud of their barbecue, the Onstads entered the barbecue cook-off at the Houston Rodeo and Livestock Show and won in

Rating: 9

3714 FM 359 (4 miles west of 90A), Richmond, Texas 77469

Phone 281-342-4758

Fax 281-342-7591

E-mail swingdoor@ neosoft.com

Menu order, take-out, catering, dancing, banquet rooms. Serves beer, wine. Brisket plate $9.95.

Opens at 11 A.M. Closes at 9 P.M. Wednesday, Thursday and Sunday, 12:30 A.M. Friday and Saturday. Closed Monday and Tuesday. Checks and credit cards accepted.

'79 and '81. With the title of World Barbecue Champions, they quit cook-offs and began adding to their business one room at a time. The latest addition became Behind the Door, a Saturday night dance hall that features live music by a six-piece band called "Brazos." On big nights, around three hundred people pound the floor.

My visit brought back old memories. Ward and I were classmates at Lamar High School in Houston. We sat and talked old times as I tested his barbecue. I wrote in code so he did not know how I rated his food. After eating, he showed me around. He called his décor "country." We went into an add-on room that had a large stained glass window. Ward bought the window from a dealer who said it came from a Waco Methodist church blown apart by a tornado. As we walked, he told me business was great. I asked him if any celebrities ate here. He nodded. "Bum Phillips, Dan Pastorini, Gifford Nielson, Farah Fawcett, the Osmonds, Earl Campbell, and the whole cast of the movie *Rush*, which was made here."

"The whole cast?"

"Including the producer Richard Zanuck. I distinctly remember Gregg Allman, Sam Elliott, Jennifer J. Leigh, and Jason Patric."

That shows you that old geezers can remember.

He showed me his barbecue pits. Made of steel, they had a firebox in the middle. He used pecan wood and diverted the smoke over the meat and out exhaust stacks located below the grills. The grills sloped so the grease ran off. "Depending on the humidity, we smoke brisket eighteen to twenty-four hours. We know it's done when we can twist a fork in it."

He admitted to using a rub. The ingredients remain a secret. No sop. He said his barbecue sauce was sweet and sour. I detected vinegar,

Worcestershire sauce, lemon, and butter.

"We do a lot of mail order, especially during the holidays. Our turkeys sell out." He proceeded to tell me that a Bohemian lady taught him how to cook turkey. "You get a pot of vegetable oil and season it. Then you immerse the turkey in it. You coat it. The oil keeps the turkey from getting burned. It gets dark but does not char."

We said our good-byes.

That night in a motel, I typed on my laptop: The brisket had a large pink ribbon. The aroma sparkled. The meat fell apart with a slight nudge of my fork. It had no fat. The flavor was a 9. I gave the brisket a 9. The pork ribs had good flavor, were tender, and had some fat. I gave them an 8. Slovacek's in Snook, Texas, supplied the sausage. I gave it the squeeze test. You should have seen Ward's eyes. Two drops of fat came out. The sausage was half pork and half beef and had no fillers. The flavor was good, and I rated it an 8. The chicken earned a 9. It was moist and tender. The flavor was above average. The turkey was moist, tender, and had great flavor. *That Bohemian lady taught Ward well*. I gave it a 9.

A hot seller was a barbecue stuffed potato. The potato salad had green onions, celery, big chunks of not overcooked potatoes, and a salad dressing base. The coleslaw had vinegar, raisins, cabbage, and carrots. The pinto beans were normal.

The dessert line-up: pecan pie, fruit cobbler, and soft ice cream.

Ten o'clock. Time to hit the hay.

Robstown

The Farmhouse Bar-B-Que & Catering

Rating: 7

Five Points Shopping Center, Hwy. 624 and U.S. Hwy 77, Robstown, Texas 78380
Phone 361-242-1100
Fax 361-242-1101

Cafeteria style, take-out, catering. No beer. Brisket plate $4.99.

The Farmhouse is hard to find. I spotted the Five Points Shopping Center, but I had to drive around buildings to find my barbecue. The place is on the backside of a strip center in Five Points.

I was glad I found it, because I found some great barbecue. Entering was like going into another store in a shopping center. Inside, Jim Matthews, owner, had done everything he could to make a contemporary setting look like a ranch.

I went through the cafeteria line and ordered a small slice of brisket, a pork rib, and two inches of sausage. I got a weird look. The man behind the counter knew I was up to something.

Let's face it, ordering so little saves a lot of my money. Besides, I could not eat all the food if I bought full orders six times a day.

I got down to business. The brisket had that familiar quarter-inch pink ribbon. *Another rotisserie! I need to get that salesman's name. He could save me a lot of travel*. I gave the brisket a 7, the ribs a 7, and the sausage a 7. The sausage had two-alarm fire.

A buffet bar offers a variety of side orders.

I never got to talk with Mr. Matthews and he never returned my calls, and so the story stalls.

Opens 11 A.M. Closes 8 P.M. Monday through Thursday, 8:30 P.M. Friday and Saturday. Checks and credit cards accepted.

Joe Cotten's Barbecue

Joe Cotten's Barbecue became a Texas legend before most of today's Texans were born. The place has served past President George Bush, former Secretary of State James Baker, NCAA Basketball Champion Kentucky Wildcats, George Strait, Bum Phillips, Nolan Ryan, and four governors.

So why is this place so great? It has atmosphere, reputation, and great barbecue.

My cousin, Ken Isaacs, in Tulsa told me, "You have to eat at Joe Cotten's. Let me tell you, it's the best. Every time I go fishing at Port Isabel, I stop there. I've been doing that for twenty years."

Off I went. Coming up Highway 77 from Kingsville, I saw the sign. I observed dozens of cars in the parking lot. *Maybe Ken is right*. I parked and walked down the long front porch, passing people chatting and some sitting in large swings. All appeared to be happy. I entered a large, crowded dining room. The motif was western. I looked around and noticed three more large dining rooms—all packed with people. Friendly Jesse Pena, manager, greeted me and seated me in a dining room to the left. A waiter was right on his heels, got me a drink, and recited the menu. I found out later that no printed menus exist.

Rating: 8

Highway 77 South, Robstown, Texas 78380
Phone 512-767-9973

Menu order, take-out, catering, banquet rooms. Beer and wine. Brisket plate $7.

Open 10 A.M. to 10 P.M. Closed Sunday. Accepts cash.

I ordered a sampler plate, and it came back fast and on butcher paper. However, I need to point out that the butcher paper was on top of a tray. That set well with me. I do not like to eat where fat seeps through paper and accumulates on the tabletop. Not only was my table free of fat, the whole restaurant was spotless.

Cotten's offers four meats: brisket, pork ribs, pork roast, and sausage. They 'cue brisket from 10:30 P.M. until 9:30 A.M. I knew that was correct, because my slice of brisket had a half-inch pink ribbon. I got an end cut, which lots of folks prefer. I prefer the lean cut. The end cut causes another problem for me: Because it's cut with the grain, it resists the fork slicing test. So I sniffed it. *Nice aroma.* I popped a chunk of brisket into my mouth. *Great flavor.* I found it a little on the chewy side, so I gave it an 8.

The pork ribs were tender, had excellent mesquite smoke flavor, but contained a bit too much fat. I pinned another 8. The sliced pork comes from Boston butt. It was tender, had a mild flavor, but carried too much fat. I gave it a 7. The sausage was homemade. Its seasoning awakened my taste buds. Two drops of fat fell from the squeeze test. If it had been a little leaner, I would have given it a higher rating. As it was, I hit the sausage with an 8. The sauce had a texture like chunky soup, and it had a little fire. The chunks made it possible to taste the different ingredients. Diners used lots of it, including me.

Later, I visited with Jesse Pea. He told me that they make 1,400 pounds of sausage a week, and serve about 1,800 pounds of ribs and 6,500 to 7,000 pounds of brisket every week. That is a considerable amount of barbecue.

Cotten's potato salad had class. It's served on lettuce and had olives on top. It was creamy and not too sweet. The beans were average, and coleslaw was not on the menu. Fancy ice cream made up the dessert list.

In 1947 Joe Cotton started a beer joint where a guy could find a good dominoes game. His customers would play all afternoon and then leave at six to go eat. He came up with an idea to keep them from leaving: serve brisket. Joe served the brisket with bread, pickles, and onions. Customers brought their own knives. They took the bread, wrapped the brisket, and ate it as a sandwich. The men started bringing their wives and lady friends, one thing led to another, and now Cotten's seats 370.

Joe passed away a few years back and his son Cecil now has the reins. Unfortunately, I did not get to meet Cecil. But Jesse more than made up for it. He took me in back and showed me their pits—three large metal ones. Fireboxes had slow-burning aged mesquite shooting smoke into the pits. The wrangler rubbed the meat with salt and black and red pepper and used no sop. The kitchen was as clean as a whistle.

Jesse took pride in the fact that many employees have worked for very long times at Cotten's. "It's one of the reasons this place is so successful." He pointed to three waiters. "Johnny has been here forty years, Rudi thirty-four, and Chapa thirty-two." Seven waiters and seven kitchen workers worked over twenty years. Jesse knows because he had been here longer than the rest.

A remarkable thing about Jesse Pea: A customer named Gerald came to Cotten's. His car had a flat. Jesse was working late as he had always done and helped the man. The customer came back after seven years, and when he entered Cotten's, he saw Jesse working away. Jesse turned to him, flashed his warm smile, and said, "Gerald, it's good to see you again!" Gerald was impressed and amazed. Moreover, when Gerald left, he said, "Jesse, you work long hours. Why are you always smiling?" Jesse answered, "Because the day is getting shorter."

Rockport

Mac's Pit Barbeque

See Mac's Pit Barbeque in Gregory, Texas, on page 48 for more information.

Rating: 7.5

815 Market, Rockport, Texas 78382
Phone 512-729-9388
Menu order, drive-thru, catering. No beer. Brisket

plate $5.50.
Opens 11 A.M. Closes 8 P.M. Monday through Wednesday and 9 P.M. Thursday through Saturday. Closed Sunday.

San Benito

The Longhorn Cattle Company

If you like everything first-rate, you will like The Longhorn Cattle Company. Its huge, immaculately kept step-styled barn building shows class. The interior exudes style. Lots of longhorn heads and skulls greet you from high up on bare, unstained wood walls. Saddles and other ranch collectibles fill in the blank spaces.

I felt privileged as I walked across its concrete

Rating: 7.5

3055 West Expressway 83, San Benito, Texas 78586
Take the Paso Real exit. Located on the south frontage road.
Phone 956-399-9151

floor and took a seat among several hundred other patrons. I gave the waitress my order for one small piece of brisket with sauce on the side. She served me two pieces of meat. One cut from the top of the brisket and one from the bottom. I looked at the meat. *Not much fat.* A quarter-inch ribbon. *Could be better.* I sniffed a piece of meat. *Good aroma.* I gave the bottom cut the fork test. *A little tough.* I cut the top portion. *Tender.* I then gave it the jaw test. *Good.* I rated the brisket a 7.

Enthused, I ordered pork ribs and sausage. The waitress came back with the meats I ordered plus a slice of turkey. *Why the turkey? She must be catching on to what I was doing.* The ribs yielded a faint touch of sweetness to my chewing pleasure. *Lean. Tender.* I rated the ribs an 8. The sausage was Polska kielbasa. It was lean for sausage. Only two drops of fat fell from the squeeze test. It had a mild flavor. I gave it a 7. The slice of turkey breast had great smoke flavor but had little moisture. I gave it a 7. I sipped the sauce. It had a touch of sweetness and tasted good.

The waitress had my number. She brought me the normal side orders to taste. The potato salad was homemade. The potatoes had their skins and were not overcooked. The coleslaw had bigger pieces than most. The pinto beans came in soup. Hot and with good spices. Very delicious.

Before I could order dessert, a big guy named Bill Turner sat down with me. After introductions, I found out that he married Lisa, the daughter of the restaurant's president, Hap Fairhart, and that The Longhorn Cattle Company was a family affair. "It was my father-in-law's dream, and Lisa and I work to make the dream come true."

I asked him about his business philosophy. He said that everything is special. "If you start with a good piece of meat, you end up with a good piece of meat. Everything is made from scratch. Even our chicken is fresh, butchered every day. We don't buy any frozen products."

He confided that they 'cued with rotisserie smokers. "It's a twenty-four hour process." He said that they do not use any liquid smoke or artificial ingredients.

He had the waitress bring me some banana pudding. Bill said they were famous for their banana pudding and the bean soup. I gobbled the dessert down in short order.

As I drove away, I knew I would miss the banana pudding.

E-mail: locobill@Sprynet.com

Menu order, take-out, catering, banquet facilities. Brisket plate $6.25.

Opens Tuesday through Sunday at 11 A.M. Closes at 9 P.M. Tuesday, Wednesday, Thursday, and Sunday and 10 P.M. Friday and Saturday. Checks and credit cards accepted.

South Padre Island

Rovan's Bakery, Restaurant & BBQ

Rating: 8

5300 Padre Boulevard, South
Padre Island, Texas 78597
Phone 956-761-9672

Menu order, take-out, catering, banquet facilities. Beer
and wine served. Brisket
plate $6.95.

Open 7 A.M. to 8:30 P.M. daily.
Accepts credit cards.

This place has been around awhile. A lady who served Cajun food owned the original Rovan's. The Dwyer family bought it and made it into a donut shop. People wanted coffee so they added some tables and chairs and served coffee. They kept adding on and adding on. Today it is a bit of everything. Rovan's starts serving breakfast early and later explodes into a full-service restaurant. Although they serve many other foods, it is barbecue that customers rave and crave.

One of the best things about going to Rovan's turned out to be the drive across Laguna Madre and up Padre Boulevard. Some pundit described the island as the "Texas Riviera." The ocean's surf crashes white against blue, and white sand fills wide beaches. Sea gulls and brown pelicans abound.

I found Rovan's easily. When Bill Dwyer bought this place, he had it in mind to turn it over to his three sons Chris, Eddie, and Michael. The sons have not disappointed. Everything is tidy, maintained, and clean. The décor is country. Wood paneling and high ceiling fans. A full-size stagecoach resides in the main dining room. It has been the backdrop for thousands of photos.

A waitress seated me and gave me a menu. One page listed breakfast items, the next—everything but barbecue. Barbecue showed up in a small block on the back page. I remembered what one barbecue place owner said: "If they serve something other than barbecue, they don't know beans about barbecue." When the waitress brought me my slice of brisket, a good-sized ribbon on the brisket edge surprised me. Encouraged, I applied the edge of my fork and exerted light pressure. It did not fall apart. I gave a little nudge. The fork went through. Anxious, I dispensed with sniffing and popped it into my mouth. Mmmm, mesquite. Tender. Lean. I bestowed an 8 on it. I ordered more barbecue. I rated the pork ribs an 8. They were tender, had little fat, but disappointed with mild flavor. The sausage spewed fat from the squeeze test but had good flavor. I gave it a 7. The chicken had mild flavor and some moisture. I gave it an 8.

When you get close to the Mexican border, you expect fajitas, and I got some barbecued fajitas. They were excellent and came with pico de gallo and flour tortillas.

Served with barbecue dinners are the usual side orders. The slaw was slightly sweet and had bits of pineapple. I deemed the potato salad average. The beans stole the show. They had onions, cilantro, and great flavor.

When hurricane George swept over South Padre Island, the three Dwyer sons had a scare. Water almost made it to their door. The winds did not blow them over, and they escaped unscathed.

The Dwyers keep changing to make Rovan's more appealing. They did enough for me. I can't wait until I get back to eat more of their brisket.

I bet that other Riviera doesn't have barbecue.

Sugar Land

Texas Brisket

This place came with the highest of recommendations—from U.S. Navy Petty Officer Paul Phelps, my grandson.

He aches to get back to here and gorge on Texas Brisket barbecue.

I went to Texas Brisket planning to bring my grandson down out of the clouds.

My first surprise was the owner had refurbished the place. It gleamed. I walked up to the counter and

Rating: 8.5

7822 Highway 90-A, across from the Imperial Sugar Factory, Sugar Land, Texas 77478

Phone 281-242-1200

a Tex-Mex chap took my order. He did not try to sell me all his remaining stock of barbecue. He was courteous and prompt. I took a seat and eyed a brisket with a quarter-inch ribbon. *Another rotisserie.* The meat parted with a slight push of my fork. *Wow.* It appeared to have zero fat. The aroma teased. My bite said above average flavor. I rated it an 8. *Not bad for rotisserie.*

A pork rib had fall-off-the-bone tenderness and little fat. A rub of McCormack Barbecue Spice sparked the flavor. *Delicious.* I gave it a 9. J & B of Sysco supplied the sausage. It yielded two drops of fat from the squeeze test. *Not bad for a commercial supplier's sausage.* The flavor was above average. I gave it a 7.5. The chicken had great tenderness, a small amount of fat, and above average flavor. I labeled it with an 8. The ham was slightly salty. I suspected it came from Sysco. The ham had above average tenderness, little fat, and superior flavor. I tagged both with an 8. The turkey was on the dry side. It had superior tenderness, almost no fat, but lacked flavor. I gave it an 8.

Texas Brisket served creamy coleslaw, a potato salad with some mustard in it, Ranch House beans, French fries, and a baked potato stuffed with all the regular fixings plus chopped barbecue meat.

The owner, Sei K. Jun, an Asian Texan, did a good job redecorating Texas Brisket. It has a country café look. Dozens of Tiffany-style lamps hang over red-and-white checkered tablecloths. Huge prints of John Wayne and other western movie scenes attract the eye while a large TV distracts.

I asked Mr. Jun why he went into the barbecue business. He said he got the idea from Pappas. A praiseworthy statement. Both serve good barbecue.

Counter order, take-out, catering. Serves beer. Brisket plate $5.45.

Opens 7 A.M. Monday through Saturday and 7:30 A.M. Sunday. Closes 9 P.M. Monday through Saturday and 7 P.M. Sunday. Accepts credit cards.

Texas City

Grand Prize Barbeque

See **Grand** Prize Barbeque in Galveston (page 47) for further details.

Rating: 8.5

2223 Palmer Highway, Texas City, Texas 77590

Phone 409-948-6501

Menu order, counter order, take-out, catering. Beer served. Brisket plate $6.95.

Opens 11 A.M. Closes 9:30 Sunday through Thursday and 10 P.M. Friday and Saturday. Credit cards accepted.

Victoria

Brother's Bar-B-Que

The owner looked like a giant football lineman. His wide smile put me at ease. "We almost didn't make it," said Rev. Greg Garza. "We'd been open just a few months and I was asking my help and friends, 'Where is everybody?' I asked the Lord, 'Please send me some business.' It wasn't much longer when a reporter from *Texas Monthly* showed up. We got a write-up and the cars started coming. They made a long line all the way to the side street." He pointed to a spot about 100 yards away. "They had to wait two to three hours to get barbecue. They must have liked our cooking, because they kept coming back and so did their friends."

I arrived at Brother's a little after one. Cars flooded the parking lot. I entered through a storm door and then through a real honest-to-goodness screen door. It slammed behind me and rattled an attached cowbell. I thought I heard two cowbells but saw one. Then I observed a string going from the top of the door, across the ceiling, and into a hole leading to the kitchen.

Garza later explained that he had a lady working in the kitchen who was hard of hearing.

I walked up to the counter. A sign said, "This is not a fast food place. Please be patient. Thank you." I ordered a small slice of brisket with sauce on the side. The lady behind the counter gave me a stub with my number on it. "We'll call when it's ready."

In minutes I had my order, and I put the brisket to the test. The meat yielded with a nudge of my fork. The aroma urged me on. I chewed the bite and enjoyed very good flavor. I knew the reverend had a strong relationship with the Lord, so I figured I had better rate it right. I gave the brisket a 9.

I went back for the rest. My new plate had a big beef rib, a pork rib, sausage, and a beef fajita. The

Rating: 8

2106 Port Lavaca Drive, Victoria, Texas 77901
Phone 1-888-832-4599 or 512-575-9091

Menu order, take-out, catering. No beer. Brisket plate $5.75.

Open 11 A.M. Closes 8 P.M. Monday through Wednesday and 9 P.M. Thursday through Saturday. Closed Sunday. Credit cards and checks accepted.

beef rib received a 6. It had tender meat but too much fat and too little flavor. I dug into the pork rib. It had fantastic tenderness was also short of flavor and had too much fat. I rated it a 7. The sausage came from V&V out of Cistern, Texas. Brother Garza had it smoked just right. I gave it an 8. Then came the surprise: beef fajitas. They melted in my mouth. If the flavor had been a little stronger, I would have given them a 10. As it was, I gave them a 9. You try them. Tell me what you think.

The employees wore aprons that read, "There's no other like Brother's." That slogan also applied to the side orders. The pinto beans contained bell peppers, bacon, and chili. The potato salad had sweet pickle, salad dressing, mustard, and pimento. The stuffed potato bulged. Garza said he'd seen only one man eat all the stuffed potato, and that man was a skinny guy. It had chopped beef, cheese, chives, barbecue sauce, sausage, and butter.

If that did not inspire your taste buds, the pies, cakes, and cobblers did.

At the end of a day, Garza puts all leftovers in a freezer. When he has enough, he packs it in boxes and sends it to Crisis Kitchen (for indigent folks). This gift is your assurance that all food served is fresh every day.

Vidor

Wright's Bar-B-Q & Catering

Prepare for a surprise. Found inside Wright's Bar-B-Q is a 10 rating for pork ribs. You have seen television shows rate the best, but more than likely, you never had the chance to partake of the cuisine because it emanates from Brussels, Rome, or Paris. Now you have your chance. Cancel all other plans and head for barbecued pork ribs at Wright's.

Wright's doesn't have the ambience of Joe's in Alvin, or County Line restaurants, or Joe Cotten's in Robstown, or Mikeska's in El Campo (I could go on with this list). It does have the best ribs in the state of Texas (that's a pretty big statement).

Wright's has a steel building and looks more like a warehouse than a barbecue place. However, the interior exudes country. I walked up to the counter and ordered a sampling of meats. The server gave me more than I could consume. I sat down at a table

Rating: 8.5

1096 North Main, Vidor, Texas 77662 (off I-10)
Phone 409-769-3812

Menu order, take-out, drive thru, catering. Dry county. Brisket plate $3.99.

Open 10:30 A.M. to 7 P.M. Closed Sundays. Credit cards and checks accepted.

beneath a wagon wheel chandelier and dug in. The brisket had about a quarter-inch of ribbon, and I liked its aroma. It took a hard push with my plastic fork to slice through the brisket. It was lean and flavorful. I gave it an 8.

As is my custom, I went to the pork rib (due to its strong taste, I save the sausage for last). I saw no sign of fat. I wasted no time taking a bite. That bite was pure heaven. The meat wanted to fall off the bone. Instead of my usual two bites, I devoured it. I gave it the aforementioned 10. Then I looked at the sausage. It received a 6. Bought from a major meat packer, it had good flavor, but a puddle of fat oozed out when I gave it the squeeze test.

The potato salad, pinto beans, and coleslaw tasted good, but the jambalaya (dirty rice) stole the sideshow. This dish reminded me that this is bayou country and I was close to Louisiana.

My stomach said, "Stop," but I ignored it and dug into some superb banana pudding.

Past the repast, I studied the surroundings. It felt cozy. The tables had green tablecloths. Locals ate, chatted, and laughed. The walls had hundreds of pictures of classic cars, and toy cars sat on every ledge.

Later, Jack Wright, the owner, conversed with me. He related that he had been doing barbecue for twenty-two years. He took me out back and showed me three big brick commercial size barbecue pits that had homemade rotisseries with hickory churning smoke. I told him his brisket rated higher than other rotisserie smoked briskets. He said his homemade rotisseries cooked slower and longer.

Wright's is growing fast, thanks to good food, good service, and good prices.

And the best ribs.

Webster

Grand Prize Barbeque

Has interesting NASA collectibles and pictures dating back to 1965.

See Galveston for further information (page 47).

Rating: 8.5

938 East NASA Rd. I, Webster, Texas 77598

Phone 281-333-3451

Menu order, counter order, take-out, catering. Beer

served. Brisket plate $6.95.

Opens II A.M. Closes 9:30 Sunday through Thursday and 10 P.M. Friday and Saturday. Credit cards accepted.

Luther's Bar-B-Q

See Houston for further information (page 60).

Rating: 7.5

20794 Gulf Freeway, Interstate 45, Webster, Texas 77598
Phone 281-332-1285

Counter order, take-out, catering. Beer served. Brisket plate $7.59.

Opens 11 A.M. Closes 10 P.M. Sunday through Thursday and 11 P.M. Friday and Saturday. Accepts credit cards.

Welasco

The Barbecue Warehouse

Five years ago Bobby McNabby decided to open a barbecue place in the citrus capital of Texas, Welasco. "There wasn't a barbecue place in town," Bobby said. "Six months later there were five. Now, five years later, there are two."

Bobby must be doing something right because his place was the only Welasco barbecue place recommended to me.

He started out with an operation on top of a gooseneck trailer. One side served walk-ups, and the other side served cars. Today, it's dine in and the dining room looms big. It seats about 120. The decor says farm and ranch. Collectibles and rare Indian artifacts swarm. The interior has a cathedral ceiling finished with number three 1x12 yellow pine planks. The walls have natural finished plywood, custom-made with Mexican pine.

I sat down and ordered my usual everything. The brisket evinced a quarter-inch ribbon and had good flavor, but it took some doing to slice through with the fork edge. In the mouth, the brisket was a delight. I gave it a 7. The sausage was not home-made but had a good hickory smoke flavor. It had a little grease, and I rated it a 7. Then came a thrill:

Rating: 8

108 North Border, Welasco, Texas 78596
Take Business 83 to North Border. Building is across from courthouse.
Phone 956-968-8888

Menu order, take-out, drive through, and catering. Dining room available for parties. MC, Visa, Disc, and Amex. Beer, wine coolers, strawberry daiquiris, margaritas. Brisket plate $5.25.

Opens 7 A.M. Closes 8 P.M. Tuesday through Friday, 9 P.M. Saturday and 3 P.M. Sunday. Closed Monday.

premium cut, baby-back pork ribs. Great flavor. No visible fat. Very tender. I honored it with a 10. The finale was barbecued fajitas. Mine were tender and flavorful. I gave them an 8.

The sauce is Cattleman's Barbecue Sauce. You can buy it at the grocery store. Bobby likes it the best and sees no reason to fool around trying to come up with a secret sauce.

Sides had style. The pinto beans had small amounts of jalapeño, onions, bacon, and cilantro. Potato salad had fine flavor with sweet relish mixed with mustard and mayo. No coleslaw, but they served Spanish rice (made with chicken bouillon) and thick, soft flour tortillas. Most folks wrapped barbecue in the tortillas, creating a savory sandwich.

Bobby McNabby is a tall guy, and as he talked to me, he stood in front of a ten-foot-high cedar rocker. The proportions of the rocker's construction appeared to be perfect. Bobby's shoulders were about even with the rocker's seat, and I asked him who sat in it. "The rocker is for picture taking." Truly, it is one of the biggest attractions in the Valley, and I wished I had my camera.

The Barbecue Warehouse gets rockin' with country music starting at 5:30, Monday through Saturday, and from 12 to 3 on Sundays. Paul Martinez, a member of the Country Music Hall of Fame, performs frequently as does world champion yodeler Paul Ballinger.

Next April, when Welasco hosts its annual Onion Festival, give yourself a real treat and eat fantastically sweet onions at the Barbecue Warehouse.

Fat Daddy's

If it's four o'clock, it's Fat Daddy's. At that time, retirees and Winter Texans flock to this place for fun. They talk shop. "I got a seventy-eight," said the man in the bright red knickers. Another quipped, "And what did you shoot on the back nine?" Food and fun. That's what Fat Daddy's is. A sign inside reads, "No dancing on tables." A big jukebox looms in one corner, and perhaps the sign is necessary when the retirees are home asleep and the younger generation romps. The next morning, the younger bunch goes back to work and the retirees head for the golf course and tell their friends they were at Fat Daddy's the evening before.

Since I am a senior citizen, I did not need a disguise to be one of the four o'clock gang. I sat down,

Rating: 8

1322 South International Blvd., Weslaco, Texas 78596

Phone 956-969-3668

Menu order, take-out and catering. Serve beer and wine. Beef (top sirloin butt) plate: $6.50.

Open 11 A.M. to 8 P.M. Monday through Thursday, 11 A.M. to 9 P.M. Friday and Saturday. Closed on Sunday. No credit cards.

ordered everything, and while waiting for grub, admired the ranch decor. Unstained wood paneling. Stools at a long bar. Cattle skulls painted with Indian designs composed a remarkable display in the apex of one wall. The dining room tables had blue-and-white checkered tablecloths. Some tables had natural stained park-type seats and benches. The place was trim and tidy.

The food came and I munched away. The barbecued beef served was not brisket. It was top sirloin butt. *Not bad.* The cook cut it lengthwise, ruining the fork test. It was easy to cut off strings of meat going with the grain, but it was difficult to cut against the grain. I pushed hard and sliced off a piece. I sniffed it. *Light aroma.* I chewed. *Very mild smoke flavor, very lean, little fat.* I rated it a 7. The pork rib had a mild flavor, was tender, but had a little too much fat. I rated it a 7. Then I ate some sausage. *Wow. Fantastic seasoning. A little on the hot side.* No drops of fat fell from the squeeze test. I bestowed a 10 upon it. *A 10, on sausage, no less.*

Two surprises remained: sliced ham and turkey. The ham fell apart with slight pressure from the fork. It had been grilled, and I found the flavor mild. I gave it a 7. The sliced turkey was moist and tender, had good flavor, and was easy to cut. I gave it an 8.

Remember, these ratings are mine. What are yours?

The menu lists many sides including Texas Toothpicks—shredded jalapeños and onions, battered and deep fat fried and served with ranch sauce. The potato salad potatoes were not overcooked. I detected salt, onion, and barbecue bits in the pinto beans. Amazingly, no coleslaw.

If you can handle it, choose from peach or apple cobbler, Blue Bell ice creams, or a coke float for dessert. I tried the cobbler. Glad I did. It had pie-crust type dough. Flavor was great.

When I finished my tests, Fat Daddy's Roy Parker took me behind the scenes and showed me Fat Daddy's double brick barbecuer. He confided that they smoked the sirloin eight to ten hours and used no sop or rub. I asked him how they got started. He said that his partner Mike Real and he liked to barbecue. One thing led to another, and they started Fat Daddy's. I asked him about the fantastic sausage. He said they found the sausage maker in Karnes City, but the lady died (not from sausage). Now the lady's son lives in Rockport, Texas, and supplies Fat Daddy's. "Customers love it. We sell about four hundred pounds in two to three weeks." He said the folks from up north like pork and really go for the ribs. "We sell about five hundred racks of ribs a week."

Do you suppose Roy was pulling my rib? I don't think so.

Trivia time. In the Valley, a "two brick Norther" means a stiff, cool north wind, and it takes a brick in each of your back pockets to keep your feet on the ground.

West Columbia

Hardtack Café

Columbia is the capital of Texas. If you want to see the capital, you had better hurry. Due to a lack of accommodations in Columbia, it is to be moved to Houston, November 30, 1836.

That situation has not changed much except for the Hardtack Café. Columbia is now West Columbia. A man by the name of Josiah Hughes Bell, a friend of Stephen F. Austin, developed Columbia as a port on the Brazos River. Sugar and cotton plantations shot up all around it. Three years later, just when things were going good, he started another Columbia three miles to the west.

This guy needed a shrink.

The former town became known as East Columbia and the new one West Columbia. After the Civil War, East Columbia declined, and today we have only West Columbia. So time proved Bell right. His dad must have advised him, "Go southwest, Bell."

One might ask, "Okay, so you have a great barbecue restaurant in West Columbia, but, other than that, why would anyone go there?"

Many visitors come to this town to see the Varner-Hogg Plantation. Governor Hogg lived there in 1901, and his children restored it in 1920. Another big reason is the famous Columbia Lakes golf course.

I came to West Columbia to find a recommended barbecue place by the name of Taste of Texas. I was told to drive out Highway 35. I did, and I couldn't find it. I finally saw an old faded sign with Taste of Texas on it. The sign was part of a building built one room at a time. A new sign declared it the Hardtack Café.

Rating: 7.5

817 South 17th Street, Hwy. 35, West Columbia, Texas 77486
Phone 409-345-6162
Fax 409-345-6152
Hotmail MR_BBQMAN.com

Menu order, take-out, catering, banquet facilities. Dry county. Brisket plate $6.50.

Opens 11 A.M. every day. Closes 8 P.M. Tuesday through Thursday, 9 P.M. Friday and Saturday and 2 P.M. Sunday and Monday. Checks and credit cards accepted.

The outside was ranch style, and the inside was "antique," according to partner Mark Rikard. It had a concrete floor, and the walls and ceiling had natural-finished light wood paneling.

I walked up to the counter to order.

An attractive lady took my order, a small slice of brisket. I knew she took me for a cheapskate. I took my piece of meat and sat down at one of many tables. I gave the brisket the shear test. It took a couple of good slices with the fork edge to slice through. It had good flavor and was extra lean. I gave it a 7. That meant the place was going to be in my book.

I went back to the counter and ordered pork ribs and sausage. The lady noticed that I had only nibbled at my brisket. She knew something was askew. As soon as I started on the other barbecued meats, partner Mark Rikard introduced himself to me. As he talked, I ate and jotted down the rest of my ratings. I gave the ribs an 8. Good flavor, tender, but a little too much fat. The sausage came from Home Smokehouse. It was half pork and half beef and had good seasoning. The squeeze test produced a small puddle of fat. I gave it a 6. Hardtack also served me barbecued chicken, ham, and turkey. All tasted great.

The sides were Texas standards: potato salad, pinto beans, and coleslaw. Other specialties included a salad bar, homemade bread, Texas chicken salad made with barbecued breast, and Texas sandwiches made with their homemade bread. Cobblers and chocolate and coconut pies made up the dessert list.

Sated, I then met the other partner, Scott Leopold. I complemented Mark and Scott on their pork ribs. Scott was proud of them, took me out back, and showed me their pits, two 4'x16' steel pipe casings with fireboxes stuffed with burning live oak wood. He 'cued the ribs at 300 degrees for one hour and twenty minutes, then stuck them in an Igloo cooler. Two hours prior to serving them, he steamed the ribs. "Then they're ready to serve." He said with a grin. He had a right to smile. The ribs are so good that they have attracted such famous eaters as Astro Jeff Bagwell and ex-Astro Darryl Kile, Bum Phillips, and Rice coach Ken Hatfield.

I asked if anything unusual happened here, and I got the low-down on their annual "KIDFISH" tourney, which occurs around the end of March. They have a small lake on their property, and every year they stock it with catfish and invite kids to participate in the fish tourney. It doesn't cost the kids anything to fish, but donations are accepted. Money raised goes to Parks & Wildlife Foundation of Texas.

If you wish to participate in this event call toll free 1-877-733-5646.

Declare your independence this weekend and head for Hardtack Café.

Wharton

Hinze's Bar-B-Que & Catering

"**Mommy! Mommy!** Look at the trees growing out of the building!"

"Nonsense."

"Mommy, I'm hungry. Can we eat at the place with the trees? Please?"

The little girl is not alone. Thousands stop to eat at the barbecue place with the trees growing out of it. Two trees to be exact. The pecan trees dwarf the building huddled around their trunks.

"Hadn't you heard," said the lithesome waitress, "everything's going to go wrong in 2000 or 2001? But we are prepared. We will not run out of pecan wood for our pits."

Amused, I ordered the Deluxe Lunch. Waiting, I looked around. People of many lifestyles jammed the place. I studied the room with the tree trunks. It had a wood plank floor with openings for the trunks. The ceiling hugged the bark. I continued my survey, noting Hinze's rustic interior loaded with stuffed animals. A huge moose had the eyes you see in paintings where they always seem to be looking at you no matter where you are in the room.

Lunch arrived, and I knew the waitress was on to me. I got a sample of every meat. *How do they know what I am up to? Is it my notebook? Do they have a network and call ahead?* I stared at the brisket. *Someone is staring at me.* I looked around. It was the moose. The brisket had the familiar quarter-inch pink ribbon. *Rotisserie pits are taking over.* The aroma encouraged me. I pressed hard to slice the meat with my fork. The flavor was above average. Very little fat. I gave the brisket a 7.

The pork ribs had black pepper, above average flavor, and were very tender. Alas, too much fat. I gave them a 7. Janak's of El Campo makes the half pork, half beef sausage. The seasoning clanged, and

Rating: 7.5

3940 U.S. Hwy. 59 Bypass, Wharton, Texas 77488
Phone 409-532-2710
Fax 409-532-2800

Menu order, take-out, drive thru, catering, banquet facilities. Serves beer. Brisket plate $5.50.

Opens 10 A.M. Closes 9 P.M. Monday through Thursday, 10 P.M. Friday through Sunday. Checks and credit cards accepted.

the meat was tender. Two drops of fat came from the squeeze test. I gave the sausage an 8. Next, I tasted a slice of Boston butt pork. It was tender for pork, had superior flavor, and was extremely lean. I rated it an 8. The chicken was moist, had excellent flavor and little fat. I bestowed an 8 upon it. A slice of ham was a welcomed change from a steady diet of brisket, pork, sausage, and chicken. The ham tasted better than the chicken. I gave it a 9.

The last test involved a slice of turkey. *That moose was still staring at me. Suppose management has a hidden camera behind an eyeball?* I gobbled the turkey. I covered my writing with a napkin. I gave it a 9. It was very moist for turkey and had great flavor. I waved my napkin aside and showed my rating to the moose.

People may have thought that I had gone around the bend. I quickly put the napkin back on my lap and ate the side dishes. I detected mustard, salad dressing, pickle relish, and onions in the potato salad. The coleslaw and pinto beans were traditional. Hinze's offers a long list of other vegetables and salads, the kind of stuff the ladies like.

The eyes of the moose bulged as the waitress placed a big slice of pecan pie in front of me. I am a nut over pecan pie. It was gone in seconds.

I talked with Rosemary Hinze afterwards. Her husband and partner, W.C., was off premises. She said they 'cued the brisket from fourteen to sixteen hours at 190 degrees. She showed me two long barrel pits and two rotisserie pits. *Rotisseries. I knew it! The quarter-inch ribbon gave it away.* They used pecan, smoked for eight hours, and then every two hours they turned the meat and sopped it.

The sop is a giant secret. I asked her about the sauce, which I liked a lot. She said its ingredients were a secret. I said I detected black pepper, onion, vinegar, ketchup, and Worcestershire sauce in it. She smiled. The sauce is still a secret.

Bum Phillips, Nolan Ryan, and Ray Childress frequent this place.

In my earlier days, I handled the advertising for a cafeteria in Houston, and we used Bum to endorse the food. He would talk football and then say, "Ask me something I know something about." He would look at his bulging waistline. "Ask me about food!" He knows food, and if Bum eats here, so should you, trees or no trees, moose or no moose.

How do you tell a moose to go away? VAMMOOSE.

Part Four

Hill Country

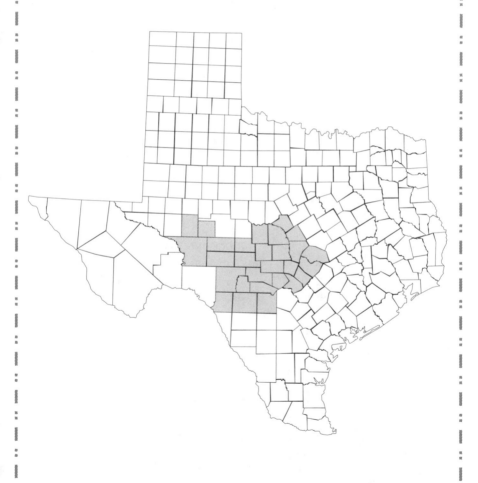

Austin

The County Line Barbecue

See San Antonio County Line on page 292 for more information.

The County Line also has locations in El Paso, Houston, Lubbock, and San Antonio.

Rating: 9

6500 West Bee Cave Road, Austin, Texas 78746-5002
Phone 512-327-1742
Open 5 P.M. to 9 P.M. daily.

Décor: exploded attic. Great mountain view. Ask to sit near the talking deer or the chicken with horns.

Lake Austin, 5204 FM 2222, Austin, Texas 78731-6516

Phone 512-328-2599
Fax 512-328-7752

Open Saturday and Sunday 11:30 A.M. to 3 P.M. and 5 P.M. to 9 P.M. (Saturday until 10), Monday through Thursday 11:30 A.M. to 2 P.M. and 5 P.M. to 9 P.M., and Friday 11:30 A.M. to 2 P.M. and 5 P.M. to 10 P.M.

5 Star Bar-B-Que & Grill

5 Star Bar-B-Que and Grill has an appropriate name. The food is 5 star—if you can find the restaurant. The place resides in a part of town that restricts signboards to diminutive proportions and subtle appearance. A man told me to watch for a small stone sign that read "Drug Emporium." He said I would find 5 Star in a strip center behind Drug Emporium.

I found it. The entrance to 5 Star exuded charm. A bridge-like ramp through massive canna lilies led me to a large deck with white patio furniture and various bright-colored umbrellas. On the right stood a smokehouse and directly ahead a small amphitheater. Across the deck, I spotted the entrance to the air-conditioned dining room and serving counter. I went to the counter and ordered my usual sampler.

The brisket had a quarter-inch ribbon. *Suspicious. Could it be another rotisserie?* The aroma was good, and it appeared to have little fat. I took a bite and found it to have superior flavor. I gave the brisket an 8. A sopped and rubbed pork rib was tender,

Rating: 8.25

3638 Bee Cave Road #104, Austin, Texas 78746
Phone 512-328-2599

Counter order, take-out, catering, banquet facilities. Serves beer and wine. Brisket plate $7.45.

Open 11 A.M. to 9 P.M. Monday through Saturday. Accepts credit cards.

had little fat and superior flavor. I rated it an 8.5. Elgin supplied the pork sausage. It yielded three drops of fat from the squeeze test, had mild flavor, and I rated it a 7. The hot sausage had less fat and one-alarm fire and I gave it a 7. A piece of pork loin also showed a quarter-inch pink ribbon. It was very lean and had superior flavor. I rated it a 9. Turkey stole the show. It had wonderful 5-star flavor, moisture, and tenderness. I gave it a 10.

I found the barbecue sauce to be sweet. It rang one-alarm fire. I detected vinegar, ketchup, and Worcestershire sauce among its ingredients.

The side orders scored above average. They made each side fresh every day with fresh ingredients. The potato salad really reflected the freshness. The coleslaw had red cabbage, vinegar, real onions, salad dressing, and a touch of Tabasco sauce. A large two-inch-wide onion ring had a thin, crispy crust on the outside and a cooked-just-right onion on the inside. The beans were different. Alex Duran, partner of 5 Star, called them "Borracho Beans." Borracho means "drunken" in Spanish. Added to the beans were onions, bacon, peppers, and beer.

If you plan to fix this, cook it slowly.

Another favorite side order was fresh garden salad.

Alex talked shop with me. He took me to the smokehouse and showed me his rotisserie smoker. He said he rubbed brisket with secret seasoning and then barbecued it fourteen to fifteen hours. He used only I.B.P. center cuts, which had less fat. He bought two-and-a-half-pound chickens and smoked them an average of three hours. I asked him if anything unusual happened here. He said, "Scarface."

"Scarface?"

"Yes. A squirrel. Been in some fight with a dog and has a bad scar. He sneaks into my smokehouse and attacks my bread supply. I chase him with a broom and we run all around the place. He somehow slips out and always makes his escape. I love animals so much I wouldn't hurt him, so I don't know what to do."

Such is life in the big city.

Every Friday night, 5 Star hosts live bands of country western or blues music.

Alex and partner Susan Provenzano were partners with two other people in the Good Eats Café. When the other partners insisted on frozen vegetables, Alex and Susan bolted and bought 5 Star. Their determination is your reward. Alex said, "I put my name on what I put out."

Jim Bob's Barbeque

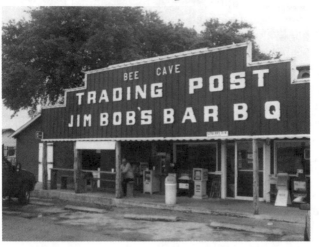

Rating: 7

12701 Hwy. 71 at Bee Caves Road, Austin, Texas 78736

Phone 512-263-3041

Fax 512-263-7300

Counter order, take-out, catering. No beer. Brisket plate $6.03.

Open 6:30 A.M. to 8 P.M. Monday through Saturday and 8 A.M. to 2 P.M. Sunday. Accepts credit cards.

What could be more Texan than the name Jim Bob's? For one thing, the looks of a place. This restaurant building could pass for an Old West saloon. Inside, it is a Texas country café with long pine plank tables and matching benches. I moseyed up to the counter, got my order, took a seat on a wood bench at a long picnic-type table, and looked at a plate of Texan barbecue.

The brisket had that encyclopedic rotisserie quarter-inch pink ribbon. The aroma squeaked like a new saddle. It had very little fat. It took two hard slices with my fork to part it. My bite revealed superior flavor. I gave it an 8. *That's pretty high for a rotisserie. Barbecuers should move outside a town's city limits so they can be out of reach of city health inspectors, have a pit, and be able to serve exceptionally good barbecue.*

The pork rib had too much fat, above average flavor, but lacked tenderness. I rated it a 6. A slice of pork roast had above average tenderness, flavor, and almost no fat. I gave it an 8. The sausage was homemade. The regular sausage yielded two drops of fat from the squeeze test and had above average flavor.

I gave it a 7. The hot sausage had two-alarm fire. Three drops of fat came from the squeeze test. The heat overpowered other seasoning. I gave it a 6. The turkey was slightly on the dry side, but the flavor sparkled. I gave it an 8.5.

The pinto beans had chili powder, black pepper, garlic powder, and Lone Star beer (I told you this place was Texan). The potato salad had Seasoning Supreme in it, and the coleslaw was traditional.

Owner Robert "Bob" Sansom took me behind the building and showed me his pride and joy: an Oyler rotisserie mounted on a trailer. It had size, like Texas. He said they rubbed the brisket with a secret mix and then smoked it for twenty hours at 250 degrees. *Maybe that's why his rotisserie smoked meat had more flavor than others?*

Back inside, blues music playing in the background I asked him about his barbecue sauces. He said the regular had the standard ingredients—vinegar, ketchup, liquid smoke, and Worcestershire sauce. The hot sauce had chili arboles peppers. He roasted the peppers and then mixed them with vinegar, garlic powder and his regular sauce. It had three-alarm fire.

Tom Landry and Jimmy Vaughn frequent this place.

The Iron Works

Smack dab in the heart of downtown Austin, a red barn-like structure with a large sign that reads The Iron Works contrasts with skyscrapers. The building used to be the historic Weigl Iron Works. Cars jam the parking lot (better get there early or late).

The place came highly recommended, so I sauntered through the doors. Inside, the place shined like the sun. Bright lights beamed on a local station reporter interviewing Stephen Yuill, son of owner Charlotte Finch, about barbecue. I stood beside another lady and commented, "Next thing you know, they'll sell barbecue on the Internet."

The lady smiled. Later I discovered why she smiled—she owned The Iron Works which already takes orders on the Internet with www.citysearch.com/aus/ironworksbbq.

I wandered up to the counter and ordered the usual: everything. I rated the brisket an 8. It took a slice with my fork edge to cut through. It possessed

Rating: 8

100 Red River, Austin, Texas, 78701

one block from I-35

Phone 512-478-4855

toll free 1-800-669-3602

Fax 512-478-2272

Counter order, sit down, take-out, and catering. Beef plate $6.

Opens at 11 A.M. Closes at 9 P.M. Monday through Friday and 3 P.M. on Saturday.

a mild flavor and less fat than most. They 'cued the brisket in two Southern Pride pits for sixteen hours, and the ribbon was wide.

The dry seasoning used to rub the meat is packaged for sale and makes a great gift. Enormous beef ribs were tender, slightly sweet, and had good flavor. I rated them a 7. The pork ribs had mild taste, superior tenderness, and less fat than the beef ribs. I gave the pork ribs an 8. The sausage had good flavor from teasing spices and from a little "fire." I graded the sausage an 8. The chicken checked out a little short on flavor—but tender—and I rated it a 7. I gave the ham and turkey an 8. Both had superior tenderness and flavor.

I sipped some barbecue sauce. The waitress said the ingredients were a deep, dark secret. Its robust flavor revealed ample portions of vinegar and Worcestershire.

The sides almost stole the spotlight from the meat and the bright TV lights. The beans were not too sweet and the spices were just right. The potato salad and cole slaw smacked good.

If you are watching your waistline, you will love The Iron Works' long salad bar with twenty selections. They serve some real Texas chili and offer baked potatoes with all the stuffings.

A nice touch to my dining experience was the bread from the bread warmer.

If you have room, try a piece of pie or one of their cobblers.

You can order barbecue by the plate or by the pound. NBC's Jay Leno orders frequently through Federal Express.

As we ate, the staff kept busy, constantly cleaning up and taking care of customers.

Dozens of tables sat on a concrete floor. A larger dining room had old-fashioned wood planking for its floor. It's décor said rustic country through and through.

Ruby's B-B-Q

University of Texas students call Guadalupe Street the "Drag." It runs past the main entrance to the UT campus, and when a blue norther howls, campus folks whiff some hunger hustling barbecue smoke from Ruby's.

The one-story building has two brick chimneys and two brick barbecue pits. You go to the counter, order, and take a number. An employee calls your number, and a waiter brings the grub to you.

Rating: 7

512 West 29th Street at Guadalupe Street, Austin, Texas, 78705
Phone 512-477-1651
Fax 512-474-4294

I found the surroundings very casual. It looked like a cozy college gathering place with a southwestern flare. Folks sit inside and out. Late at night, I am told, many blues greats from Antone's hang out here.

Luke Zimmermann and Patricia Mares started this place in 1988 with the idea of providing quality barbecue. Their menu reads, "The only barbecue place in Texas serving all natural Texas beef." The beef comes from the Bradleys, who have been ranching near Childress since 1875.

Menu order, take-out, catering, cash and checks. Beer and wine. Brisket plate $6.95.

Opens 11 A.M. Closes at midnight Sunday through Thursday; closes 3 A.M. Friday and Saturday.

"Most of our competition serves Iowa Beef Packers meat. What does that tell you?" said Pat Mares. "Bradley's brisket is lean and tender. The cattle eat only quality grain, hay, and no animal by-products. Antibiotics are never used."

That information capped off a zestful taste testing. The pink ribbon on the edge of the brisket measured a quarter of an inch. The meat was 'cued twelve to twenty-four hours depending on the dryness of the mesquite. A cook rubbed the meat with salt, black pepper, garlic salt, allspice, Hungarian paprika, and 80,000 BTU cayenne pepper. Does that sound good? Wait until you taste it.

I later noted that the brisket could have been more tender (I probably got a piece cooked in shorter time). It had good flavor and little fat. I gave it a 9. The pork ribs got an 8. They possessed good flavor but were not as tasty as the brisket. I think Ruby's cook did a good job of reducing the fat.

Ruby's barbecued and served Elgin Hot Sausage. It was a slightly warm Polish sausage. I frankly prefer sausage with more seasoning. I gave the sausage a 7. The chicken lacked flavor and was dry so I gave it a 6. The sauce was two-alarm and had a lot of vinegar.

A surprise was Ruby's "Spicy Chopped Brisket." More than chopped, it was shredded. They combined other ingredients with it and served it in a cup. I found it slightly sweet and mild and a nice and delicious variation.

Side orders included chunky mayonnaise potato salad, chunky creamy mustard potato salad, B-B-Q beans (hot and spicy), vinaigrette coleslaw, and creamy coleslaw with poppy seeds. Ruby's also had some fancy salads, hot all-beef Texas chili, and a slew of sandwiches. A special item was Ruby's Home Fries—pan fried with rosemary, bell pepper, onion, mushroom, jalapeño, and topped with mozzarella cheese.

Ruby's stays open until 3 A.M. If you think that's strange, you must remember that Ruby's commands a prime position on the Drag and caters to blues artists and 50,000 plus students who do not keep the same hours as most folks.

Parking is a problem, but the inconvenience is worth the trip. I suggest you park along the right side of the building.

Boerne

The Back Porch of Texas

Remember "Alice" (Ann B. Davis) in the Brady Bunch? She likes this place. So do I. Order anything here. You cannot go wrong.

The building's outside and inside walls are stone precisely set between large planed timbers. A huge Remington sculpture of a cowboy riding a wild one greets you at the entrance. You pick up your food and sit at one of dozens of tables beneath ceiling fans and an unpainted pressed metal ceiling. An impressive hearth with a roaring fire commands the end of the dining area. If the weather's right, you can eat on the back porch.

The mesquite-smoked meats were full of flavor. I gave the brisket a 10. It fell apart when I touched it with the plastic fork. It was lean and the flavor yodeled. It was perfect. The chicken was a 10 plus, had good flavor, and was moist and tender. The ribs earned an 8 and the sausage an 8. The turkey got an 8 and the ham a 9.

The potato salad, pinto beans, and coleslaw were well above average in taste. Consider the French fries. Reader, if you go to the Back Porch and fail to eat the French fries, you're never going to know what real living is.

Business owners John and Linda Necker have taken on a new partner, John Paul Dejoria, founder and CEO of Paul Mitchell Hair Styling products. As far as I know, the barbecue did nothing for my hair. But in time—who knows?

To visit The Back Porch, take Exit 542 off I-10, and go a quarter mile east. It is on the right.

Rating: 9

27 U.S. Hwy. 87 Business, quarter-mile east from exit 452 on I-10 and quarter-mile south of Hwy. 46, Boerne, Texas 78006

Phone 830-816-2782

E-mail backporch23@hotmail.com

Cafeteria style, take-out, catering, banquet facilities. Beer served. Brisket plate $5.45.

Opens at 11 A.M. Closes at 8 P.M. Sunday through Wednesday and 9 P.M. Thursday through Saturday. Checks and credit cards accepted.

Riverside

"Do we need gas?" Bee asked as we pulled into the Texaco station.

"No. That real estate guy said there's a barbecue place inside."

"This is a gas station. It smells like a gas station. Can't we eat at The Back Porch?"

"It's my job. I have to put the place to the test."

Reluctantly, Bee followed me through store gondolas, past some tables with green plastic tablecloths, and to a meat market counter. Looking over the top, I saw a big brick barbecue pit and a man working away. He noticed me, stopped what he was doing, and said, "Yessir?"

I ordered a sampler, and Bee requisitioned a rib plate.

Bee beamed when he presented the food on Styrofoam plates. She repeated her conviction, "Barbecue is better on plates."

We sat in captain's chairs beneath long fluorescent bulbs attached to a water-stained, suspended ceiling. We dug in. The brisket would not yield to hard pressure from my fork. I had to wriggle the fork to separate the meat. The aroma was average. The ribbon measured a quarter inch. *Not cooked long enough.* It chewed easily and yielded a good oak flavor. I gave it a 6.

Bee handed me a rib. It had some fat and a hard crust. *They cooked it too fast.* The flavor was satisfactory. I gave the rib a 7.

The sausage stole the show. I squeezed it and a couple drops of fat oozed out, but the resulting aroma chirped. I greedily gobbled it up. The seasoning was out of this world. It had half beef, half pork and, as far as I could tell, no filler. I said, "Bee, you have to taste this!" She did, and we agreed, the sausage got a 9.

As a reader, you probably surmised by now that I think more of brisket and ribs than sausage and rate

Rating: 7

Inside the Texaco station, 491 S. Main Street (Haupstrasse) and River Road, U.S. Hwy 87 Business, Boerne, Texas 78006

Phone 830-249-2546

Counter order, take-out. Beer available. Brisket plate $4.49.

Open 8 A.M. to 8 P.M. Accepts checks and credit cards.

sausage low. Therefore, this was a high mark from me. Good news: They make the sausage in the back of the meat market and sell it by the pound.

The beef jerky was also a winner.

The side orders were average. As far as I could tell, the barbecue sauce had lemon, Worcestershire sauce, and vinegar, among other ingredients. It also had big chunks of onion. Bee liked it.

If you wanted dessert, you bought candy or ice cream in the store part of the service station.

Mary Lou Zoeller owns the entire complex. It has been serving the folks around Boerne for over fifteen years.

You need to order some of her sausage, and that's no bull.

Brady

Lone Star Barbecue

When I saw the Lone Star flag, I pulled in and parked between two Ram pickups. *This place has to have barbecue*. It did. I spied two pits beneath a canopy next to its entrance. A man stood at the closer pit and asked me if he could cut me a slice of barbecue. He lifted up the lid. I selected the pieces, and he cut me what I needed. We thanked each other, and he motioned me to the entrance door. I took my tray and sat down at one of many picnic-style tables. A lady asked me if there was anything else I wanted. I asked for and received a glass of water.

I began to probe. The brisket possessed superior tenderness, above average flavor, and little fat. I rated the brisket an 8. The beef rib was very tender, had a little too much fat, and the flavor whispered. I gave it a 7. The pork ribs, rubbed with salt and pepper—no sop—had zero fat and above average tenderness and superior flavor. I rated the pork ribs an 8. The pork chop had no brown sugar like Cooper's in Llano. It had salt and pepper, moist and tender, and had good flavor. I gave it an 8. The sausage came from City Market in Schulenburg. When I squeezed it, only three drops of fat came out. Seasoning trilled. The half beef and half pork mix induced good

Rating: 8

2010 Bridge Street, U.S. 87 South and U.S. 377 South, Brady, Texas 76825
Phone 915-597-1936

Cafeteria style, take-out, meeting room. No beer. Brisket plate $6.95 per pound.

Open 11 A.M. to 9 P.M. Sometimes 8 P.M. if sold out.

Accepts checks and credit cards.

flavor. I gave it an 8. The chicken had out-of-this-world flavor, tenderness, and little fat. I gave it a 9.

Lone Star had two sauces. The regular was CD Brand Barbecue Sauce. The other was a thin, vinegary sauce.

Side dishes consisted of pinto beans, potato salad, coleslaw, and a green salad. For dessert, I had to decide on peach or cherry cobbler and/or ice cream.

The décor said ranch style. The walls had raw plywood, two large deer heads, and one elk head. It was the perfect setting for a Ward Bond or Ben Johnson movie fistfight.

The owners, Chuck and Sally Dalchau, had gone to the big city for the weekend. I asked the cook, Harold Allgood, if any celebrities ever came here. He said the whole *Star Trek* crew ate here including the leading actress. He could not remember the lady's name, but from his description, it must have been Marina Sirtis a.k.a. Commander Deanna Troi, Ship's Counselor, USS *Enterprise*.

Harold did remember that the largest deer rack in the state of Texas came from Ford Ranch, just outside of Brady. "Hunting is big business here," he said. "This place is packed in deer season."

My hunting for good barbecue paid off in Brady, Texas.

Mac's Bar-B-Que

You might say that Mac's draws attention.

It has two old-fashioned barbecue pits puffing smoke right by the highway in front of the restaurant. Trucks have hit the pits three times. One was a Portland cement bottom-dumping truck. Another was a lumber truck. And, another time a state highway truck hit a pickup truck that hit another pickup truck that rolled into a policeman and broke his hip, and the truck broke the pits.

Each time, owner Arlan (Mac) McBee—with help from his son Shannon—rebuilt the pits. Now they ask customers to park carefully, walk in, and sit down.

Mac built his two long pits with concrete block walls, firebrick floors, and metal lids. He spliced a large firebox between them, and the mesquite smoke smothers the meat on metal grills and exits

Rating: 7.75

1903 South Bridge, U.S. 87 South and U.S. 377 South, Brady, Texas 76825
Phone 915-597-2164

Menu order, take-out, catering. No beer. Brisket plate $4.50 for lunch or $6.59 per pound.

Opens 10:30 A.M. to 7 P.M. Closed Thursday (boss's farm and ranch day). Accepts checks.

through stacks at each end. The firebox is metal, and Mac boils potatoes and other vegetables on it.

I went inside and entered a dining room on the right that had what I called real country decor. I ordered small portions of barbecue and got down to business. The brisket had about a 1/16-inch pink ribbon. The aroma said "Ahhhh." The fork went through the brisket with a gentle shove. The flavor said "Ummm." It had very little fat, and I rated it an 8. The only thing that Mac added to the pork rib barbecuing was salt and pepper. The pink went to the bone. It had very little fat. The flavor was superior, and I gave it an 8. Opa's of Fredericksburg supplied the sausage. Opa's had too much fat and not enough flavor. I gave Opa's sausage a 6. The chicken had superior tenderness, above average flavor, and little fat. I gave it a 7.

The menu presents two sides: potato salad and pinto beans. The potato salad is homemade.

Dentists would be pleased to know that no desserts graced the menu. My preacher would be happy to know that no beer made the menu.

Mac wanted me to see his pits. We left the main dining room and passed a smaller room. Inside, a number of men sat around tables, drank beer, and shot the bull. Mac told me that they can bring beer in, but he does not sell any. He called it the "B.S. Room."

We made it to the outside pits. Arlan lifted the lid, and I viewed an old-fashioned long pit in action. Mac (Arlan) said he smoked the meat until the fork went in and out easily. He rubbed brisket with his special seasoning, smoked it, and when it was done, sopped it with his sauce.

Mac admitted to barbecuing cabrito once in a while but did not have any the day I showed up. He said I needed to come back the Friday and Saturday before Labor Day when Brady had its annual World Championship Goat Cook-off.

Put it on your calendar. More than two hundred entrants cook cabrito more than two hundred ways.

Driftwood

The Salt Lick

The Salt Lick is a ranch turned barbecue restaurant. The Roberts family settled here right after the Civil War. Onion Creek runs through the property, and Thurmond Roberts, founder of the restaurant, picked the site. Early family members set salt in rock hollows by the creek for the animals, and that is how the restaurant got its name. Way back when they started in the barbecue business, they dug a pit and lined it with rocks and concrete, then welded a grate for the top. "People would drive by and smell the barbecue smoke, stop, and take some home," said Scott Roberts, Thurmond's son.

Today, The Salt Lick can serve 920 people at one time and 3,700 in a day. They average barbecuing 15,000 pounds of meat a week, and the restaurant seats up to 900 people.

Eagerly, I sampled their stock in trade: brisket, pork ribs, and sausage with sauce on the side. The brisket had a half-inch ribbon, a sign that promised and delivered good flavor. It had a touch of sweetness which I later found out came from a sop. It severed with a little pressure from my fork and had little fat. I gave the brisket a 9. The pork ribs had good flavor but too much fat, so I gave them a 7. The sausage came from J Bar B in Waelder, Texas. It was Polish style, almost like bologna. It had a little pepper but not much in the way of spices. I gave it a 6.

The sauce had thirty-six ingredients, according to the waitress. Plenty of vinegar and little—if any—tomato. Habanero peppers delivered some slow heat to the mix.

The pinto beans had some zing. The potato salad had no mayo or mustard. Scott's mother, Mrs. Hisako Roberts, invented the secret recipe. The coleslaw was not sweet and had a very good twang.

I had to choose from superb cobblers (blackberry

Rating: 8

FM 1826, one mile east of Driftwood (going toward Austin), Texas 78619

Phone 512-858-4959

Fax 512-858-2038

Web site
www.saltlickbbq.com

Menu order, take-out, catering, mail order catalog, banquet rooms. Beef plate $9.95.

Open 11 A.M. to 10 P.M. Cash only.

or peach), chocolate pecan pie, and/or ice cream for dessert. I went for the peach cobbler.

Scott said they 'cue the brisket twenty to twenty-four hours. They cook it for twelve hours, chill it, and then cook it again for eight to twelve hours. The cook sops with their secret sauce. Scott pointed out that the brisket 'cues right over the coals. "That's why we use a vinegar based sauce, because a tomato based sauce burns."

The Salt Lick has an idyllic setting. Eventually, they will have a walk-through garden of twenty-two acres. "We'll be planting more than four hundred rose bushes, eight hundred gladiolas, and lots of lavender. A lantana bush will be planted in each angle of the split cedar fence."

Good taste.

Dripping Springs

Hart's of Texas Bar-B-Q

Rating: 8

Highway 290, Dripping Springs, Texas
11 miles west of Dripping Springs and 14 miles east of Johnson City. Located inside Friday's General Store.
Mailing address: Rt 1, Box 225, Johnson City, Texas 78636
Phone 830-868-9014
Fax 830-868-2544

Counter order, take-out. Catering. Beer available. Brisket plate $6.

Open Tuesday from 11 A.M. to 2:30 P.M. Wednesday through Sunday from 11 A.M. to 8 P.M. Closed Monday. Checks and credit cards accepted.

"You go 'round the bend and you come back again, just a smellin' that ole barbecue," I sang to the tune of "That good ole Mountain Dew."

I came around the bend, and, sure enough, I saw the barbecue sign. I pulled in and parked in front of a huge farm tractor that had been converted into a barbecue pit. The firebox occupied a position beneath the tractor seat, and a barrel pit took the place of the tractor engine. Heavenly smoke came from its stack and encouraged me to enter Friday's General Store.

The barbecue place took up the left side of the store and looked inviting with its fancy handcrafted cedar furniture. I sauntered up to the counter and ordered my usual.

Melinda Price handed the order to her partner Jimmy Hart, who does the serving. I congratulated her on the nice furniture. She said Rob Eberle of Wild Woods of Texas handcrafted the counter, tables, and chairs from cedar and that Rob's store was a couple doors down.

I got my food and nudged the brisket with my fork. The plastic fork went through on the second nudge. Picking up a tidbit of brisket with my fork, I sniffed it. Good aroma. I put it in my mouth and slowly ate it. Fantastic flavor. I gave it an 8.

I gave the pork ribs an 8. They had great flavor, and were lean and chewy. I had two sausages on my plate: regular and hot. Jimmy Hart makes the seasoning for the sausage and takes it to a butcher in Dripping Springs who blends it with pork. I was disappointed with its lack of flavor. I gave both 6's. Then came the treat, a chunk of barbecued pork shoulder. It was super tender and possessed superior flavor. I gave it a 9. Included on the plate was a slice of barbecued turkey. It was moist, had great flavor, and almost melted in my mouth. I gave it a 10.

The sauce had a lot of Worcestershire, ketchup, and spices, but no vinegar—other than the vinegar found in the Worcestershire sauce.

The sides were average. The potato salad had a mayonnaise base, and the cole slaw had a creamy garlic base. The beans were normal.

If you have room, try Hart's peach or cherry cobbler.

Partners Melinda and Jimmy said they 'cued the brisket twenty-four to thirty hours, using live oak wood. And, yes, they used the tractor pit, but showed me a 25-foot-long black barrel pit in back. They rub spices on the brisket and pork and sop the chicken and turkey. Like some other owners, they would not tell me their formulas.

Hart's seats about twenty inside and another twenty outside.

Elgin

Meyer's Elgin Smokehouse

Rating: 7.5

188 U.S. Hwy. 290, Elgin,
Texas 78621-3216
Phone 512-281-3331

Counter order, take-out,
catering, banquet facilities.
No beer. Brisket plate $6.89
per pound.

Opens 10 A.M. Closes 7 P.M.
Sunday through Thursday
and 8 P.M. Friday and Saturday. Accepts credit cards.

Meyer's distributes sausage all over Texas and sells sausage via mail order all over the United States. The company started making sausage in 1949, and it was not until 1998 that they went into the barbecue restaurant business. Gary and Greg Meyer bought Biggers Barbecue after James Biggers passed away. But had James Biggers gone away?

Biggers was a hard-working owner. He toiled all hours of the day and night. He pinched every penny. He turned off lights to save on the electric bill, etc. After the Meyer purchased the business, partner Greg Meyer worked one night at the restaurant by himself. He went into the sausage making room and, unlike Biggers, turned on the light to see where he was going. He went back to his office and did book work for several hours. He needed a break so he got up, stretched, and walked back through the building. It was pitch black. The light was off. Had the ghost of James Biggers flipped the switch?

Others thought that brother and partner Gary, who likes hijinks, sneaked in and turned off the light.

But Gary was out of town.

Now, when anything without explanation occurs, they blame it on the ghost of James Biggers.

No need to be frightened. This must be a friendly ghost because spirits are high at this restaurant.

When I entered Meyer's Elgin Smokehouse, I found myself in a cafeteria line that directed me through the sausage processing room of white ceramic tile (the room of the light switch). I viewed their sausage making machinery and a meat counter loaded with packaged sausage. The path led me to a food service counter in the main dining room. I ordered my usual sampler, took my food to a table, and began my tests.

I observed the oft-repeated quarter-inch pink ribbon. The aroma lured me on. It had fantastic flavor, very superior tenderness, but a little too much fat. I gave it an 8. A pork rib was extremely tender, had above average flavor, but a little too much fat, and I gave it a 7. I tried two Meyer's sausages, pork/garlic and beef. Both had slightly above average flavor, but when I gave them the squeeze test, too much fat came out. I gave them both a 6. A slice of turkey had excellent flavor, was tender but a little on the dry side. I bestowed an 8.5 on it.

The side show featured pinto beans with black pepper and one-alarm heat, sweet coleslaw, and a slightly sweet potato salad with fresh potatoes.

Dessert selections consisted of small miniature pies and Blue Bell ice cream.

I asked Greg about their sauces. His grandmother invented the recipe for the regular sauce. It had a little vinegar, ketchup, Worcestershire sauce, corn syrup, and garlic powder in it. The hot had quite a bit of hot pepper and vinegar. A taste of the hot sauce scorched my tongue with three-alarm heat. Water did not make the heat go away, but bread helped.

He showed me their two Southern Pride rotisserie pits. One had ten racks and the other eighteen. Then he showed me his secret weapon, a tumbling machine. He put the brisket and the secret seasoning in the machine, connected the machine with a vacuum hose, and then he turned it on. It tumbled, rubbing and sucking the seasoning into the meat. I had to admit that it ingrained very good flavor. I asked him to describe the décor and he said, "It's everything out of Grandma's barn."

Southside Market & Barbecue

Texans frequently butcher the English language. Settlers turned Tejas into Texas. In Elgin, they changed the soft "g" into a hard "g." However, some things do not change. Barbecue is barbecue even if they spell it occasionally with a "q." The folks at Southside Market & Barbecue have been 'cuing since 1882. The original place had a fire in 1992. They fixed it up, but owners Ernest and Rene Bracewell decided to move to the highway where more people could find them. The new place has a huge feeding area. Customers pack it. On a Saturday, Southside serves 2,000 pounds of homemade sausage, 500 pounds of other meats, and fifty to seventy-five chickens.

If they sell that much, it ought to be good, right? Frankly, I determined to prove them wrong. You see, this was the fifth barbecue place for me that day. I had barbecue up to my ears. I tired of all the song and dance of how good everything was.

When I entered the cavernous dining room, I was impressed. I walked through the crowd and got into the left queue of two cafeteria lines. Service flew. I had my usual everything handed to me on butcher paper, which I plunked down on my tray. Sides came in cups. I paid and fetched my utensils and napkins. I picked up a knife, thinking I would have to saw my way through the brisket. Was I wrong. I had no need of a knife. The fork did the job with a little added pressure. The brisket had a mild flavor, and I had to admit that it was pretty good for a large operation like Southside. I gave it a 7.

Huge beef ribs, a 7, tasted mild and had a little fat, but were good. Elgin Hot Sausage stole the show. Surprisingly, it had a mild flavor. It tasted great and contained less fat than most. I gave it an 8. The server had surprised me by giving me some steak and mutton. The beefsteak was tender and possessed a good warm flavor. I gave it an 8. The

Rating: 7

109 Central (U.S. Highway 290), Elgin, Texas 78621
Phone 512-285-3407

Cafeteria style, take-out, catering, banquet facilities. Serves beer. Beef plate is $5.25.

Opens 8 A.M. Monday through Saturday and 9 A.M. Sunday. Closes 8 P.M. Monday through Thursday, 10 P.M. Friday and Saturday, and 7 P.M. Sunday. Accepts credit cards.

mutton came in the form of a rib and could easily fight pork ribs for top honors anywhere. All previously devoured mutton had too much fat and slipped around on my fingers. This did not. It was tender and had good flavor. I bestowed it with a shining 9.

The sauce veiled a myriad of secret ingredients. I tasted a dash of vinegar, a hint of sweetness, but never figured out what spices and other flavorings were present. The sauce was outstanding, and you should try this place for its sauce if for no other reason.

Then came a surprise: fantastic potato salad. The components were not overcooked, and the flavor was perfect. It had a touch of mustard and, I guessed, a touch of mayo. I gobbled it down. The beans were gratifying.

The only other side dish was Blue Bell ice cream. They have a regular ice cream counter, and an employee scoops the ice cream for you.

A framed reprint from a defunct magazine of years ago reported that LBJ frequented this place.

Southside packages and sells Elgin Hot Sausage all over Central Texas.

Yellow paper table napkins read, "We could circle Texas in Elgin Hot Sausage."

Fredericksburg

Ken Hall & Co. Barbecue

Ken Hall never did anything average. He set the national high school football rushing record of 4,045 yards in 1953. Today he serves above average barbecue.

And, if you don't serve above average barbecue, you are not going to be in this book.

You want to eat chicken and turkey here.

I rated them a 10. Moist, tender, and full of flavor, you cannot beat Ken's birds. Brisket had good flavor but did not do well on the fork test. I gave it a 7. Ribs—tender, good flavor, and a little fat—earned a 7. Sausage came from Dutchman's Market in Fredericksburg. It had good flavor and was leaner than most. I gave it a 7.

The sauce was as secret as Ken Hall football plays. I tasted some vinegar and maybe beef broth among other ingredients. The potato salad had a

Rating: 8

Hwy. 87 South,
Fredericksburg, Texas 78624
Phone 830-997-2353

Cafeteria style, take-out, catering. Serves beer. Brisket plate $5.95.

Opens 11 A.M. Closes 3 P.M. Tuesday through Friday and Sunday; 4 P.M. Saturday. Accepts out of town checks.

mayonnaise base and unique seasoning. The beans were mild and had a trace of sweetness.

You need to get to Ken's before noon. That's when patrons storm the place.

The place had a country rustic atmosphere. Ken Hall memorabilia and other collectibles decorated the walls.

Everything I needed was upright on the table: brown paper towels, salt, pepper, Cajun Chef Sport Peppers, Cajun Chef Hot Sauce, and elbows.

What you won't find is Ken Hall. I was told he comes in early, does the barbecuing, and leaves early. Too bad. I'll bet I'm not the only disappointed fan.

Folks sat together at seven tables with benches. The place was as clean as a whistle. I rated the place a touchdown and a two pint conversion.

R&L Barbeque

Over a million people a year visit Fredericksburg. The town has around fifty top-notch restaurants, but only one R&L Barbeque. To make matters worse, R&L can only seat sixty.

I got the last table at lunch. Folks at the table next to me spoke German. *This is a German town.* The brisket had a disappointing quarter-inch pink ribbon. I knew it was not a rotisserie because, earlier, I observed their barbecuing method, which was smoking with smoldering mesquite coals in a pit.

The brisket emitted very little aroma. *Sehr bose.* I barely pressed the edge of my fork against the meat and it fell apart. *Das ist sehr gut.* It had little fat, and the flavor sang "wunderbar." Ah, "himmel" in Fredericksburg. I crowned it with a 9.

The pork rib had good appearance. It had some fat. The crust was crisp, and the inside meat was very tender. The flavor was double-wunderbar. The cook rubbed it with salt, pepper, garlic powder, and onion powder. I gave it a 9. A chunk of barbecued pork roast melted in my mouth. It was fall-apart tender. I gave it a 9. The sausage hailed from Austin. It yielded two drops of fat from the squeeze test. The seasoning was light and had some black pepper. I

Rating: 9

338 West Main Street, Fredericksburg, Texas 78624
Phone 830-997-6953

Counter order, take-out, catering. No beer. Brisket plate $4.24 (small) and $5.85 (large).

Open 11 A.M. to 5:30 P.M. Tuesday through Saturday. Accepts checks.

gave it a 7.

R&L's barbecued pork chop was fantastic. They let me pick my chop. It was thick and moist. They used their rub on it, and the flavor yodeled with glee.

The coleslaw had a very light oil base and contained a small amount of pepper. The ingredients were fresh. The potato salad was traditional. I helped myself to the pinto beans. They were in a large pot with a big serving ladle. Other than bacon, a large, whole pickle swam in it. The beans tasted good.

Bee, my wife, likes to put barbecue sauce on her beans. Have you tried it?

I chose between cherry and peach cobbler for dessert. Sometimes they have apple. It depends on a lady in town who makes them. The crust is light and flaky.

The décor said "country." A ceiling fan with tulip light shades hung over a pine floor. Tables and chairs were wood. The soft blue tablecloths added color. A wooden wainscot met white walls that displayed framed original oil paintings—some done by the owner's great-grandmother.

I talked with owner Russell Cooke (perfect name for a restaurant owner). His partner and wife, Lynne, was out of pocket. He told me that his grandfather taught him barbecue. In fact, the sauce they used was his grandfather's but without the beer.

Russell said they did cook from mesquite coals in a pit. They rub the meat and smoke it for about eight hours, depending on humidity and size of the meat. The barbecue sauce contained something a little sweet, black pepper, a tad of Tabasco, chili powder, a small amount of Worcestershire sauce, lemon juice, and the magic ingredient, beer.

I asked him how he developed his barbecue style, and he said he used to do competition cooking. He learned what to do to come up with winning barbecue.

Let it also be said that he came from Llano and worked for Cooper's at one time. "I saw what Cooper's did and I knew I could do better. So, I opened up my own barbecue place."

His mother, Petreta—but called Tita—worked the cash register. Her wide smile and bright eyes matched her son's.

Kerrville

Big Earl's

Imagine The Platters singing "The Great Pretender" while you gobble some of Texas's best barbecue. It was a long story, and it happened here. And another good thing happened. Dennis Rodman, while playing for the Spurs, made Big Earl's famous by including the place in a quote in *People Magazine*. The day the article came out, Big Earl (Earlie Williams—and he *is* big), after the lunch crunch, around 2:30, saw a steady stream of cars coming his way. He thought they were headed for DPS next door, but they turned into his place! The cars kept coming for three and a half months.

Big Earl's stories go on and on and so does the barbecue.

This is a family business. Big Earl's parents were in the barbecue business when he was born. He's a single parent, and his son and two daughters work here when not in college. Grandmother arrives early and makes three large batches of peach cobbler. By the end of lunch, the cobbler is gone.

The order counter looked like a cafeteria, but it wasn't. I told the server what I wanted, and they loaded it onto a plastic plate. The brisket had lots of flavor and a half-inch pink ribbon. It was fork cutable. I rated it a 9. If it had been just a touch more tender, I'd have given it a 10. The meat was 'cued by Big Earl for eighteen hours and rubbed with salt, pepper, and two secret ingredients. Ribs were tasty and fairly tender, had a little fat and good flavor. I gave them an 8. An outside supplier made the sausage according to Big Earl's recipe. I knew it was his recipe because it had more spices than your regular brand sausage. It had less fat and was tender. I gave it an 8. The chicken tasted great, its meat tender and juicy, and I gave it an 8.

The sauce was not too sweet and not fiery. It was

Rating: 8

401 Sidney Baker South, Kerrville, Texas 78028
Exit 508 south off I-10, 62 miles west of San Antonio. Phone 830-896-5656

Counter order, take-out, drive thru, and catering. No beer. Beef plate $4.80.

Opens 11 A.M. Closes 7 P.M. Monday through Wednesday, 8 P.M. Thursday through Saturday and 2 P.M. Sunday. Accepts checks.

just good old barbecue sauce. The formula was a secret, but I could taste a little lemon added to normal makings.

After wishing Big Earl the best, I sneaked around back and saw a lot of oak and mesquite, and two long barbecue barrels.

Big Earl does everything right.

Buzzie's Bar-B-Q

Rating: 8

213 Schreiner Street,
Kerrville, Texas 78028
Phone 830-257-4540
Other location in Comfort,
Texas.

Cafeteria style, take-out, catering. Serve beer. Brisket plate $5.25.

Opens 11 A.M. Closes 8 P.M. Tuesday through Saturday, and 3 P.M. Sunday. Closed Monday. Accepts checks.

Are you ready for a 9-rated beef brisket? Head for Buzzie's. With the usual furnished plastic fork, I used the edge to cut the meat. I pressed gently and the lean meat fell away. The pink belt was deep and the taste unforgettable. Buzzie and Brenda Hughes run a clean, first-class joint. Brenda said the meat is 'cued with mesquite and oak for eighteen hours. Rub and/or sop stuff is a closely guarded secret. Their delicious, mild barbecue sauce has unique ingredients: lemon, onion, and butter.

She shared a secret with me—how do you find good brisket at the meat counter? You pick it up, bend the ends, and if the ends can touch, you have excellent lean brisket.

I gave the ribs a 7. They had a little fat, great flavor, and were not sweet. Their sausage hailed from Opa's in Fredericksburg, had mild flavor, and received a 7. They cooked other meats including rib eye and filet steaks.

Now it only gets better when you sample the side dishes. They make everything from scratch. I gave the potato salad a 10, the coleslaw a 9 (slightly sweet), and the beans a plus 10. Folks, you don't know what good pinto beans taste like until you eat Buzzie's.

If you have room left, try some peach, cherry, or blackberry cobbler.

The Hughes family started cooking BBQ in their backyard, and it got out of hand. They opened in Comfort, Texas (a few miles east on Highway 27), over five years ago and the Kerrville place a year ago. Movie stars Madeline Stowe and Brian Benben, and Minnesota Viking Joe Jackson have frequented this place, so it must be good (who would argue with Joe?). Live music revs up the place on Thursday nights. To get there, take Kerrville exit from I-10, go south, turn right at Schreiner Street.

Lampasas

Circle H Bar-B-Q & Catering

Owners Kay and Ray Bocanegra purchased the Circle H one week before I arrived. The place was in great shape and clean as a whistle.

The brisket had a 5/16-inch pink ribbon. *Encouraging.* The aroma beckoned me onward. It took two pushes with my fork to part the meat. The brisket appeared to have little fat. *They probably did not cook it long enough*. My bite revealed above average flavor, and I gave the brisket a 6. Since a 6 qualifies a barbecue restaurant for a place in my book, I went on with my tests. A pork rib had good appearance but had some fat, which also meant they did not cook it long enough. When I bit into it, I had the surprise of the day—superior tenderness and a fantastic flavor from a secret rub. I gave it an 8.

Slovacek furnished the half beef and half pork sausages. The regular Polish sausage had garlic and black pepper and yielded four drops of fat when I squeezed it. The flavor was good, and I gave it a 6. The jalapeño sausage had almost no fat and three-alarm fire, and I gave it an 8.

Pinto beans had some chili powder and a little

Rating: 7

1799 Hwy. 281 South,
Lampasas, Texas 76550
 Phone and fax 512-556-4133

Counter order, take-out, catering. No beer. Brisket plate $5.35.

Opens 11 A.M. Closes 8 P.M. Monday through Thursday, 8:30 Friday and 8 P.M. Saturday and 3 P.M. Sunday. Accepts checks and credit cards.

sweetness. The coleslaw was creamy and sugary. Macaroni salad and potato salad were traditional. Circle H made the side orders every day with fresh ingredients.

For dessert, I had a choice of banana pudding, peach cobbler, or pie—pecan, lemon meringue, chocolate meringue, or coconut meringue.

I called the décor "cozy country kitchen." Collectibles were everywhere. A very clever idea was small vegetable baskets turned upside down to make lampshades.

They put in some new bathrooms outside. You think you are going to an old-time outhouse or Elmer, but inside they are sparkling modern and clean.

Circle H is directly across the highway from a golf course, so naturally they get a lot of 19th hole trade. But the Trevino who turned up here to eat was Rick Trevino, the country western music star.

Mason

Cooper's Pit Bar-B-Q

Cooper's brings the biggest barbecue argument to mind: barbecue is or is not grilling. Cooper's has a huge furnace where they burn mesquite down to charcoal. Cooks shovel coals from the furnace to the pits, and they grill the meat 28 to 30 inches above the coals. Owners Duard and Yvonne Dockal maintain that their way is real barbecue. "The other way is just smoking," said Duard.

The finished product on my plate had my attention. The server asked me if I wanted my brisket dipped in a light, vinegary sauce or not. I thought it might tarnish the true flavor of the meat, so I said no.

The slice of brisket had a 3/16-inch pink ribbon. *Less than a rotisserie.* Intriguing wafts of pleasurable aroma caught my attention. It took two slices of my fork to part it. *Same as most rotisserie smoked brisket.* It had a little fat, and my bite had excellent flavor. I rated it an 8. *One point higher than most rotisserie-smoked barbecue.*

A pork rib showed quite a bit of fat but had fall-off-the-bone tenderness and superior flavor. I

Rating: 8

U.S. Hwy. 87 South,
P.O. Box 732, Mason, Texas 76856
Phone 915-347-6897
Toll free 1-800-513-6963
Web site
www.sig.net/~nasoncoc

Pit order, take-out, catering. B.Y.O.B. Brisket plate $6.99 per pound.

Open 10:30 A.M. to 5 P.M. or earlier if sold out. Accepts checks and credit cards.

gave it an 8. A commercial meat company supplies the sausage according to Cooper's recipe. It seeped four drops of fat from the squeeze test, but, thanks to generous chunks of meat, had superior flavor. I tagged it with a 7. A piece of chicken breast was semi-moist and tender, had little fat and above average flavor. I gave it an 8.

Then came one of the biggest surprises of the entire barbecue search: cabrito. They served me a small rack of ribs. It had the same pink ribbon of the brisket, but way too much fat. The flavor delighted, but it must have been an old ram because the meat was on the tough side. I gave it a 7.

The barbecue sauce had a tangy flavor. I liked it. It had the basic ingredients in good proportions.

Cooper's coleslaw was creamy and slightly sweet with a touch of vinegar. The potato salad was creamy and had big chunks of potato. The pinto beans had some chili powder.

Yvonne made the desserts. I had to choose from cobblers, pies, cheesecake, bread pudding, rice pudding, and lemon, pineapple-upside-down, and German chocolate cake. *A line-up like that every day, and I would end up at the psychiatrist's office.*

The original Cooper's started two doors away in 1953. Duard said, "My dad was in the barbecue business before then but quit to do some ranching. When he heard Mr. Cooper was retiring, Dad went to work for Mr. Cooper and eventually bought the place January 1, 1983. We moved to our new place in November of 1985."

The "new place" has a rustic look. Customers sit at long picnic tables and chat or watch TV.

Mel Tillis is a big fan of Cooper's barbecue. He ate here many times when he was on the road. Movie star Ben Johnson and character actor Dub Taylor also ate here.

San Marcos

Fuschak's Pit Bar-B-Q

San Marcos, gateway to the Hill Country, has Southwest Texas State University, the Aquarena Springs, and Fuschak's Pit Bar-B-Q.

Rating: 7.5

920 Hwy. 80 just east of I-35, San Marcos, Texas 78666-8124
Phone 512-353-2712

Fuschak's building resembled a large dining hall in a major national park. It had rough, dark stained wood siding, and tourists were packed inside and out. A half dozen cars lined up at the drive-thru window, and a dozen or more people waited in line inside the front door. The place was so busy, I knew I might never get small samples of everything, so I took a seat and waited for the line to let up. I waited two hours. Of course, I kept busy writing and editing. Finally, an employee brought me small pieces of brisket, pork rib, and sausage. "Sorry, Mr. Troxell. We just had a huge order. Thanks for your patience."

Cafeteria style, take-out, drive thru, catering. No beer. Brisket plate $5.59

Open 10:30 A.M. to 9 P.M. Closed Sunday. Accepts credit cards.

I thanked him. *How did he know my name? These guys must network.* I gave the brisket the once over. The pink ribbon was small. *Cooked too fast.* The aroma waffled. The meat appeared fairly lean. It took extra effort with my fork to cut it. It was a good piece of brisket, but lacked flavor. I rated it a 7. The pork rib was extremely tender, but had a bit too much fat and needed more seasoning. I gave the rib an 8. A meat company makes the sausage according to Fuschak's specifications. I squeezed the sausage and three drops of fat oozed out. *Not lean enough.* I tasted it and thought it had above average flavor. I gave it a 7.

The sauce was sweet and warm. I detected cayenne, ketchup, and Worcestershire sauce in it.

The usual sides of potato salad, pinto beans, and coleslaw seemed normal—the way most folks like them.

Banana pudding and pecan pie comprised the dessert offering.

I sat back, sated. Looking around, I decided that the interior—like its exterior—also looked like a national park place. Rough, dark stained wood paneling covered ceiling and walls. Long stemmed fans hung from a high cathedral roof. A magnificent, huge stone fireplace ruled at the end of the hall.

Foods fit for a king or a queen or for even a tourist.

Taylor

Louie Mueller's Bar-B-Que

According to John Mueller, son of Bobby, son of Louie, 2,500 publications in the last ten years wrote about Louie Mueller's Bar-B-Que.

You can now make it an official 2,501.

What is the attraction of this place? A weathered old building? A genuine screen door that slams?

Rating: 7
206 West Second Street,
Taylor, Texas 76574-3511
Phone 512-352-6206

119

Hard wooden chairs and tables? High green walls turned grimy brown from smoke and even grimier as you get closer to the pits? Could it be the barbecue?

Cafeteria style, take-out, catering. Serves beer. Brisket plate $4.50.

I entered with a shove on my backside from the screen door. I ambled up to the counter and ordered one small slice of brisket with sauce on the side. I sat down and observed the meat. It had about a quarter of an inch of ribbon. *Not encouraging.* I sniffed it. *Mild aroma.* I placed the fork edge against the brisket. *Could 2,500 publications be wrong?* It came apart on the second slice of the fork. *Not very tender. Cooked too fast and with too much heat.* It didn't 'purr' like one publication said. The flavor was mild. I gave the brisket a 6. The sauce was vinegary and thin. It had some tomato and onions. Good for dipping.

Opens at 8 A.M. Closes 4 P.M. Monday through Friday (take-out till 6), 2 P.M. Saturday. Closed Sunday. Accepts checks and credit cards.

I went back for a rib and a piece of sausage. The rib was a different matter. It was tender, and had lots of pepper. It carried a little too much fat. I gave it an 8. The sausage was homemade, lean, and had two-alarm fire. I gave it an 8.

Other meat offerings were chicken breasts, T-bones, and pork steaks.

The potato salad had a mustard base and average flavor. The pinto beans were one alarm and had good flavor. The creamy coleslaw seemed average. They charge you for a pickle, a jalapeño, or a slice of cheese.

If you like something sweet after you eat, you can feast on Blue Bell ice cream.

Bobby showed me their two pits behind the serving area. One is brick and the other steel. "We use post oak wood and cook it four to six hours. High temperature. No thermometer. And the only thing we add to the meat is salt and pepper."

This business started in the early forties. *They must be doing something right.* The place packs in barbecue lovers, and according to Bobby Mueller, they sell out every day.

Rudy Mikeska's Bar-B-Q

I arrived at a slow time. Most lunchtime folks had already gone back to work. I decided I would only order a small slice of brisket with sauce on the side. The server carefully weighed the portion and asked for seventy-six cents. "You want bread?"

Rating: 7.5

300 West 2nd Street, downtown, Business Highway 79, Taylor, Texas 76574

I guess he felt sorry for me. "Please."

I observed a quarter-inch ribbon. *Look's promising*. I ordered a rib and two inches of sausage. I thought the pork rib was tender, and had a little too much fat and mild flavor. The rib got a 7. I tested the sausage. I squeezed it, and very little fat dropped out. It had a good beef taste with a little warmth to it. I gave it an 8. I gave the chicken a 9 and the lamb ribs an 8.

The serving counter was cafeteria style, and Rudy Mikeska's Bar-B-Q presented a number of good side dishes: stew, creamed peas, creamy fruit salad, mashed potatoes, peaches along with the regulars, potato salad, coleslaw, and pinto beans. I ordered the latter three and found them good but average.

Dessert had big winners: banana pudding and peach cobbler.

The manager showed me a twin brick pit in back. He said they 'cued the brisket over eight hours at 209 degrees.

That accounted for the quarter-inch ribbon (low heat—like 190 degrees—and longer smoking with many lid openings and closings—to let the oxygen in—result in a wider ribbon and more tender and flavorful meat).

Rudy Mikeska founded the business in 1952. He converted an old Safeway store into his restaurant. Like all Mikeska barbecue places (El Campo, Columbus, and Temple), Rudy hung hunting trophies everywhere. Today Rudy hunts for bigger game in the sky, and his son Tim has the reins.

Phone 1-800-962-5706
E-mail mikeskaBBQ @aol.com

Cafeteria style, take-out, catering, banquet facilities. Brisket plate $5.65.

Opens 10 A.M. Closes 8 P.M. Monday through Saturday and 2 P.M. Sunday. Checks and credit cards accepted.

The Taylor Café

In an old red one-story metal building facing the highway overpass next to the railroad tracks stands the old Taylor Café. Neighboring stores have long since emptied. I had no problem finding the place because it had cars parked all around it. I must admit that, at first glance, I thought I had the wrong place because it looked more like a beer joint than a barbecue place. Like Louie Mueller's, I walked through a screen door with a strong spring. The force from the spring physically encouraged me to enter.

The first thing I saw was a long bar with a smiling señorita waiting on customers. A sign behind her

Rating: 8

101 North Main, Taylor, Texas 76574
One block south of Business Route U.S. Highway 79 at State Highway 95 (northeast of Austin).
Phone 512-352-2828

Menu order, take-out, and catering. Beef plate $4.50.

read, "Never trust a skinny cook." A jukebox played, and neon beer signs beamed. Boldly I sat down on a stool and asked, "Got any barbecue?" She pointed to a menu posted on the glass door of a large, vertical cooler filled with beer. I ordered every meat on the menu. When she left, I questioned my sanity for coming here and thought that

Open 7:00 A.M. to 10:00 P.M. Monday through Saturday and 11:00 A.M. to 10:00 P.M. Sunday. Accepts cash and checks.

the people who recommended this place made a mistake—probably gave me the wrong name and address. I looked around. Some guys were playing pool at one end of the place. The pool table looked solid and above it hung a long, rectangular multicolored imitation Tiffany lamp, another beer sign. Other guests ignored the players and kept busy downing their food and beer.

The waitress placed a big platter of barbecue in front of me. It looked inviting, and, despite the saloon decor, I decided to be fair while testing it. I touched the fork edge against a slice of brisket and nothing happened. *Aha!* I gave it a nudge. The meat fell apart. Now what am I going to say to all the experts who rated the two other places in Taylor so much higher? I shrugged and gulped the bite down. I found great flavor, and just a little too much fat. I gave it an 8.

I gave the pork ribs an 8. They had a mild flavor, were tender, but had a little too much fat. The sausage was homemade. It tested like the ribs, and I gave it an 8. Then I looked at the next piece of sausage, and it appeared darker in color. It smelled good. I ate it. I found out that it was turkey sausage, the specialty of the Taylor Café. It was lean and the taste was keen. It had a little fire and a wonderful blend of spices. I gave it a 10.

They served three sides the day I dined. The potato salad and the beans were average but good. I didn't have room for chili which was "Today's Special" for $3.35. And, like most Texas barbecue places, pickles and onions were offered.

Through testing, I found the owner, Vencil Mares. I congratulated him on his fine barbecue, and he took me into the kitchen to show me how he did it. He had a long brick pit with large iron lids. He lifted one, revealing a dozen or so beef briskets. The chestnut colored beauties looked ready to eat. He said, "I cook my brisket a little differently than most. I rub the meat with a dry seasoning of black pepper, salt, and garlic. I add a touch of chili powder to give it color, and then I let it set overnight. It barbecues for eight to ten hours. I never turn the meat. If you do that, the juice goes down the drain. I cook the meat in its own juice." He took a big fork and tested the meat. "If the fork slips out, it's done. If it grabs, it isn't done." He let me try poking the meat, and I declared the brisket done. He smiled and nodded. "I've been doing it like this since forty-eight."

Maturity etched his rugged face. He read my mind and said, "I'm seventy-five." He went on to tell me how he had served in the Army as a medical aide in World War II. He landed at Normandy and took part in the Battle of the Bulge.

I wanted to stay and listen to old war stories, but I had to make one more barbecue stop before the night was over. As I drove away, I did a little mental arithmetic. Vencil Mares' Taylor Café has been in business for over fifty years.

I urge everyone to try it. Gobble up some turkey sausage.

Uvalde

Haby's BBQ

First, the Comanches drove off the Apaches. In 1790 Captain Juan de Ugalde ran the Comanches out. Then Texans moved in, bringing such people as King Fisher, Pat Garrett, and John Nance "Cactus Jack" Garner. Fisher, an alleged cattle rustler and murderer, was found innocent on charges and later became acting sheriff of Uvalde County. Pat Garrett, slayer of Billy the Kid, lived here a few years, and John Nance Garner lived here his entire life. Garner served as vice president under Franklin Delano Roosevelt.

Unfortunately, none of the aforementioned had a chance to eat at Haby's BBQ.

I arrived at Haby's at one o'clock, missing the big lunch crowd and also missing the sold-out pork ribs (I cannot be at every barbecue place at noon).

I ordered a small slice of brisket and took a seat at a table with benches. I placed my Styrofoam plate on top of the red-and-white checkered tablecloth.

Somehow, red enhances the looks of food.

Looking around, I thought the owner had done a good job of decorating the place ranch style. A stuffed bobcat looked down at me.

I commenced the plastic fork test. I nudged the meat with the edge of the fork. Nothing happened. I

Rating: 7

529 East Main Street, U.S. Hwy. 90, Uvalde, Texas 78801-5714
Phone 830-278-5746

Cafeteria style, take-out, drive thru, catering. No beer. Brisket plate $5.75.

Open 10:30 A.M. to 5 P.M. Closes sooner if they run out of barbecue. Stays open until 9 P.M. on Friday night for catfish fry. Accepts checks and credit cards.

pushed harder. I made an indention. I gave it a final shove and the meat parted. I looked at the pink ribbon with suspicion. It measured one-quarter of an inch. *Could be another rotisserie*. The meat lacked aroma and, when I chewed it, the flavor squeaked. Too much fat. I rated it a 6.

Since a brisket rating of six qualifies a barbecue place to be in my book, I went back for a two-inch section of sausage. I squeezed it and one drop of fat fell out. *That's pretty lean*. The half beef, half pork sausage had above average flavor. I gave it an 8. Later I found that the sausage came from Eckridge Farms, a commercial meat supplier.

Side dishes included coleslaw and potato salad. No beans. The slaw was creamy and sweet and contained carrots. The potatoes in the potato salad were not overcooked. However, I thought the potato salad was too creamy and sweet.

Pecan pie made up the entire dessert list.

I met with owner Jesse Haby, and he said they used a stainless steel rotisserie to smoke the meat. *Ah ha. I knew it.* He said they smoked the brisket fourteen hours, and the only thing they added was salt. I asked him about his barbecue sauce. He said that it came from an old family recipe and contained garlic, salt, pepper, mustard, Worcestershire sauce, and other mysterious ingredients.

The barbecue place began about one hundred years ago. Mr. Denmark acquired it a way back when. In 1971 Mr. Denmark, tired of running two locations (the other in Del Rio), told Dan Haby, Jesse's brother, he wanted to sell the place right away and did he know someone who would like to have it. "He won't have to pay much down," Mr. Denmark said.

Dan remembered that Jesse had a lot of barbecue experience. He introduced Jesse to Mr. Denmark and, that day, Jesse became the new owner. "I got the whole place—furniture and fixtures, and stocked with food," Jesse said. "Best deal I ever made."

When in Uvalde, thanks to Ugalde, you can eat at Haby's.

Part Five

Panhandle Plains

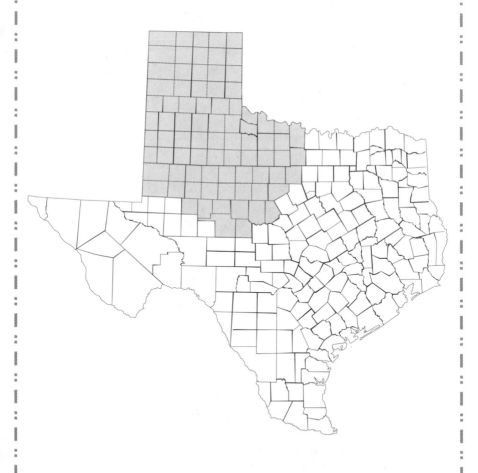

Abilene

Harold's World Famous Pit Bar-B-Q

Taylor County has six noteworthy barbecue places, five in Abilene and the sixth in Buffalo Gap. No doubt, the county has the most barbecue eaters per capita and should claim the title of barbecue capital of Texas.

Harold Christian, owner of Harold's, is a big black man with a big baritone voice. An accomplished singer, he will burst into song to entertain. The customers love it.

Are you going to sing today?" I asked.

"Only if the customers stop coming in." He flashed a teasing smile that almost went from ear to ear.

"What songs do you like to sing?"

"Gospel, 'How Great Thou Art,' 'Amazing Grace,' but my favorite is 'I Won't Complain.'"

"I don't know that one."

"Most people don't. It's a new song. One you hear in black churches."

I actually hoped customers would stop coming through the door, but they did not.

The place was small, packed, and forte. I got my order and took a seat at a bench with several other eaters. I looked at a 5/16-inch pink ribbon. It had a smidgen of fat. In the shear test, it parted after three slices with my fork. The aroma was pianissimo. The flavor was not glorioso. I scored it a 7.

A pork rib had some fat, excellent tenderness, and above average flavor. I gave it an 8. A chunk of barbecued roast beef had some fat, superior tenderness, and average taste. I tagged it with a 7. Harold's Polish pork sausage yielded only two drops of fat from the squeeze test and had superior flavor. I gave it an 8. A slice of ham had some salt, but the smoke flavor won out. The ham had a little fat, excellent tenderness, and the flavor sang "How Great Thou

Rating: 8

1305 Walnut, Abilene, Texas 79601-3649
Phone 915-672-4451.

Counter order, take-out, catering. No beer. Brisket plate $5.50.

Opens 11 A.M. Closes 6:30 P.M. Monday, Tuesday, Thursday and Friday; 2 P.M. Wednesday and 5 P.M. Saturday. Closed Sunday. Accepts credit cards.

Art." I christened it with a 9.

The barbecue sauce had some sweetness, probably from brown sugar. I detected ketchup, Worcestershire sauce, some chili powder, bits of onion, barbecue, vinegar, and a little heat from perhaps cayenne.

The place was so busy, I did not get a good look at all the veggies. I tried the coleslaw. It was creamy and contained some mustard.

Harold put some deep fat fried corn bread on top of my plate. It was sweet and delicious. If I lived in Abilene, I think I would come back here just to eat the corn bread.

Harold offers peach cobbler, apple cobbler, and ice cream for dessert.

The interior looked like a typical small town café. Long and bare fluorescent bulbs lined the ceiling. The floor had a vinyl tile brick design. Concrete block walls had light gray paint. Harold used red to add color to the scene, red Naugahyde benches, booths, and tablecloths. Memorabilia dotted the walls and shelves.

Harold told me that he custom built his metal barbecue pit. He uses oak wood and smokes up to 500 pounds of brisket twelve to fourteen hours. No rub. No sop.

Suddenly, Harold went over to a lady and sang "Happy Birthday" to her. The customers gave them both a big round of applause.

Joe Allen's

Joe Allen's is big-time barbecue, and little guys like me are lucky to get to eat it. I know from experience that they treat the little guy with as much respect as they treat the big guy.

Their banquet room seats 500. They catered 30,000 skiers at Copper Canyon, Colorado, and 450 business people at Myrtle Beach, South Carolina, last year, and they did a great job of taking care of me.

Joe Allen's brisket had a quarter-inch pink ribbon. *Could it be another rotisserie?* It had little fat, superior tenderness, and very good flavor. I gave it an 8. *Couldn't be a rotisserie.* A pork rib was very lean and had above average tenderness, and the flavor shouted, "Ti yippee yay." I rated it a 9. The sausage yielded three drops of fat from the squeeze test. Black pepper clobbered the rest of the sausage

Rating: 8.5

1233 South Treadway, Abilene, Texas 79602
Phone 915-672-6082
Fax 915-672-3015

Cafeteria style, take-out, catering, banquet facilities. Serves beer. Brisket plate $5.49.

Opens 11 A.M. Closes 9 P.M. Monday through Thursday and 9:30 P.M. Friday through Sunday. Accepts checks and credit cards.

127

seasoning and the meat flavor. I hit it with a 6. A piece of chicken had superior tenderness, very little fat, and above average flavor. I tagged it with an 8. The salt in a slice of ham overpowered the smoke and pork flavor. It was tender and very lean. I gave it an 8.

The barbecue sauce had a heavy tomato base. I detected black pepper, maybe a little cayenne, some Worcestershire sauce, and what was it? Lemon? Pickle juice?

Joe Allen served the regular sides. Coleslaw had a light sauce and was slightly sweet. Creamy potato salad had mashed potatoes and a little relish. Pinto beans came with onion and bacon. Also available were French fries and green salad.

Dessert was "Just Like Home Peach Cobbler" and ice cream.

The interior said "cabin." Walls and ceiling had dark walnut stained wood paneling. A fan spun beneath a cathedral ceiling, and some very nice framed Western art prints decorated the walls.

Joe Allen knows meat and knows all the sources for meat. He acquired that knowledge while working as a county agent for years. He shops around and buys the best. He does not depend on one supplier like his competitors do.

They barbecue on a long brick pit, the old-fashioned way. The wrangler in charge starts mesquite smoking the briskets at 8:30 P.M. At 8 A.M. the next morning he throws on three or four small sticks. It's ready to go at 10:30.

Be sure to eat some homemade bread.

Ronnie Ingle's Pit Bar-B-Q

Rating: 8.5

3910 South Treadway,
Abilene, Texas 79601
Phone 915-695-9924

Counter order until 5 P.M., then menu order. Take-out, catering, banquet facilities. Outdoor facility accommodates 300 people. Serves beer and wine. Brisket plate $5.60.

Voila. I found some great barbecue brisket. It practically melted in my mouth. The flavor said yippee! When I touched it with my fork, it fell apart. *That's tender.* It had a 5/16-inch pink ribbon and very little fat. I rated it a 9.

Open 11 A.M. to 9 P.M. Monday through Friday and 5 P.M. to 9 P.M. Saturday. Accepts checks and credit cards.

Later, I found out why the brisket was so good. Ronnie and his son Layne do all the barbecuing. They mesquite smoke the brisket for twenty-four hours with low heat. They use a homemade barrel pit. *What a difference.*

Ronnie started this business in 1985. He tired of his former work and wanted to do something different. He liked to barbecue, so he decided to make it his career. Ronnie found a vacated antique store, bought it, fixed it up, installed his barrel pit, and began corralling customers.

I asked Layne if they used a rub or a sop on the brisket. "Only salt and pepper. I guess you could call that a rub."

They serve ribs only on Fridays. Unfortunately, I arrived on Tuesday. Layne did cut me off a piece of pork sausage. It had too much fat but above average flavor, and I gave it a 7.

Unlike many others in the business, Ronnie Ingle's barbecues their hams and turkey breasts. A slice of ham was extremely tender, a little short on flavor, but was very lean. I gave it an 8.5. A piece of turkey breast had above average tenderness, a touch of fat, and excellent flavor. I labeled it with a 9. It was the best turkey since a month before when I had some at Goode Co. in Houston.

Ingle's served the standard sides. The pinto beans had traditional flavor; the potato salad had chunks of potato. They marinated the coleslaw with a sweet and sour sauce.

Dessert: peach cobbler and/or ice cream. They add cheesecake to the dinner menu.

The decor came from the country, befitting the original antique store. Raw wood shutters closed on the inside. I asked Layne if there was a reason for that, and he didn't know of any. Ingle's added a large dining room, which looked like an old western saloon. A long bar went across one end of the room, and an albino longhorn head loomed over it. The steer stared at a large elk trophy at the other end of the room. The ceiling was corrugated metal. The walls had some very interesting framed photo enlargements of scenes at a working ranch. I took a close look and spotted Ronnie and Layne on horseback in several pictures. One photo I admired depicted a round-up scene. It looked like a Remington oil painting with its light colors and sunlit dust.

Betty Rose's Little Brisket

A statewide magazine publicized Betty Rose's Little Brisket. An onslaught of business ensued. They had to open two new locations to take care of the customers.

How good is Betty Rose's?

The beef brisket had a 1/8-inch pink ribbon. *Not much to show for flavor*. It displayed very little fat. I had to push hard with my fork to cut the meat. The aroma murmured. The flavor was above average, but it took a long time to chew it. I rated it a 7. A pork rib had too much fat but was very tender and tasty. I gave it an 8. Eckridge, an excellent commercial meat processor, supplied the sausage. It oozed three drops of fat from the squeeze test and hit superior on the taste scale. I gave the sausage a 7. A piece of ham was slightly salty, but not salty enough to overpower the smoke taste. It had very little fat. I gave it an 8. A slice of turkey had excellent tenderness and little fat and possessed superior flavor. I tagged it with a 9.

The barbecue sauce was sweet and vinegary. It had some black pepper for warmth. I detected, I think, pickle juice.

The potato salad consisted of mashed potatoes and relish. The coleslaw was creamy. The pinto beans had a traditional flavor. Betty Rose's also served macaroni salad and homemade banana pudding.

Becky, employee in charge, showed me their barrel pit. She said that each store had the same pit—all built by Betty Rose's son.

They use mesquite and smoke briskets eighteen hours. No electronics. No gas. No electricity. All manual. And the cook rubs briskets and ribs with Betty Rose's secret spices.

Betty Rose no longer has anything to do with the business, but all the recipes are hers. Today, a triumvirate of couples—Rick and Carolyn Daffron, Kyle

Rating: 7.5

2402 South 7th Street, Abilene, Texas 79605-3149
Phone 915-673-5809

3362 Rebecca Lane, Abilene, Texas 79606-3228
Phone 915-698-8000

1055 N. Judge Ely Boulevard, Abilene, Texas 79601-3853
Phone 915-672-3500

Counter order, take-out, catering. B.Y.O.B. Brisket plate $5.50.

Open 11 A.M. to 8 P.M. (South 7th); open 11 A.M. and close 9 P.M. Sunday through Thursday and 10 P.M. Friday and Sunday (Rebecca Lane and Judge Ely locations). Accepts checks and credit cards.

and Cherry Johnson, and Pat and Harvey Jackson—owns and runs the restaurants.

Becky said, "Betty Rose's secret ingredient is T.L.C."

Square's Bar-B-Q

Rating: 8

210 North Leggett, Abilene, Texas 79603
Phone 915-672-6752
Fax 915-673-7184

Cafeteria style, take-out, drive thru, catering, banquet facilities. Serves beer. Brisket plate $6.50.

Open 11 A.M. to 9 P.M. Closed Sunday. Accepts credit cards.

A Kiowa Indian legend tells of a giant cave that extends from Abilene to the Caprock to the Canadian River. At the appointed hour, a weird herd of sixty million red-eyed buffalo will emerge. A shaggy white-haired bull, mighty and terrible, will lead them. The enemies of the Kiowa will be trampled, and the Kiowa nation will rise again.

No one has found the cave because most people in the area are too busy working and trying to pay taxes.

At 11 A.M., I, the incarnation of the white shaggy-haired buffalo, led a herd of hungry animals into Square's. Fortunately, I was first in the cafeteria line. I picked up my usual barbecue samples and took a seat.

The brisket had a 1/16-inch pink ribbon. The aroma was as silent as a Kiowa Indian walking on polished marble. My plastic fork parted the meat with one firm slice. The brisket had as much fat as the white buffalo story had credence. The flavor did not make me yelp. I graded it an 8. A sopped pork rib had very little fat and superior tenderness. The added sauce detracted from the smoke flavor. I gave it an 8. Dankworth Sausage, a fifty-year-old firm in Ballinger, Texas, supplied the sausage. It yielded four drops of fat from the squeeze test. It had above average flavor, and I rated it a 5.5. The salt in a slice of ham overpowered the smoke flavor. It had tenderness and was very lean. I tagged the ham with a 7.

Then came the treat of treats, barbecued turkey breast. Square's marinates the breast for twenty-four hours. They rub it with a seasoning and smoke it with mesquite. It was moist, tender, and had excellent flavor. I gave it a 10.

Square's potato salad had sour cream and tasted like a stuffed baked potato. The beans had bits of bacon and barbecue sauce mixed in. The coleslaw had a generous amount of coleslaw dressing. The broccoli and rice salad was a winner.

Desserts: banana pudding and peach cobbler.

The interior reminded me of a rustic western hunting lodge. The walls and ceiling had rough wood 1x12's. Huge wooden crossbeams bolstered a cathedral ceiling. Mounted deer and elk trophies overlooked the crowd of diners.

Square's resulted from a collapse in beef prices in the seventies. Back then, Grandfather Callaway sold the ranch and bought the barbecue place. His grandson Al worked at the place, and eventually, Grandfather sold the business to him.

Al showed me his Oyler rotisserie barbecue pits. *Another rotisserie. No wonder the pink ribbon measured only 1/16th of an inch.* He said they mesquite smoked the brisket sixteen to eighteen hours at 225 degrees and dipped the ribs in a sauce.

Turnerhill's

Wilton Turnerhill began business in 1964. An enterprising young man, he started the pit fire at night and placed brisket in the pit, then Wilton went home and slept. At 4:30 A.M., he went back to the pit to check the meat and the fire. He added the right number of sticks and made the place ready for the day's upcoming business. Then he went to his regular job at the bank at 7 A.M. Throughout the day, he called to tell his employees what to do. After work, Wilton rushed back to his barbecue place, took care

Rating: 7

1881 North Treadway,
Abilene Texas 79601
Phone 915-672-5811

Cafeteria style, take-out, catering. No beer. Brisket plate $4.95.

of business matters, and started the whole proce- | Open 10:45 A.M. to 8 P.M.
dure all over again. This went on for a long time. | Closed Sunday. Accepts

In 1998 he sold the business to brother-in-law | checks and credit cards.
Clyde Davis. Clyde does a good job running the
place, and Wilton, who cannot sit around doing noth-
ing, works a couple of hours every day and assists as needed on catering
jobs. Clyde's daughter, Beverly Lavender, helps her dad. The day I visited,
Clyde had the day off, and Beverly answered my questions.

Turnerhill's brisket had a 1/8-inch pink ribbon. The aroma sang some
slow blues. The meat showed a little too much Fats Domino and was as
tough as George Foreman. When I took a bite, I heard the "saints come
marching in." I rated it a 7. A pork rib had above average tenderness, superior flavor, and a little too much fat. I gave it a 7. The sausage oozed four
drops of fat from the squeeze test, but the flavor was superior. I tagged it
with a 7. A slice of ham had a slightly salty flavor that did not override the
smoke flavor. It had above average tenderness and very little fat. I gave it a 7.

Clyde serves three barbecue sauces. They shared a common tomato and
vinegar base. The original sauce had a small amount of red and black pepper.
The sweet sauce had brown sugar or plain sugar added to it, and the hot
sauce had a generous supply of red and black pepper.

The cafeteria line presented a number of vegetable dishes. Of note was a
mind shattering dish entitled, "Butter Rolls." It was not an oven-baked roll.
It was cobbler crust without fruit. It had come-back-again-and-again
ingredients.

Beverly makes the Butter Rolls and all of the desserts. The day I visited,
she made cherry, sweet potato, buttermilk supreme, and pecan pie, and blueberry cobbler.

The place looked like a utilitarian café of the forties. Bare fluorescent
bulbs hovered over a vinyl tile floor. Two ceiling fans spun slowly. Simulated
wood paneling had an off-white finish. Rose-colored Naugahyde tablecloths
added color.

The place did have a woman's touch. Hanging baskets had plastic flowers,
and ruffled curtains ran across the tops of the windows.

Amarillo

Cattle Call

You should be able to find this place. It is at the main entrance of Westgate Mall, facing Interstate 40, west of downtown Amarillo, on the way to barbecue desolation (land outside of Texas).

I went through the doors and found the restaurant on the immediate right. A pretty hostess seated me, and I gave a waitress my order. Waiting, I studied a large longhorn mural, photos of working ranch cowboys, and Western art. Walls of boxes and sacks of foodstuffs created a feed store effect.

Owner David Wilson did a good job of converting a mall setting into a barbecue place.

My slice of brisket had a quarter-inch pink ribbon. It had the qualities of a rotisserie pit, little fat and little aroma. In the shear test, it parted with the second slice of my fork. Above average flavor. Above average barbecue. A 7. A chunk of shoulder clod beef had a strong sweet sauce that clobbered any smoke flavor. It tasted good if you like that sort of thing. However, it suffered as barbecue. I gave it a 4. A pork sparerib was a different matter. It had a little too much fat but above average tenderness and flavor. I gave it an 8. A piece of pork sausage oozed a puddle of fat and had very little flavor. I gave it a 4.5. A slice of ham contained a little salt and had superior tenderness, little fat, and average flavor. My turkey came grilled. It was good, but it was not barbecue so I passed on judging it.

The barbecue sauce had the basics (ketchup, vinegar, and Worcestershire sauce). I detected black pepper, garlic, a touch of liquid smoke, and some sweetness.

They sprinkled the potato salad with paprika, the coleslaw snapped with light vinegar, and the ranch style beans had chili powder. Other sides were corn on the cob, baked potato, and stewed apricots, the

Rating: 7

7701 Interstate 40 West, Suite 398, Westgate Mall Amarillo. Texas 79160 Phone 806-353-1227 or 1-800-658-6097

Menu order, take-out, catering. No beer. Brisket plate $7.39.

Opens 11 A.M. Closes 9 P.M. Monday through Thursday, 9:30 P.M. Friday and Saturday, and 6 P.M. Sunday. Accepts checks and credit cards.

darling of the Panhandle.

Dave was born and raised in Borger, Texas. After graduating, he worked in the oil fields and at a Borger barbecue place at night. He moved to Amarillo and labored at several restaurants including one owned by Scott Sutphen, a barbecuer of note from times past. He finally gave in to his calling and opened Cattle Call in 1985.

He admits to using a rotisserie pit, a J&R from Dallas. He smokes brisket for seventeen hours at 250 degrees and uses hickory wood.

Warning: They slop everything with sauce unless you ask them not to do it. I recommend you ask for sauce on the side.

Cattle Call barbecues 2,800 to 6,000 pounds of brisket a week.

Desperado's BBQ & Steaks

Desperado's wins the looks parade of barbecue places in Texas. Of adobe construction, it has a southwestern theme, inside and outside. When you walk in the front door of Desperado's you "step into the real Texas," according to Richard Dyer, owner. A beautiful and enlarged color photograph of cowboys and their horses in an aspen quaky in the middle of winter hangs behind the cashier's counter. It is worth a good look. Walls have photos of ranch scenes and displays of ranch paraphernalia. The large dining rooms seat 275 and appointments are tasteful and elegant.

Seated at a table, I read my menu:

A Poker Player's Menu
One Pair:
One meat, 2 pieces
Two pair:
2 meats, 2 pieces of each
Three of a kind:
Choice of one meat, 3 pieces
Straight:
One piece of 5 barbecue meats
Flush:
5 spare ribs

I went for the Straight. The menu had a

Rating: 9

1503 South Madison, downtown, Amarillo, Texas 79101
Phone 806-372-3030
Fax 806-372-3082

Menu order, take-out, catering, banquet facilities. Serves beer. Brisket plate $5.50.

Summer hours: opens 11 A.M.; closes 10 P.M. Monday through Saturday and 9 P.M. Sunday. Winter hours: opens 11 A.M.; closes 9 P.M. Sunday through Thursday and 10 P.M. Friday and Saturday. Accepts checks and credit cards.

Desperado design and several bullet holes through it. The slogan read, "Shoot…that's good BBQ!"

Desperado's brisket had a quarter-inch pink ribbon. *Another rotisserie?* The aroma tantalized. I quickly touched the meat with my fork, and it parted without pressure. It showed no fat. The flavor zinged. I awarded it a 9. *Could not be a rotisserie.*

At this point, I began to realize because of the high altitude of this country (3,000 to 4,000 feet) that I would not see the same pink ribbons I saw in lower climes.

A pork rib was a big surprise—not that it had great tenderness and little fat, not that it had shoot-'em-up flavor, but because it had an unusual ingredient in the sweet rub, cinnamon. It was delicious. *I could eat pork ribs like this all day and all night.* I rated it a 9. A chunk of beef shoulder clod had zero fat, above average tenderness, and almost zero smoke flavor. I gave it a 5. A piece of pork tenderloin possessed superior tenderness and very little smoke flavor. It was quite lean. I rated in an 8. Old Smokehouse (Hormel) supplied the pork and beef sausage. It oozed a puddle of fat from the squeeze test, and the flavor hummed. I tagged it with a 6.

The barbecue sauce was sweet, rich, and tangy. *Seems to be that way everywhere in the Panhandle.*

Desperado's coleslaw was creamy and contained some unusual ingredients. I asked Richard Dyer about it. He said they added buttermilk, garlic powder, Miracle Whip, black pepper, and a tiny amount of salt to the cabbage.

Potato salad consisted of mashed potatoes made from boiled potatoes and not instant potatoes. Chuck Wagon beans had a small amount of chili powder. Other sides were corn on the cob, French fries, Texas toast, and chunky applesauce.

Desserts: peach, blackberry, or cherry cobbler and ice cream.

Richard Dyer comes from the famous Dyer family, owners of barbecue restaurants in Texas for several generations. Richard started working in Dyer's in the seventh grade. When Richard finally had his chance to open his own place, he made many changes, which resulted in better barbecue. For example, the pit. He said they used a long, flat metal pit that had four big lids on top. They can smoke sixty-three slabs of brisket at one time. They start smoking at 8 P.M. and let them 'cue all night. The cook takes them out of the pit at ten in the morning.

I asked Richard if any celebrities ate here. "Teresa Parker, the granddaughter of Comanche chief Quannah Parker, comes in quite often."

Teresa gave Richard a picture of Quannah Parker's house. It hangs on a wall in the restaurant. The house has seven stars on it. Teresa said he had a star on the roof for each of his seven wives. "And that's why everybody calls it the *Star House*," Teresa said.

Every summer, the Indians have an annual powwow at the Tri-State Fairgrounds. Quannah Parker used to attend. *With his seven wives?*

Dyer's Bar-B-Que

See Dyer's Bar-B-Que in Wichita Falls (page 165) for more information.

Rating: 8

2927 SW Parkway, Wellington Square, Amarillo, Texas 79102-2239

Phone 806-358-7104

Menu order, take-out, drive thru, catering, banquet

facilities. Serve beer and wine. Brisket plate $6.99.

Opens 11 A.M. Closes 9 P.M. Sunday through Thursday and 10 P.M. Friday and Saturday.

Robinson's Bar-B-Q

As the address implies, Robinson's is on the southwest side of Amarillo. Take the Western exit off I-40 W near Westgate Mall and head south.

Your perseverance in finding Robinson's pays big dividends in barbecue.

I went to the counter and met Keva, the daughter of Carol and Worlan Robinson, owners of this place and a new location at 6th and Maryland, old U.S. Hwy. 66 in downtown Amarillo. Keva dished out a plate of barbecue samples, and I began my tests.

A slice of brisket had a small pink ribbon. *Strange. Must be the high altitude.* A good aroma urged me on. The meat parted with one hard slice of my fork. It had some fat and I rated it a 7. A chunk of pork butt melted in my mouth and had excellent flavor and no visible fat. I gave it a 9. A pork rib had above average flavor, some fat, and average tenderness. I tagged it with a 7. Black Oak Meat Company supplied the sausage. It yielded four drops of fat from the squeeze test. It possessed above average flavor, and I gave it a 6. The barbecue sauce had the standbys of ketchup, vinegar, and Worcestershire

Rating: 7.75

7012 South Western, Amarillo, Texas 79110

Phone 806-356-9662

Counter order, take-out, catering. BYOB. Brisket plate $5.50.

Opens 11 A.M. Closes 8 P.M. Monday through Friday and 6 P.M. Saturday. Accepts checks.

sauce. Black pepper and Tabasco gave it a little snap.

The coleslaw was creamy. The pinto beans had great flavor, and I found the potato salad sweet and chunky.

For dessert, I had the only dessert, cobbler a la mode.

Robinson's looks like your typical country café on the side of the road. They painted everything white, inside and out. Splashes of color come from red Naugahyde padded chairs, motorcycle pictures, a TV, and motorcycle collectibles.

Take time to examine a cabinet packed with miniature motorcycles.

Worlan worked as a butcher all his life before taking the big plunge to own a barbecue place.

Keva said they use a barrel pit and smoke the brisket five to six hours at 180 to 200 degrees. *Those are small numbers. With higher altitude, I expect numbers to increase, not to decrease.* She said they use mesquite wood and apply a secret mix of seasoning to the ribs.

Sixth (6th) Street Station

Rating: 7.75

3514 West 6th Avenue at Maryland on old U.S. Hwy. 66, west of downtown, Amarillo, Texas 79106
Phone 806-342-0150

Menu order, take-out, catering. Serves beer. Brisket plate $5.50.

Open 11 A.M. to 2 A.M. (if no one's here at 10 P.M., they close). Accepts checks and credit cards.

Sixth Street Station is a motorcycle haven for barbecue heaven. During Memorial Day weekend, over four hundred bikes jammed the parking lot. If you do not have a motorcycle, keep cool. You will receive friendly smiles and good service.

This is a second location for the Robinson family. Daughter Keva assists at the South Western Street restaurant, and daughter Dana helps out here.

On weekends, bands provide entertainment. One

week it might be blues, another jazz, or rock, or country western.

See Robinson's Bar-B-Que in Amarillo (page 137) for more information.

Wesley's Bean Pot

Wesley's is a sweet little deal on Amarillo's north side. Working men jam the place at noon to get a full plate of barbecue and sides for $4.90.

I received a plate of barbecue samples, and the man behind the counter asked me what I would like to drink.

"Water, please."

He motioned toward the glasses and a water cooler. "I don't make any money on water." He flashed a big smile. I later found out that he is not only the owner, but the entertainment as well. Although I did not hear any of his jokes, he had customers laughing all the time.

I took my water and tray of food to a table and began my tests. A slice of beef had a small pink ribbon and a little fat. Discouraged, I administered the shear test. The meat parted with the third slice of my fork. No aroma stirred. The decision to put Wesley's Bean Pot in my book weighed on the flavor of the brisket. I took a bite. The flavor mumbled.

Laughter came from another corner of the store. *Folks love this place. I cannot let their happiness affect my decision.* I gave it a 6. Since a 6 qualifies, I tested a pork rib. It had a vat of fat, excellent tenderness, and very good flavor. I rated it a 7. Polish sausage oozed five drops of fat from the squeeze test and had average flavor. I tagged it with a 5. A piece of hot link seeped three drops of fat and had three-alarm fire that clobbered any other flavor. I gave it a 5. Jalapeño sausage yielded three drops of fat and had two-alarm fire. I gave it a 7. The salt in a slice of ham was too strong. The only smoke flavor came from the outside edge. It had excellent tenderness and almost no fat. I rated it an 8. A moist piece of turkey had almost no fat, excellent tenderness, and little smoke flavor.

Rating: 6.5

400 East Hastings Avenue, Amarillo, Texas 79108-5264
Phone 806-381-2146

Counter order, take-out, catering. Beer. Brisket plate $4.90.

Opens 11 A.M. Closes 8 P.M. Tuesday, Thursday and Friday and 3 P.M. Wednesday and Saturday. Closed Sunday and Monday.

I labeled it with an 8.

The barbecue sauce ran on the sweet side like most Panhandle barbecue sauce.

Wesley's does everything from scratch. They even pick the beans. The beans had some chili powder and tasted good. The coleslaw had a very light dressing. They picked the potatoes, washed them, boiled them, peeled them, and made a better-than-average potato salad.

The place looked like a hundred other roadside cafes. Inside, a bright Coca-Cola border ran around the room at the ceiling. The walls displayed many funny sayings. One read, "Some people are alive simply because it is against the law to kill them."

Big Spring

Al's and Son Bar-B-Q

The Sulphur Draw is the longest dry draw in Texas. It runs through a gorge in the Caprock escarpment at Big Spring. The draw did in fact have a spring-fed watering hole that attracted buffalo, wild mustangs, Indians, Forty-niners, stagecoaches, military men, and settlers. Comanches thought of it as a place of peace and war. Early pioneers named it the Big Spring.

In June of 1999 I passed through here, not looking for water but barbecue. Everyone I asked said I should try Al's & Son Bar-B-Q. I did.

Al's brisket had a 1/8-inch pink ribbon. *Ouch*. It had a little fat. In the shear test, it gave with the second slice of my fork. My bite revealed above average flavor. I graded it a 6. They rubbed the pork rib with a sweet seasoning. It had superior tenderness and flavor but a little too much fat. I rated it an 8. Opa's of Fredericksburg supplied the pork and beef sausage. It seeped five drops of fat from the squeeze test, but the flavor was above average. I gave it a 6. A piece of chicken breast was moist and had above average flavor, good tenderness, and almost zero fat. I gave it an 8. A slice of ham was slightly salty. It had very good tenderness, little fat, and superior flavor. I

Rating: 6.5

1810 Gregg Street, U. S. Hwy 87, south of Interstate 20 and a half block north of the H.E.B. Food Store, Big Spring, Texas 79720
Phone 915-267-8921
Fax 915-267-6567
E-mail cscom@crcom.net

Cafeteria style, take-out, drive thru, catering. No beer. Brisket plate $5.79.

Opens 11 A.M. Closes 8 P.M. Tuesday through Friday and 3 P.M. Saturday. Accepts checks and credit cards.

labeled it with an 8.

The barbecue sauce had the basic ingredients of ketchup, vinegar, and Worcestershire sauce. I tasted some chili powder and a little red pepper in it.

Sides: ranch house beans, coleslaw with a light dressing and pimento bits, and potato salad with a touch of mustard. Al's serves other vegetables.

Desserts: apple and cherry cobbler, pecan pie, and banana pudding.

The décor looked country to me. It had a red-and-white vinyl tile floor, red Naugahyde tablecloths, pink ruffled curtains ran across the tops of windows, and shelves held dozens of interesting collectibles.

Chuck and Sue Bagwell (no relation to Astro Jeff) own Al's & Son. Chuck is the son of Al, who started this business back in 1964. Al sold it to Chuck in 1991.

I asked Chuck what kind of pit he had. He confessed that they used an electric Cookshack smoker.

Note: The electric smoker uses electric heat as well as heat and smoke from a few logs. Since logs cost more than electricity, the electric smoker saves the owner money, but costs him less flavor in his barbecue. Anytime you see a piece of meat with less than a quarter-inch pink ribbon, you can expect less flavor from the meat. This type of smoker works well in restaurants that smother their meat with barbecue sauce.

Al's & Son smokes brisket for eighteen hours at 190 degrees. Those numbers accounted for the tenderness of their brisket.

Country western star Jodie Nix ate here.

An interesting trivia item is the electric eye operated paper towel dispenser in the restroom.

I never saw the Big Spring.

Buffalo Gap

Perini Ranch Steak House

The New *York Times* ranked the Perini Ranch out of Buffalo Gap (pop. 499) at the top of their "best mail order" list. The *Times* said, "...with his mesquite-smoked peppered beef tenderloin, Tom Perini ate the competition for lunch."

I went to Perini Ranch because many Texans from my polling said they had great barbecue. The road to the Ranch is on the west side of FM 89 just south of Buffalo Gap. Keep a sharp eye for the sign.

Rating: 8

FM 89 off Hwy. 89 south,
PO Box 728, Buffalo Gap,
Texas 79508
Phone 1-800-367-1721

Menu order, catering, picnic and banquet facilities. Full bar with one dollar membership fee. Brisket plate $8.95.

Open 6 P.M. to 9:30 P.M. Wednesday and Thursday and 12 noon to 10:30 P.M. Friday and Saturday. Accepts checks and credit cards.

Buffalo Gap derived its name from a geological slash through the Callahan Divide where buffalo once roamed. Bison came through the gap on their way to the high plains for the summer or to South Texas for the winter. Buffalo hunters picked them off as they passed by.

This action wrote an important page in Texas history. President Mirabeau B. Lamar of the Republic of Texas determined to kill off the buffalo to rid the nation of Comanches. Buffalo Gap provided the opportunity to do that.

Driving to the Ranch on a lonely road surrounded by live oaks, I thought the barbecue restaurant part of the Ranch must be a fun thing for Mr. Perini. Who would go this far out of the way to eat his barbecue? Soon I saw the entrance, and the sight of motor buses erased all speculation from my mind.

The building had the look of a dude ranch dining hall. Inside looked more country than outside. It had old rusted corrugated metal panels in the ceiling. Walls looked sturdy with large hewed planks sealed with mortar. A big brick fireplace held a longhorn skull, and ceiling fans stirred above a red painted concrete floor.

I took a seat and placed my order with a waitress. Waiting, I noticed a number of folks chose to eat and socialize outside under arbors and oak trees.

My Perini slice of brisket had a smallish pink ribbon and a lot of fat. A waft of smoke aroma twitched my nose. In the shear test, the meat parted with slight pressure from my fork. *Promising.* To prime my taste buds, I sniffed it closely. *Very good.* I took a bite, and the flavor yodeled victoriously all the way to New York and back. *If only it had been a little leaner.* I rated it an 8. The pork rib fared the same as the brisket, too much fat but great flavor. I gave it an 8. The sausage oozed five drops of fat from the squeeze test and had above average flavor. I tagged it with a 6.

The barbecue sauce was sweet, and I detected perhaps a little lemon in it.

Two sides came with my meat order, potato salad and pinto beans. The potato salad had big clumps of boiled potato with a touch of mustard blended into the salad dressing, and the pinto beans contained chunks of barbecue.

The sides did not last long on my plate.

The waitress asked me if I would like a dessert.

"What do you have?"

"Bread pudding, cheesecake, *and...*" She smiled.

"And?"

"And jalapeño cheesecake."

I fell. I ate the whole thing.

Later, I met with the head wrangler, Dale Cronk, whose in-laws live in my hometown, Fredericksburg. Dale showed me their barbecue pits. It was a Cooper's type setup, or maybe I should say Cooper's had a Perini-type setup. They reduced the mesquite wood to charcoal and grilled the meat over the coals (see my Introduction). Several hands worked full time manning the pits on restaurant days. Dale said they smoked brisket twelve to fourteen hours at 250 to 275 degrees.

Perini caters barbecue all over the world. It's a big business.

Childress

J.T.'s Drive In

Normally, I poll an area in advance to find prospects for my book. J.T.'s is an exception to the rule.

This time I stopped because of its steam engine locomotive barbecue pit puffing smoke. I took a photo of it and thought, "What the heck. I should at least try the brisket."

I entered a plain, plain, plain converted mom and pop hamburger stand and ordered a slice of brisket with sauce on the side.

For some reason, it is difficult for waitresses to accept an order for such a small amount of barbecue. To help them understand, I said, "If you give me a big pile of meat, I can't eat it. I eat at six or seven barbecue places a day, and I do not have any more room in my stomach. You will be wasting food if you give me more than one bite of each piece of meat."

"Well, okay," she said and brought me one small

Rating: 8

406 Avenue F NW,
U.S. Hwy. 287, Childress,
Texas 79201
Phone 940-937-2688

Counter order, take-out,
drive thru. No beer. Brisket
plate $5.20.

Open 11 A.M. to 8 P.M. Monday
through Saturday. Accepts
checks.

slice of brisket.

I looked at the slice in admiration. It had a 3/8-inch pink ribbon. The meat parted with a slight touch of my fork. The aroma warbled. It had very little fat, and my bite evinced superior flavor. I rated it an 8.

Well! I was ready to try some more barbecue. Guess what? They only do brisket.

The barbecue sauce had a tangy taste, and J.T.'s makes it from scratch. I detected Tabasco sauce, tomato, chili powder, and maybe a little Worcestershire sauce.

The waitress did not know how the boss made the sauce or how long he barbecued the brisket.

Johnny Longbine started this business in 1992. One wag at a service station said, "The barbecue place is Johnny's hobby. He has another full-time job."

The place seats twenty-four people, and you do get to eat on a plate atop a bright green Naugahyde tablecloth. You can see what you are eating because of large windows and two scrawny circular, bare bulb, fluorescent light fixtures.

The waitress did not know who made the locomotive barbecue pit.

I chugged on down the road.

Clarendon

Sam Hill Pit BBQ

They named Clarendon, "Saint's Roost," because cowboys had to check their guns at the general store. No liquor. No gambling. No nothing. Back in 1878, a Methodist preacher by the name of Lewis Henry Carhart started Clarendon. He wanted a peaceful town that would attract families. It worked.

The only shoot-'em-ups in Clarendon these days is the "Bible Shoot." The event is held every other July 4th unless it's Sunday, then they defer to an adjacent year. They place a Bible on a post with two nails. You shoot the Bible. The Bible verse that stops your bullet applies to you. Of course, they do more than shoot the Bible. Better call Sam Hill Pit BBQ and verify time and date if you want to participate.

Rating: 7.5

614 West 2nd Street, Hwy. 287 West, Clarendon, Texas 79226

Phone 806-874-3358

Toll free 1-888-874-3358

Fax 806-874-9608

E-mail
womackl@gojuno.com

Counter order, take-out, catering, banquet facilities. No beer. Brisket plate $6.95.

Inside Sam Hill's, I ordered my usual sampler of barbecue.

My slice of brisket had a small 1/16-inch ribbon. *Not encouraging.* In the shear test, the meat parted with the second hard-pressed slice of my fork. A little whiff of aroma teased me. *Encouraging.* My bite revealed very good flavor. I rated it an 8. A pork rib had very little fat, above average tenderness, and above average flavor. I gave it a 7. The sausage seeped four drops of fat from the squeeze test and had very good flavor. I gave it a 6.5. The salt in a slice of ham wiped out any smoke flavor. The ham had excellent tenderness and little fat. I tagged it with an 8. A slice of turkey had little fat, extreme tenderness, and superior flavor. I gave it an 8.

The barbecue sauce was sweet. They served the standard sides of potato salad, pinto beans, and coleslaw. Desserts were cobbler and ice cream.

Suzanne and Kent Womack own Sam Hill's.

Sam opened it in 1987, and the Womacks bought it in 1995. Suzanne was out, but we did get to talk with Kent. He showed us their unusual brick pit that steams water to make the meat tender.

I did not tell him, but he can read it here. I have yet to see where steam made barbecue more tender. What I have seen is less flavor.

Kent said they smoke brisket overnight and use mesquite wood.

The last hanging in Texas took place in Clarendon on June 3, 1910. Judge J. N. Browning ordered G. R. Miller of Childress executed for his crime spree that left four men dead and four wounded. Lewis Henry Carhart probably turned over in his grave four times.

Open 11 A.M. to 8 P.M. Tuesday through Sunday. Closed Monday. Accepts checks and credit cards.

Colorado City

Nix's Bar-B-Que & More

The first Colorado City was laid on the west bank of the Colorado River and lasted less than a decade. The first Texas Legislature voted to make it the capital of the Republic of Texas, but President Sam Houston vetoed it. So the promoters went west and started another Colorado City on the Llano River. They billed it as The Mother City of West Texas.

Folks visit the new Colorado City to see the Colorado City Historical Museum and eat barbecue at Nix's.

Rating: 8

Fort Woods Complex, Interstate 20, exit 217, Colorado City, Texas 79512

Phone 915-728-3000

Menu order, take-out, catering. No beer. Brisket plate $5.95.

Driving along Interstate 20, you can't miss it. It occupies the center portion of a stockade fort known as Fort Woods Complex on the south side of the highway.

I parked and stepped onto the big wooden porch in front of the shops in the Complex and entered Nix's. I took a seat and a waitress took my order.

Waiting for my food, I cased the joint. I dubbed it rustic western. Quaint photos taken in the 1930s decked the walls.

My order arrived, and I began my investigation. The brisket had a half-inch pink ribbon and very little fat. *Wonderful, but where was the aroma?* A slight nudge with my fork parted the brisket. Alas, it had little flavor. I gave it an 8. The pork ribs were very lean and tender, but the flavor, again, was lacking. I gave the ribs an 8. I squeezed two drops of fat from the half beef sausage, and the flavor, this time, was above average. I gave the sausage a 7.5. The chicken was moist and tender and had little flavor and little fat. I gave it a 7. A slice of ham was lean and tender and had above average flavor. I rated it an 8.

Corn on the cob and French fries plus the regular sides of potato salad, coleslaw, and pinto beans made the veggie list. Cobbler makes up the entire dessert list. Owner Doyce Nix decides which cobbler flavor on which day.

Nix worked for a large national bakery before his brother persuaded him to buy a barbecue place in Andrews. He did and in five years lost his lease. He opened a place in Colorado City, sold it, opened one in Snyder, sold it, and ended up with this place.

I asked him if anything exciting ever happened here, and he said that every Friday night Nix's serves all the pork ribs and trimmings you can eat for $6.95.

Not bad.

Opens 11 A.M. Closes 8 P.M. Monday through Wednesday, 9 P.M. Thursday and Friday, and 8 P.M. Saturday. Closed Sunday. Accepts checks.

Dalhart

Hodie's Bar-B-Q

Dalhart used to be a part of the three million acres of the XIT Ranch. The spread ran 200 miles north and south in Texas along the New Mexico border and averaged 30 miles east and west.

In 1882 the land had no value, and the State of Texas offered the three million acres in exchange for

Rating: 8

U.S. Hwy. 87 South at 7th Street, Dalhart, Texas 79022
Phone 806-249-6773
Fax 806-244-3773

a state capitol building. The state specified that the capitol had to be larger than the one in Washington and at least one foot higher.

Chicagoans Abner Taylor, A. C. Babcock, and John V. and Charles Farwell of the Capitol Syndicate made the deal. They found financing for the project in England. The Syndicate agreed with their financiers to eventually sell off the land as small farms and ranches. In other words, the Syndicate acted as developers.

Menu order, drive thru, take-out, catering. No beer. Brisket plate $6.25.

Open 6 A.M. to 9 P.M. Monday through Saturday. Accepts checks and credit cards.

At its peak, the XIT had 125,000 head of cattle and 150 cowboys. It never made money, but Texas garnered a state capitol building, one foot taller than D.C.'s. The XIT was sold off, bit by bit. The empire lasted twenty-seven years.

Dalhart hosts the XIT Reunion on the first Thursday, Friday, and Saturday of August. Up to 20,000 people jam the streets for the festivities. A riderless horse commemorates the cowboys who have passed on. Among the notables who participated in last year's event was World Champion All-Around Cowboy and movie actor Larry Mahan.

Fortunately for me, I arrived in June and avoided the only crowd during that month, the lunch crowd at Hodie's. A waitress brought me my usual order of barbecue samples, and I began my tests.

Four waitresses watched my every move.

I observed a slice of brisket with a 1/16-inch pink ribbon. *Oh no*. A smoky aroma teased my nose. *Ah ha*. It took two hard slices of my fork to part the meat, and it had too much fat. My bite delivered very good flavor, and I graded it a 7. A pork rib showed more fat than a Reserve Champion at a Fat Stock Show, but flavor and tenderness received blue ribbons. I gave the pork rib a blue ribbon (9) for all-around brisket (a 10 would be Grand Champion).

A slice of pork received a yellow ribbon for leanness, a gold ribbon for above average tenderness, and a red ribbon for superior flavor. I awarded the slice of pork a 7. A slice of turkey was very dry and a little on the tough side. I gave it a gold ribbon for flavor and a red ribbon for little fat. I awarded the rib with a 7 for all-around pork rib. A thin slice of ham had too much salt. I gave it an orange ribbon for flavor, a red ribbon for tenderness, and a gold ribbon for less fat. I gave it a 7 for all-around ham. Hillshire Farms supplied the sausage. It seeped a puddle of fat from the squeeze test. It ran out-of-the-money on that test. The flavor won a green ribbon. I gave it a 6 for all-around sausage.

Dianne and Charlie Hodo own Hodie's. Both had other business elsewhere the day I arrived, so I talked with the cook. She said they had a

Southern Pride rotisserie smoker. *That accounted for the 7 rating for the brisket.* They smoked the brisket for twelve hours at 175 degrees and rubbed the ribs after smoking.

The twelve hours seemed like a short time for an elevation of 3,985 feet.

Charlie's "elsewhere" may have been a fishing spot. A sign in Hodie's read, "A wife and a steady job have ruined many a good fisherman."

Dumas

Roots Bar-B-Q

A year after the town of Dumas organized, grasshoppers devastated the area and almost every person left. Those who stayed believed that things could only get better, and they had it right. It became an agricultural center and then the home of major natural gas and helium fields. In fact, most of the nation's helium comes from the Dumas area.

Little wonder I felt lightheaded as I pulled into the parking lot of Roots Bar-B-Q.

The lady at the counter fixed up a plate of barbecue samples for me, and I began my tests. The brisket had a quarter-inch pink ribbon. *Another rotisserie.* The slice had almost zero fat. It took a good shove with my fork to part the meat. My bite revealed heavenly flavor. I gave it a 9.

A pork rib had almost no fat and up-in-the-clouds flavor. It was a little on the chewy side, and I gave it an 8. Hillshire supplied the sausage. The squeeze test produced a puddle of fat, and the flavor was very good. I tagged it with a 6. A slice of ham was slightly salty, but the smoke flavor came through. It had great tenderness and very little fat. I rated it an 8.

Roots had two barbecue sauces. I noticed some sugar or brown sugar, vinegar, lots of ketchup, and maybe a little Worcestershire sauce in the regular sauce. The "Tangy" sauce contained the regular sauce plus Tabasco. Generated heat hit the fire bell twice.

The decor said ranch. An interesting collection of

Rating: 8

324 South Dumas Avenue, U.S. Hwy 287 South, Dumas, Texas 79029
Phone 806-935-7425
E-mail jdr@arn.net

Counter order, take-out, drive thru, catering. No beer. Brisket plate $5.49.

Open 11 A.M. to 8 P.M. Monday through Saturday. Accepts checks and credit cards.

ice tongs (Dumas gets awfully cold) hung on one wall, Roy Lee Ward prints of renditions of cowboys in the winter graced another wall, and early photos of Panhandle scenes decorated yet another wall. Of note was a photo taken during a dust storm in Oklahoma in 1935 entitled, "A Face in the Dust." I studied the picture and found the eerie face. In the corner, a set of horns hovered over an old Regulator wall clock.

Owner Ray Root and his son John manage the business. The day I visited, I talked with John. Ray was out. He said they had a Southern Pride gas-fired rotisserie. *Of course. I knew it.* They barbecued the brisket with mesquite wood for twelve to fourteen hours at 175 degrees. I found that perplexing. Dumas is 3,500 feet high, and the higher you are, usually higher temperature and longer cooking time is needed. In lower climes, most Southern Pride smokers run fourteen hours at 250 degrees. Could it be lack of humidity up here?

They rub ribs with Cain's. Coming out of the pit, they sop the ribs with a sweet tomato-type sauce.

Country western stars Toby Keith, Clint Gregory, and Michael Martin Murphy ate here—but not together and at different times. Dallas Cowboys Tony Hill and Michael Downs also chowed down.

Lubbock

Bigham's Smokehouse

Besides providing good barbecue, Bigham's on 82nd Street has an artistic mural of old downtown Lubbock and another mural of a wrangler feeding cowboys from a chuck wagon. Many devotees of barbecue argue that barbecue began with the cowboy—out on the range.

City dwellers hunger for outdoor cooking. Cowboys hanker for a nice comfortable, air-conditioned place like Bigham's.

I went through the cafeteria line and picked up my usual samples of barbecue.

I stared at a slice of brisket with a quarter-inch pink ribbon. *Another rotisserie.* It took two slices of my fork to cut the meat. The brisket emitted little aroma and my bite produced above average flavor. I rated it a 7.

Rating: 7.5

4302 19th Street, Lubbock
Texas 79407-2407
Phone 806-793-6880

3310 82nd Street, Lubbock,
Texas 79423-2011

Cafeteria style, take-out, catering. Serves beer. Brisket plate $3.50 to $6.25.

Open 11 A.M. to 9 P.M. Accepts checks and credit cards.

A pork rib had superior tenderness, little fat, and very good flavor. I tagged it with an 8. I had two Hillshire sausages to test. The regular yielded five drops of fat from the squeeze test, but the flavor was above average. I gave it a 6. The jalapeño sausage gave up four drops of fat from the squeeze test. It had two-alarm fire that did not kill the other seasoning. I gave it a 7. The salt in a slice of ham almost overpowered the smoke taste. It had very little fat, good tenderness, and superior flavor. I rated it an 8.

A slice of turkey breast won the day. It was moist and very tender. It had little if any fat and excellent flavor. I gave it a 9. The barbecue sauce was sweet and vinegary.

The pinto beans were good and so was the coleslaw.

They had apple, peach, and cherry cobblers. I selected the peach with no ice cream and a glass of milk.

The owner, Joyce Bigham, was at the other restaurant, so I talked with Christina Edwards. She said they had J&R rotisserie smokers. *I knew it.* They used white oak wood. They put the brisket on in the evening around eight and set the thermostat at 200 degrees. The logs burn down in the middle of the night, so at 7:30 in the morning, they throw on some more sticks and up the temperature to 300 degrees. Bigham's applies their secret rub seasoning to ribs, turkey, and chicken. *No wonder they rated so high.*

Christina said that Don Bigham started the business in 1978. He died in a car accident in 1995. His wife Joyce took the reins and has done a very good job.

The County Line

See **San** Antonio's County Line on page 292 for more information.

Rating: 9

FM 2641, half mile west of U.S. 287 North, Lubbock, Texas 79401-2217

Phone 806-763-6001

Menu order, dine in and out, take-out, catering, banquet facilities. Full bar. Brisket plate $10.95.

Open 11 A.M. to 2 P.M. Monday through Friday, 5 P.M. to 10 P.M. Friday and Saturday and 5 P.M. to 9:30 P.M. Sunday through Thursday. Accepts credit cards.

Whistlin' Dixie Barbeque & Grill

Rating: 7.5

3502 Slide Road, Lubbock,
Texas 79414-2500
Phone 806-795-9750
Fax 806-795-4759
E-mail
wdmanagers@aol.com

Menu order, take-out, catering, banquet facilities. Full bar. Brisket plate $5.99.

Opens 11 A.M. Close 9:30 P.M. Sunday through Thursday, and 10:30 P.M. Friday and Saturday. Accepts checks and credit cards.

When I found Whistlin' Dixie, I discovered a little bit of the French Quarter deep in the heart of Lubbock, Texas. I entered a large, shady courtyard and found trumpet vines, trees, and all the posh greenery you would expect to find in New Orleans. Even the interior of the restaurant looked more like crepes suzettes than barbecue. The walls had New Orleans Mardis Gras posters, and the windows, carpet, and furniture said French Quarter. But the food said Texas.

A hostess seated me and handed me a menu. The back cover had an interesting essay on the derivation of the word "dixie." One historian said that before the Civil War the Citizens Bank of Louisiana issued ten-dollar bank notes inscribed with the French word dix (ten). These notes became known as "dixies." The folk song "Dixie's Land," by Daniel Decatur Emmett, became popular in 1859, and the word dixie fell into use. The *Charleston Courier* on June 11, 1885, explained that the word dixie had now become synonymous with "an ideal location, combining ease, comfort, and material happiness of every description." Naturally, Whistlin' Dixie goes along with the latter description.

I asked for my usual plate of barbecue samples, and they brought me a platter with ten different barbecued meats.

The brisket had a quarter-inch pink ribbon. *Another rotisserie*. In the shear test, the meat parted with a second slice of my fork. The aroma was feeble. It possessed a little fat and had above average flavor. I graded it with a 7. A pork rib had superior tenderness, superior flavor, and a smidgen of fat. I tagged it with an 8. A large beef rib had black pepper and other seasonings. The flavor *c'est magnifique*. The beef rib had superior tenderness and little fat. I rated it an 8. A big chunk of brisket end, a favorite at Whistlin' Dixie, had above average flavor, little fat, and was on the tough side. I gave it a 7. A Louisiana riblet had the same black pepper and other seasonings of the beef rib. It retained superior tenderness and flavor and had very little fat. I gave it an 8.

Some stringy meat on my plate happened to be what Whistlin' Dixie called "pulled pork." It possessed superior tenderness, very good flavor, and some fat. I graded it with a 7. Sausage gave up a puddle of fat from the squeeze test, but the flavor was very good. I gave it a 6. A piece of chicken had too much grease but was extremely tender and had above average flavor. I gave it a 7. A slice of honey smoked ham was slightly salty. Despite the salt, it had superior flavor and little fat. I tagged it with an 8. A slice of turkey breast was slightly salty. It had above average tenderness and flavor and little fat. I gave it an 8.

Whistlin' Dixie served three sauces. Each sauce came with a different colored tape on its bottle so I wouldn't get confused. Tennessee Honey sauce tasted like Cattleman's barbecue sauce with extra sugar. The Original Dixie sauce tasted like Cattleman's with extra vinegar. The Louisiana Fire barbecue sauce tasted like Cattleman's but contained a big slug of Tabasco. It bristled with four-alarm fire. It took several mouthfuls of coleslaw to douse the flames.

The coleslaw was slightly sweet and creamy. The pinto beans and potato salad came from traditional recipes. The Whistlin' Dixie menu also listed corn on the cob, spicy fries, and a stuffed baked potato. The potato came with a pile of honey-kissed ham, smoked turkey, or shredded beef. It went for $4.99.

One of the owners' moms made the cheesecake. *C'etait formidable*. Other desserts were peach cobbler, with or without ice cream, and ice cream by itself.

Owners Tom Hardin and Kent Lyon were not at the restaurant when I dropped in, so I asked my waitress a few questions. She said that Whistlin' Dixie used an Oyler rotisserie. They smoked the meat with mesquite from ten to twelve hours at 225 degrees.

She would not give me the secret recipe for the black seasoning I mentioned earlier.

Maybe you can figure it out.

Pampa

Dyer's Bar-B-Que

Dyer's Bar-B-Que originated in Pampa. Grandpa and Grandma Dyers opened the business in 1964.

See Wichita Falls for more information (page 165).

Rating: 8

Hwy. 60W, Pampa, Texas 79065

Phone 806-665-4401

Menu order, take-out, catering, banquet facilities.

Serves beer and wine. Brisket plate $6.95.

Open 11 A.M. to 9 P.M. Monday through Saturday.

Plainview

Chuck Wagon Bar-B-Q

Plainview is on slightly higher ground than the rest of the area and affords a splendid view of the plains. The Chuck Wagon is in plain view. Just follow the signs to Wayland Baptist University, and you will see the Chuck Wagon on the south side of the street. Plainview is the headquarters for this expanding university, which now has campuses in Alaska, Hawaii, Lubbock, Amarillo, Arizona, Fort Huachuca, Glorieta, Cannon Air Force Base, San Antonio, and Wichita Falls.

Chuck Wagon is a good name for a barbecue place. Many argue that barbecue started with early cowboy chuck wagons. This Chuck Wagon has ruffled red calico curtains, red Naugahyde booths, and some nice Western art, very different from what the cowboys had. I suspect today's barbecue is also better than way back then.

My slice of brisket had almost zero fat and a

Rating: 8.5

2105 Dimmitt Road, Plainview, Texas 79072-2001

Phone 806-296-9907

Menu order, take-out, catering. No beer. Brisket plate $5.99.

Open 11 A.M. to 9 P.M. Closed Sunday. Accepts credit cards.

5/16-inch pink ribbon. In the shear test, it parted with the second slice of my fork. The aroma meowed, and the flavor hummed. I rated it an 8. A pork rib stole the show. It had some fat, but it also had excellent tenderness and above average flavor. I gave it a 9. The German pork and beef sausage came from Swisher Meats in Tulia. It only gave up two drops of fat in the squeeze test, and it had superior flavor. I labeled it with an 8.

The barbecue sauce tasted like Cattleman's with a little Tabasco thrown it for some warmth. It tasted good.

The coleslaw was very creamy. The potato salad had some mustard. Beans had the biggest demand. They had lots of bacon.

Ladies flock here for the big salad bar.

I had to choose from fried pies, pecan pie, chocolate or coconut meringue pies, and soft frozen yogurt for dessert. I went for the yogurt.

Arriving after the lunch bunch, the place seemed reasonably quiet when I finished my repast so I talked with owner Sally Parks. She said they used a homemade long barrel pit and mesquite wood. "I wrap the brisket in foil and leave an opening in the top. I smoke it about twelve hours."

"Do you have a thermometer or a timer?"

"No. It's done manually."

"How do you know when the brisket is done?"

"By pressing on it."

"Your ribs were great. Do you rub or sop your ribs?"

"I put a little Lowry's Seasoning on and some barbecue sauce."

Country western stars Joe Stampley, Troy Bates, Davis Daniel, and Johnny Paycheck chowed down here.

Bill Parks started this business in August 1988. In 1998 the *Plainview Herald*, in a people's choice contest, proclaimed the Chuck Wagon had won the title of "Best Barbecue," bar none.

An old Panhandle witticism: "My honey bathes in *Sweetwater* but dresses in *Plainview*."

Ropesville

Bevers Crossing Bar-B-Que

Rating: 10+

U.S. Hwys. 82 and 62 at Hwy. 41, 14 miles southwest of Lubbock, Ropesville, Texas 79358
Phone 806-562-4412

Counter order, take-out, catering, party facilities. No beer. Brisket plate $6.95.

Daylight Savings hours: Opens 11 A.M. Closes 3 P.M. Tuesday and Wednesday and 9 P.M. Thursday through Saturday. Winter hours: opens 11 A.M.; closes 3 P.M. Tuesday through Thursday and 8 P.M. Friday and Saturday. Accepts checks.

The Santa Fe railroad came to this spot in the South Plains. Cowboys shipped cattle, and the train brought goods. How the town acquired the name "Ropes" stirs debates. One story says that because wood and wire were scarce, the men used rawhide ropes to herd the cattle onto the trains. The cowboys fondly called the spot "Ropes." The other story says that Santa Fe named it after Horace Ropes, a company engineer. Either way, it became Ropes, Texas, but the U.S. post office refused to accept the name because of address confusion with Roper, Texas. The post office named it Ropesville, but denizens still call it Ropes.

You pass through Ropes on the way to Hobbs, New Mexico, or Midland and Odessa. The traffic is light, and a great deal of that traffic only goes to Bevers Crossing to get the best barbecue in the state of Texas.

You heard me—number one. I will put up Bevers against any other barbecue place in the Lone Star State, and once you eat barbecue at Bevers Crossing, you will be roped in too.

Bevers is a family affair. Buddy Bevers learned how to barbecue from his cousin, Jack Bevers, who owned Cowboys Barbecue in Angleton, Texas. Jack left the barbecue business for fishing, but Buddy carries on the family tradition. Wife Delores Bevers and daughter Rose contribute mightily with their charming smiles, cooking, and service.

I ordered my usual sampler. Delores brought my plate. I looked at the prettiest piece of slice brisket in the state of Texas—a slice of brisket with a 5/8- to 3/4-inch pink ribbon. *Hosannah.* The aroma added fuel to the fire. *This can't be true. I'll bet it's tough.* I pressed the fork against the meat, and it fell apart. *Something has to be wrong. It probably has no flavor.* I took a bite. It possessed fantastic mesquite smoked flavor. I awarded it the Grand Prize: 10 plus.

The appearance of my pork rib showed class. *Very little fat.* They seasoned it with special spices and lots of black pepper. My bite rang with gusto and superior tenderness. I gave it a 10. The sausage came from Slaton. It yielded five drops of fat, but the flavor was beautiful poetry. I gave it a 7.

They served pinto beans and potato salad. The beans had bits of green beans and onion. Bevers Crossing did not list coleslaw on the menu.

Dessert consisted of peach cobbler and Blue Bell ice cream.

Buddy came over to our table and we had a friendly chat. "The building says 'Depot' and the railroad tracks are on the other side of the highway. Did they change the tracks?"

"No," answered Buddy. "We restored the station master's house. It was a shambles, but it was available." The humble abode had smooth wood floors, wood wainscot and wallpaper with a steam engine train border on the walls, and a pot-bellied stove. Outside, Buddy built a bed and breakfast cabin.

The front porch of the cabin serves as a stage for Western music and poetry on Saturday nights. It costs $5 for adults and $2.50 for children 10 or under. Shows run from 7:30 P.M. to 9:30 P.M. and play during the months of April through October.

I asked Buddy if the poetry was free verse. He smiled and said, "Free verse is for intellectuals. With us cowboys, it's gotta rhyme or we don't understand it." He handed me a cassette tape. "Now this young fella, Andy Hedges, is going to be one of the best Western poets. This tape is 'Rawhide Rhymes.' I want you to have this."

Driving down the road, I listened to the tape. I liked it. Bet you would too.

Santa Anna

Dub's Bar-B-Q

Rating: 7.5

619 Wallace, U.S. Hwy 67,
Santa Anna, Texas 76878
Phone 915-348-3191
Fax 915-348-3161
E-mail
fklnliquidators@webtv.net

Menu order, take-out, catering. No beer. Brisket plate
$5.95.

Open 7 A.M. Closes 9 P.M.
Sunday through Thursday
and 11 P.M. or so on Friday
and Saturday. Accepts checks
and credit cards.

When you go through downtown Santa Anna slow down and look for the old two-story opera house on the corner with the sign "W. R. Kelley & Co." Above that sign is a smaller sign that reads "Dub's Bar-B-Q." Below the sidewalk canopy is a gun that barbecues. It's called "The Smokin' Gun." Pull in for some good grub and some fun.

William B. "Dub" Franklin is a look-alike for Willie Nelson. He and Willie are friends and have a lot in common. Both are talented guitar picking, singing, and writing music men. Both love country western. Both are professional musicians. When the IRS came after Willie Nelson for back taxes, Dub put on a concert to pay off some of Willie's debt.

Dub did music for forty-six years on the West Coast and got tired of the drinking and the druggies. "Fortunately," Dug said, "I never did drugs." Dub came back to his native state Texas. "I'd done cooking all my life. Cooked in the Army during the Korean War. I got this call from a man who fixed up the old opera house here in Santa Anna. He wanted me to come down and do some cooking for him. When I got down here he wanted me to run this place. I balked. Then I delivered a load of mesquite to Joe Saladino, owner of Joe's Barbeque in Alvin, and Joe talked me into the barbecue business. I came back here and leased this place for five years and then bought it."

The opera house isn't what it used to be, but Dub does everything he can to fix it up. The old opera room is on the second floor and is not open to the public—yet. The main dining room is on the first floor and has a fourteen-foot-high ceiling. On the walls are hundreds of pictures of country and western entertainers and movie stars. On the back wall over the service area and cash register is a loft with music stands and chairs. Musicians come on weekend nights, and this place takes on a different look.

Dub brought me a plate with a slice of brisket, a pork rib, and a piece of chicken. The brisket had a 5/16-inch pink ribbon. It had little fat. The aroma did not stir. In the shear test, it parted with the second slice of my fork. The flavor shined. I gave it an 8. The pork rib showed some fat, had above average tenderness and superior flavor. I rated it a 7. A piece of chicken had a little fat, was tender, and had superior flavor. I tagged it with an 8. The barbecue sauce had a heavy tomato base and was on the sweet side.

The pinto beans had a little garlic and bits of bacon. The potato salad had a traditional recipe. Dub was proud of his dinner salad that came with his homemade dressing he called "Farm aid."

For dessert, he occasionally serves ice cream.

I asked him if anything unusual happened here.

"Do you believe in spirits?"

"What do you mean?"

"Well, my wife and I hear ladies talking in back."

"Behind the building?"

"No. In the building. We have customers who hear them."

Suddenly, absolute silence prevailed and lasted what seemed like a long time.

No lady voice.

I asked Dub to pose for a picture by the Smokin' Gun. He obliged.

I said, "You ought to play that ghost thing up big time."

"I do." He flashed his Willie Nelson smile.

Snyder

Red Barn Bar-B-Que

W. H. "Pete" Snyder, for some unknown reason, opened a trading post at this spot in 1877. Settlers built buffalo hide dwellings and dugouts. The place became a home for desperados and fugitives, and cowboys called it "Robber's Roost."

J. Wright Mooar, a famed Kansas buffalo hunter, came to Texas and slaughtered buffalo including a white one. He claimed he killed 20,000 buffalo in his lifetime. A statue of a white buffalo stands in Snyder's town square.

Could that white buffalo be the one the Kiowas thought would lead the great stampede and wipe out their enemies?

I entered the Red Barn and found a country restaurant with a Western flair. A waitress brought me a plate of barbecue samples, and I looked at a slice of brisket with a 5/16-inch pink ribbon. The aroma was faint. It separated with one extra hard push from the edge of my fork. It had some fat, and the flavor was above average. I rated it an 8.

A pork rib had superior tenderness and flavor but too much fat. I gave it a 7. Regular sausage yielded four drops of fat from the squeeze test. Its black pepper seasoning tasted great. I tagged it with a 7. A cut of hot link yielded three drops of fat from the squeeze test. It had two-alarm flavor that did not overpower the other lighter spices. I labeled it with a 7. I saved the best for last. A slice of ham had mouth-watering smoke flavor, was extremely tender, and possessed little fat. I bestowed it with a 9.

The barbecue sauce had the basic ingredients of ketchup, vinegar, and Worcestershire sauce, and it had a little warmth—maybe from cayenne.

Sides: potato salad had a little mustard, dill pickle relish, and chunks of potato; coleslaw was creamy; the pinto beans came from a traditional recipe.

Rating: 7.5

U.S. Hwy. 84 at Huffman Avenue, Snyder, Texas 79549
Phone 915-573-2291
Web site www.bbq.snyder.net
Menu order, take-out, catering. No beer. Brisket plate $5.95.
Opens 11 A.M. Closes 9 P.M. Monday through Saturday and 2 P.M. Sunday. Accepts credit cards.

Other sides were French fries, corn on the cob, giant onion rings, and fresh salads.

Dessert: cobblers, banana pudding, pecan pie, and coconut "crème" pie.

Owner Daren Hopper uses a 36-inch wide barrel pit. It has three lids with counterbalances, which makes the pit easy to handle. The grate measures 36 inches wide by 16 feet and came from a heavy-duty oilfield catwalk from a drilling rig. The firebox belches mesquite smoke. Daren said he smokes his brisket nine to twelve hours, depending on the size of the brisket, its tenderness, ambient temperature, and humidity.

Weyland Jennings ate here. He wore a double-breasted suit, and no one recognized him until the waitress asked, as he was finishing his meal, "Are you Weyland Jennings?"

"My mother thought I looked like Elvis Presley."

They laughed, and Weyland burst into a created-on-the-spot song about the waitresses and their Red Barn red T-shirts.

Sweetwater

The Shed

See "The Shed" in Wingate, Texas, (below) for more information.

Rating: 7.5

710 East Broadway, take Interstate 20 Business Route, Sweetwater, Texas 79556 Phone 915-235-1042 or 915-235-8090

Menu order, take-out, catering, drive thru. No beer. Brisket plate $5.95.

Open 11 A.M. to 9 P.M. Accepts checks and credit cards.

Wingate

The Shed

Yes, Virginia, there is a barbecue place tucked back in the wilds on a crooked little road. And, yes, it is worth finding. It's called The Shed.

This business began in "The Shed." Hollis Dean started barbecuing at home and then he did it for friends. He built The Shed in 1989 to house a big kitchen and then added a few seats outside. In December of that year he and wife Betty decided to

Rating: 7.5

Located on U.S. Hwy. 277 just south of Hwy. 153, northwest of Wingate, Texas
Mailing address: 608 CR 226, Wingate, Texas 79566

open the place up to private parties. One thing led to another, and today the Deans own two "Sheds"— one in Sweetwater and this one located in the boondocks near Wingate, Texas.

Hollis said it was difficult getting started. "It's a thirty-mile trip to get a jug of milk. You learn fast what it takes to keep a restaurant going."

Hollis was born just fifty yards from the Shed, and Betty was born in Winters, fourteen miles south.

Phone 915-743-2175 or 915-743-6142

Menu order, take-out, catering, banquet facilities. No beer. Brisket plate $5.95.

Open 5 P.M. to 9:30 P.M. Thursday through Saturday and 11 A.M. to 3 P.M. Sunday. Accepts checks and credit cards.

The Shed barbecues a come-back-again brisket. The pink ribbon measured a quarter of an inch. *Another rotisserie.* It had very little fat. I had to push the fork twice to separate the meat. The aroma was captivating, and my bite produced a fantastic smoke and rub flavor. I awarded it an 8. A pork sparerib had above average tenderness. It had that smoke and rub flavor but had excessive fat. I graded it a 7. The sausage yielded three drops of fat from the squeeze test. It had very good flavor, and I gave it a 7. The barbecue sauce was sweet from brown sugar or sugar. I detected vinegar, some ketchup, a dash of Worcestershire sauce, a little jalapeño, and maybe some pickle juice. An intriguing mix, and the recipe remains a deep, dark secret.

Sides: coleslaw had bits of carrots and a creamy base. Potato salad contained chunks of boiled potato and smaller bits of pimento. Pinto beans had a touch of chili powder. These sides went down well with some homemade sourdough bread.

A waitress said they used nothing out of a jar; they made everything from scratch including the desserts: cobblers and pie. The treat of the treats was Betty Dean's cherry, peach, or apple crisps (die-for food).

The interior looked unsophisticated rural. The walls had barn siding, and the tops of the windows had red-and-white ruffled curtains. Walls presented old license plates, advertising signs, farm implements, and ranch memorabilia. Ceiling fans lazed over a concrete floor.

Many things happened at The Shed through the years, but the one story that stands out occurred the night of the great storm. The rain came down so hard that no one could leave. The electricity went out. Hollis drove his pickup truck to the back door and flooded the kitchen with its headlights so they could keep cooking. The customers ate by flashlight. How's that for innovation?

Dallas Cowboy star Jay Novacek dined here as did country western stars Jim Gough and Don McAlister Jr.

I spoke with Byron Stephenson, the grandson of the Deans. He said that they smoked the brisket twelve hours at 225 degrees and that the recipe for the rub was a secret. He asked me if I liked their barbecue.

"I loved it."

"How did you rate us?"

"It's a secret until my book comes out."

And Virginia, if you are a good little girl, maybe Daddy will take you there some day.

Wichita Falls

The Branding Iron Inc.

William J. McDonald broke up banditry in Wichita Falls in the late 1800s. He must have done a good job. I saw no signs of banditry anywhere in Wichita Falls. Gasoline prices beat Panhandle prices by sixteen cents. Barbecued brisket sold for a dollar less than in Central Texas.

I missed the Branding Iron the first time I drove by. The surrounding commercial area slept in bleakness, and the Branding Iron sign did nothing to awaken it. Street numbers told me to turn back. I did and spotted a parking lot jammed with sporty cars and pickups. I surmised that it was the Branding Iron. It was. Upon closer inspection, the Branding Iron sign had charm but was almost impossible to read. A torch cut out the letters. The two faces had a foot or so gap between them, and the light and shadows crisscrossed to make an interesting design but not a very legible sign.

I entered and found myself in a long line. My wait passed quickly as I studied two large framed presentations of photos of the great tornado of 1979, shot by Floyd Styles.

My turn came. I told the server what I wanted, and he fixed me up.

As I went through the line, I glanced at the dining room's Western motif. Saddles hung from rafters. Walls displayed old faded prints of Western art. A

Rating: 7

104 East Scott, Wichita Falls, Texas 76301

Phone 940-723-0338

Cafeteria style, take-out, catering. Serves beer. Brisket plate $5.75.

Opens 11 A.M. Closes 3 P.M. Monday through Thursday and 8 P.M. Friday and Saturday. Accepts checks.

second dining room had a corrugated metal roof and a concrete floor. A number of life-size cutouts of John Wayne stood guard. Booths filled the sides of the room, and in the middle pushed together tables mingled elbows and conversations. I took a place in the middle row and attracted attention by testing the barbecue. I ended up passing out business cards and advising all that *Barbecuing Around Texas* would be in all the bookstores this fall.

Branding Iron brisket had a quarter-inch pink ribbon. *Another rotisserie.* The aroma drowsed. My formidable plastic fork separated the meat with little more than a touch. It had very little fat and the flavor… where was the flavor? *Maybe one of those bandits stole the flavor.* I graded it a 7. A pork rib teemed with fat. It had average tenderness and excellent flavor. Doused with barbecue sauce, the rib hid its smoky flavor. I tagged the rib with a 6. The rib was a good example of what happens when you cook a rib too hot and too fast.

I moved on to test Polish sausage and a hot link. The former oozed five drops of fat from the squeeze test but had above average flavor. I rated it a 6. The latter gave up three drops of fat and had above average flavor. I gave it a 7. I don't know why they called it a hot link because it only had one-alarm heat. A piece of ham contained little if any salt. It had better than average flavor, a little fat, and superior tenderness. I tagged it with an 8. A piece of turkey was dry yet had superior tenderness. It had almost zero smoke flavor. It was very lean, and I gave it a 7.

The barbecue sauce had a rich, tangy flavor. I detected vinegar, ketchup, Worcestershire sauce, and a little Tabasco.

Owner Ray Styles had other important business and was absent the day I called.

Later I found out that photographer Floyd was Ray's father. Floyd does not do photography for a living but had his camera in his car when the big tornado touched down near where he was driving.

The lady cashier told me they used an Oyler rotisserie and smoke brisket with oak for about eighteen hours at 230 degrees. They sopped ribs after smoking them.

Callaway's Hik'ry Pit Barbecue

Rating: 8

719 10th Street, Wichita Falls, Texas 76301
Phone 940-767-9825

While eating at another large barbecue place in Wichita Falls, I asked two diners, who happened to be policemen, if this was the best barbecue place in town. One policeman looked around, smiled, and said in a low voice, "This is good, but Callaway's

Hik'ry Pit Barbecue on 10th Street is the best."

Callaway's occupies an old twenties to thirties style one-story building. It is sandwiched between other similar buildings in downtown Wichita Falls. Inside, benches run along two sides with tables and chairs in between. Nothing fancy.

Cafeteria style, take-out, catering. No beer. Brisket plate $3.95.

Open 7:30 A.M. to 2:45 P.M. Monday through Friday. Accepts checks.

I went through the cafeteria line and picked up what I needed. I sat down at one of the side tables and prepared myself for some good 'cue.

But what is this? I looked at a small pink ribbon. *Uh oh.* The aroma mumbled. *Uh oh.* It took two good shoves of my fork to part the meat. *Oh no.* It had very little fat. *Ah ha.* The flavor was above average. I graded it a 7.

A pork rib was extremely tender, possessed little fat, and the flavor vindicated the police officer. I gave the rib a 9. *Must be what the police officer ate here.* A piece of sausage yielded three drops of fat from the squeeze test and, though slightly salty, had above average flavor. I gave it a 7. A piece of ham had great tenderness, but the salt in the ham overpowered the smoke flavor. It had very little fat, and I gave it an 8.5. A piece of turkey breast was dry, which meant it had very little fat. The flavor flew the coop, but, despite all that, it had above average tenderness. I gave it a 7.

The barbecue sauce was a little sweet. It had ketchup, vinegar, and Worcestershire sauce, plus maybe a little chili powder and Tabasco. Its flavor sparkled.

Callaway's coleslaw contained a little carrot for color, mayonnaise, mustard, vinegar, and sugar. The potato salad contained no eggs or onions. The pinto beans had bits of ham.

Dessert: homemade apple cobbler, pecan pie, and cheesecake. Pumpkin pies and other pies become available during the holidays and on special occasions.

Owner Clarence Callaway had a career in pharmaceutical sales but tired of traveling. He wanted to spend more time with his wife and children. He opened this place in 1976.

He showed me his old thirty-five-year-old brick pit. "It does the job," Clarence said. "We use oak and hickory and smoke our brisket eight to ten hours."

I asked him what he put on the ribs to make them so mouth-watering.

"Another sauce. It has some mustard, black and red pepper, vinegar, and some other secrets." He smiled.

Dyer's Bar-B-Que

In 1876 a community began on the banks of the Wichita River. The beauty of the pastoral setting was a five-foot falls. By 1881 eight families lived there. The train arrived in 1882, and the town grew rapidly. Dams sprung up on the river, and the falls drowned in a new water level.

I arrived in May, and the temperature was in the nineties. I remembered that Wichita Falls hosted the annual "Hotter'N Hell" bicycle race at the end of each August.

The waitress took my order, and I cooled down in the spacious air-conditioned dining room. I looked the place over. Dyer's had enough room to feed an army. The waitress said it used to be a nightclub. The walls had old panoramic photographs of Wichita Falls and Burkburnett, a neighboring town fourteen miles north. One photo of Burkburnett in 1919 showed oil derricks as thick as the crowd of diners here at noon.

I spotted Gene Watson, on old-time country singer. I waved, and Gene looked around to see the person I waved to.

The waitress brought my order, and I observed a slice of brisket with a quarter-inch pink ribbon. *Another rotisserie*. It had little fat, and when I administered the shear test, the meat fell apart after one hard slice with my fork. *Tender for a rotisserie job*. I sensed a small whiff of aroma and took a bite. The flavor sang a nice melody but one I could forget. I rated it an 8.

A pork rib had good appearance from a crusted sop. It had superior tenderness, a little too much fat, and the flavor sang a "sweet" refrain. I gave it an 8. The sausage won in the squeeze test. Only one drop of fat came out. It had superior flavor, and I tagged it with my next to highest sausage rating of 9 (see Fat Daddy's, page 86). A slice of ham had some salt and very little smoke flavor. It had tenderness, some fat,

Rating: 8

2917 Southwest Parkway,
Wichita Falls, Texas 76308
Phone 940-696-3300
Fax 940-691-1533

Menu order, take-out, drive thru, catering, banquet facilities. Serves beer and wine. Brisket plate $6.99.

Opens 11 A.M. Closes 9 P.M. Sunday through Thursday and 10 P.M. Friday and Saturday.

and fair flavor. I labeled the ham with a 7. A slice of turkey breast was on the dry side. It had very little fat and superior flavor but was short on tenderness. I gave it a 7.

The barbecue sauce was not too sweet and had some fire in it.

Sides: normal coleslaw, Dyer's special recipe potato salad, beans, green salad, onion rings, fried mushrooms, and a baked potato.

Desserts: cake of the day, cobbler of the day, strawberry cream cheesecake from Margie's Sweet Shop, and ice cream.

Greg Stockton liked Dyer's barbecue so much, he bought this franchise for Wichita Falls. He said they barbecued brisket with hickory smoke in an Old Hickory rotisserie pit for twelve hours at 225 degrees. "We do ribs in an entirely different manner. We smoke them in an open pit for three and a half to four and a half hours and do forty-two slabs at a time. They get a rub going in and we baste them as they come off the grate."

"We won the Texas Sesquicentennial Barbecue and Chili Cook-off and was voted Texoma's Best Barbecue in 1994, 1995, 1996, and 1998."

Ty Herndon, Tanya Tucker, Martina McBride, and Cowboys Darrell Johnston and J. C. Garret ate here.

The best way to find this place is to take U.S. Hwy. 281 South and turn west on FM 79, Southwest Parkway.

Wellington

Miss Piggie Bar-B-Q

John and Wiley Dickinson came to this part of Texas with 2,000 cattle in 1880 and started the famous Rocking Chair Ranch. In 1887 they sold it to an English company. During the reign of the Englishmen, they named the towns of Wellington (after the Duke of Wellington), Tweedy, Shamrock, Clarendon, and Aberdeen. They set up Pearl to be the county seat, but the Rocking Chair foreman moved enough cowboys so that the vote went in favor of Wellington 56 to 32. The Englishmen could not control the cowboys or the systematic stealing of cattle and sold the ranch to William E. Hughes, Continental Land and Cattle Company, in 1896. Hughes made the ranch profitable by selling off the ranch in small tracts.

Rating: 6

U.S. Hwy. 83 at Hwy. 203, Wellington, Texas 79095
Phone 806-447-2335

Cafeteria style, take-out, catering. No beer. Brisket plate $5.35.

Opens 11 A.M. Closes 7 P.M. Tuesday through Friday and 2 P.M. Saturday. Closed Sunday. Accepts checks.

Today Wellington's economy comes from agriculture, grain elevators, and small businesses like Miss Piggie Bar-B-Q.

I arrived at four in the afternoon and found an empty dining room. The place was plain but cozy. I went up to the counter and met the owner and only employee, Peggy McKinnon. I asked for a small piece of brisket, one rib, and a piece of sausage. She smiled. "The ribs sell out at lunchtime. Anything else?"

I ordered some coleslaw, potato salad, and beans.

"You need to try my stewed apricots." She quickly handed me a dish of them, my first introduction to stewed apricots, a popular side dish in the Panhandle.

My slice of brisket had some fat and a small dark pink ribbon. Negative vibes. In the shear test, the meat parted with the second slice of my fork. It had above average flavor and I rated it a 6.

A six puts a barbecue place in my book, so I proceeded to the pork and beef sausage. It oozed five drops of fat from the squeeze test and had very good flavor. I gave it a 6. The barbecue sauce was mild and sweet.

The potato salad had some sugar and a little mustard. The beans had salt and vegetable oil. The coleslaw had half vinegar and half mayonnaise. Peggy said she ground her own cabbage. Peggy also serves French fries and chili cheese fries.

She sat down with me. "How did you like the brisket?"

I told her about my book. "You will have to read the results in my book."

"You haven't tried the stewed apricots."

"Right." I dug into them. They went down fast. "Delicious."

Peggy told me that her husband built her barrel pit. She uses wood and smokes brisket sixteen hours. The only thing she put on meat was salt.

I asked Peggy why she went into the barbecue business.

"I got tired of working for another man. I was a cook at a nursing home and had nine children. I prayed to the Lord, and He led me this way."

She said the business started in 1983. "I've been running it by myself for the last seven years."

Part Six

Piney Woods

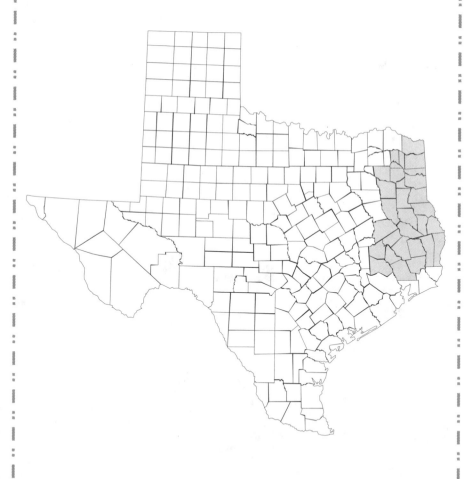

Conroe

McKenzie's Barbeque

See Huntsville for more information (page 171).

Rating: 8

1501 North Frazier, Conroe, Texas 77301-1817
Phone 409-539-4300
Fax 409-539-4300
Web site
www.mckenziesbarbeque.com

Counter order, take-out, catering. No beer. Brisket plate $6.25.

Open 10:30 A.M. to 9 P.M. Closed Sunday. Accepts checks and credit cards.

Luther's Bar-B-Q

See Houston for further information (page 60).

Rating: 7.5

1101 West Dallas, Conroe, Texas 77301
Phone 409-441-5901

Counter order, take-out, catering. Beer served. Brisket plate $7.59.

Opens 11 A.M. Closes 10 P.M. Sunday through Thursday and 11 P.M. Friday and Saturday. Accepts credit cards.

Gilmer

Bodacious BBQ

See Tyler for more information (page 189).

Rating: 8.5

1204 North Wood, Gilmer, Texas 75644
Phone 903-843-3481
Jerry Scarborough, owner.

Counter order, take-out. No beer. Brisket plate $6.75.

Open 9 A.M. to 9 P.M. Closed Sunday. Accepts credit cards.

Gladewater

Bodacious BBQ

See Tyler for more information (page 189).

Rating: 8.5

1105 W. Unsher Avenue,
Gladewater, Texas 75647-2025
Phone 903-845-2311
Jimmy Ray Eisenhood, owner.

Counter order, take-out,
catering. No beer. Brisket
plate $6.50.

Open 10 A.M. to 8 P.M. Accepts
credit cards.

Huntsville

McKenzie's Barbeque

When Kevin McKenzie started his barbecue place in Huntsville, no one gave him a chance because one of the best barbecue places in the world, New Zion Missionary Baptist Barbecue, was just down the road. He did it anyway.

The local newspaper, the *Huntsville Item*, features a reader's choice every year. Subscribers vote for their favorite restaurant. McKenzie's has received the Best Barbecue award for the last six years.

The brisket I ordered had a very small ribbon —maybe a sixteenth of an inch. *Discouraging*. The aroma mumbled. I touched the meat with my fork, and it fell apart. *Encouraging*. The cut came from the fatty end of the brisket and was extremely tender. I gave it an 8. A pork rib had fall-off-the-bone tenderness. They had rubbed it with a little sugar, white pepper, black pepper, and red pepper. It had lip smacking flavor but a little too much fat. I rated it a 9. The pork and beef sausage came from Eckermann's of New Ulm, Texas. It had no garlic. It produced one drop of fat from the squeeze test. Its flavor was superior, and I tagged it with an 8. The

Rating: 8

1700 East 11th Street,
Huntsville, Texas 77340
Phone 409-291-7347
Fax 409-291-7347
Web site
www.mckenziesbarbeque.com

Counter order, take-out,
catering. No beer. Brisket
plate $6.25.

Open 10:30 A.M. to 9 P.M.
Closed Sunday. Accepts checks
and credit cards.

171

chicken scratched for flavor. It was tender, moist, and somewhat lean. I gave it an 8. The ham was slightly salty. It had excellent flavor, little fat, and superior tenderness. I rated it an 8. The turkey possessed superior flavor, almost zero fat, excellent tenderness, and moisture. I gave it an 8.

The barbecue sauce had a tangy bite to it. I detected vinegar, Worcestershire sauce, cayenne, and garlic.

McKenzie's serves the standard sides of pinto beans, coleslaw, and potato salad.

A popular entree is a stuffed baked potato with a choice of chopped barbecue meats. It goes for $3.45.

For dessert, I had to choose between pecan and apple pie. I went for the latter. As I ate my pie I looked around. The place had a "plain country" appearance. Exposed fluorescent bulb fixtures and brown ceiling fans hovered over a vinyl tile floor and off-white walls. Western art, old photos, and ranch paraphernalia dotted the walls. After my repast, I discovered an intriguing painting by Lillian Smith entitled "Two Burros" in the men's bathroom.

Later I asked Kevin how he started. "Crazy," he said. "My brother Darin got a job with Bodacious. We lived in Longview then. When Darin announced his new employment, our father called Bodacious and told them that Kevin needed the job more than Darin. I was a sophomore in college, and Darin was a freshman in high school. Bodacious hired me."

Later Darin secured another job with Bodacious. Today, their sister owns a Bodacious in Longview, and the brothers have restaurants in Huntsville, Conroe, and Livingston.

Like Bodacious restaurants, Kevin uses Bewley pits. Unlike Bodacious, he smokes brisket twenty hours, which is six hours longer than Bodacious, and uses oak and hickory. McKenzie's puts a rub of white pepper, black pepper, red pepper, and sugar on ribs.

Ben Johnson, Earl Campbell, and Mark White ate here.

New Zion Missionary Baptist Barbecue

Whenever people talk about barbecue in Texas, they usually mention New Zion. Whenever an article about barbecue runs in a publication, the writer usually mentions New Zion.

After breaking bread with them, I understood why.

I parked my car behind the church and walked

Rating: 8

2601 Montgomery Road,
Huntsville, Texas
77340-6013
Phone 409-295-7394

around front where two large barbecue pits belched smoke. Brother Howard tended them. I asked him where I could get some barbecue, and he nodded toward the door. I entered and found myself in a very plain and humble building. No frills. I walked up to the counter, told the lady what I wanted, and she followed my instructions to the letter. I took a seat at one of the tables.

Counter order, take-out. No beer (this is a Baptist church). Brisket plate $6.00. Open 11 A.M. to 7 P.M. Wednesday through Saturday. Accepts checks.

My brisket had a 1/8-inch pink ribbon. *Shocking.* The aroma said, "Hallelujah!" The meat fell apart when I touched it with my fork. The flavor shouted, "Amen." However, the brisket had a little too much fat. Alas, we live in an imperfect world. I gave it an 8. A pork rib had praise the Lord taste, superior tenderness, but also had a little too much fat. I gave it an 8. They buy the sausage at a grocery store, and it tasted like it. It yielded a puddle of fat from the squeeze test. I rated it a 5.

With every plate, a New Zion volunteer adds generous helpings of homemade creamy sweet potato salad and traditional pinto beans.

They offer three desserts: pecan pie, sweet potato pie, and cake. Get there early for the sweet potato pie. It sells out fast.

Finished with my repast, I went back outside and talked with Brother Howard. As we chatted, the fire flared and Brother Howard reached behind without looking, dipped a tin cup in a pail of water, and in one smooth motion splashed the baffle door. The fire hissed and went to heaven. I asked him what wood he liked best. He said, "Sometimes I use pecan, hickory, or mesquite, but I really like oak. The best is seasoned oak. You know, old oak."

"Can you tell if it's seasoned by looking at it?"

"No. But I know it's seasoned because I cut it."

Good enough.

We talked about his barbecue pits. He said the small one had the meat directly over the fire, and he used it mostly for ribs and chicken. The other barbecue pit was a long pit with a firebox on one end and a smokestack on the other. It smoked the brisket. Brother Howard said he smoked the brisket four to six hours and used Reo seasoning.

It's a church affair. Members volunteer to do the work and the profits go to the church.

You receive a blessing from good food, good service, and smiles.

Jefferson

Riverport Bar-B-Que

In 1844 Jefferson, located on Big Cypress Bayou, achieved fame as a great river port when the first steam wheeler arrived. In 1873 the U.S. Corps of Engineers unclogged the Red River, causing the Big Cypress Bayou water level to go down and the steamers to quit coming. The town gradually declined.

Rating: 7.5

201 North Polk Street, Jefferson, Texas 75657
Phone 903-665-2341
E-mail rvrportl@swbell.net

Counter order, take-out, catering. Full-service bar. Brisket plate $5.95.

Opens 11 A.M. Closes 6 P.M. Tuesday through Thursday, 8 P.M. Friday and Saturday, and 4 P.M. Sunday. Accepts checks and credit cards.

In recent years Jefferson won a reputation as a fun town, a lady's shopping dream, and home of notable bed and breakfast places. That happened because citizens restored old buildings, and antique and collectibles shops moved in. That, in turn, attracted other businesses.

Now Jefferson has a new "river port," Riverport Bar-B-Que, which sits right in the middle of everything. Inside, it has a long bar on the left, tables on the right, and an order counter at the rear. The décor? Deep South café.

I selected my usual sampler, and a man brought it to my table. The brisket had a quarter-inch pink ribbon. The aroma slept. It took two hard slices of my fork to part the meat. It evinced little fat. My bite found above average flavor. I gave it a 7. A pork rib stole the show. It had fantastic flavor. They rubbed it with brown sugar and black pepper, and when it came out of the pit, they sopped it with a small amount of honey. It had some fat and fall-off-the-bone tenderness. I gave it a 9. A slice of pork loin was just what the doctor ordered. It possessed almost no fat, and the price for that resulted in tough meat. The flavor mumbled, and I rated it a 6. A slice of turkey had melt-in-your-mouth tenderness, almost no fat, and very mild flavor. I gave it an 8.

Stephen Joseph, co-owner with his father, offered no sausage. "I'm switching brands. I'm having a hard time finding good sausage."

The potato salad had real egg in it, and they used chopped whole potatoes. The coleslaw had a little sweetness and vinegar. I tasted chili powder in the beans. An onion ring had a crisp exterior and a just-soft-enough onion inside.

I had to choose from homemade buttermilk pie or pecan pie or one of many different fried pies for dessert.

Savoring the remnants of a meal in my mouth, I looked around at the interior. It had neon beer signs, miscellaneous collectibles on the walls, and a TV broadcasting ESPN for the bar occupants.

Stephen said they used a Bewley pit. For brisket, they burned pecan or hickory wood twelve hours at 250 degrees. He was proud of his ribs. He smoked them four to five hours. "Most barbecue places only smoke them three hours," he said.

I hope he will soon apply that longer smoking theory to his brisket.

I brought my wife Bee along on this trip. *Now what was the name of that antique store she said she would meet me at?*

Kilgore

Bodacious BBQ

Log cabin inside and out. Hunting trophies including a full-size bobcat.

See Tyler for more information (page 189).

Rating: 8.5

Interstate 20 at Hwy. 42, Rt. 5 Box 108 Y, Kilgore, Texas 75662-9156

Phone 903-983-1421

Billie and Pam Suggs, owners.

Counter order, take-out. No beer. Brisket plate $6.75.

Open 10 A.M. to 9 P.M. Accepts checks and credit cards.

Country Tavern

The waitress asked me what I would like. I told her. "We only serve a brisket plate, a rib plate, or a sandwich plate." Bee, my wife, was with me. She ordered a rib plate, and I asked for a brisket plate.

The waitress left. Bee and I looked around the dark, poorly lit room. A jukebox played country western music for an empty dance floor. "This looks like a honky-tonk," I said.

"Don't write that," replied Bee. "Ask the

Rating: 8.5

Hwy. 31 West, P.O. Box 973, Kilgore, Texas 75663

Phone 903-984-9954

Menu order, take-out. Serves beer and wine. Brisket plate $10.50.

waitress how to describe it."

I did. She smiled and said, "It looks like a candlelit tavern." She placed a candle on our table and lit it.

With candlelight, I could barely see my food. I think the brisket had a pink ribbon. The low light

Opens 11 A.M. Closes 11 P.M. Sunday through Thursday and 12 midnight Friday and Saturday. Accepts credit cards.

made everything appear good. *Maybe even me*. Bee took on the appearance of a temptress—and I'm 70. It took a slight push with my fork to part the meat. It was as tender as Sharon Stone's lips. *Must be the candlelight*. I could not see if it had any fat, and the flavor sang "Ela." Disturbed about the lack of light, I took a piece of brisket and a pork rib over to the entrance door and inspected them for fat. The brisket did indeed have some fat, and the rib had as much. I sat back down and ate them. The rib had out-of-this world flavor and slow-dance tenderness. I gave the brisket an 8 and the pork rib a 9. Pretty good barbecue.

The only side was potato salad, and it wasn't much to brag about. That was the end of the food chain in the Country Tavern. Not even a dessert.

One comes to the Country Tavern to play pool, party, dance, eat good barbecue, and have fun. It seats 250 people.

Kirbyville

Lazy H Smoke House

Rating: 8.5

Six miles south of Kirbyville on U.S. 96, Rt. 3 Box 155, Kirbyville, Texas 75956 Phone 409-423-3309 Fax 409-423-1114

Counter order, take-out, catering. No beer. Brisket plate $5.50, $6 on Sunday.

Open around 9 A.M. until dark. Accepts checks and credit cards.

Velma Willet is the Marjorie Main of barbecue. She's straightforward, does not mince words, and does not put on any airs.

I asked her if anything unusual happened here. She said, "Well, my husband fought behind enemy lines. Had a life expectancy of three days. He lived three months. Got tired of killin' people. For some reason, we don't have any trouble around here."

Another customer said, "Tell him about the window."

"Now that was years ago," Velma said. " I had worked late one night 'til 'bout twelve or so making sausage and was real tired. So I just went to bed. Sometime later, I was disturbed. I realized something was different, so I kept my eyes closed and listened. Well, this ol' guy had come through my window. So I snuck around and lammed into him and scratched him and hit him like a wildcat, and he realized he'd better git. So he dove through the winder. I grabbed his shoe and held him and bit his leg. His face hit that rose bush outside. Then I let him go. I found my husband's ole gun, and I shot it in the ground near his runnin' feet." She smiled. "No one's bothered me since."

"Thing is, I always thought I knew who it was, 'cause this guy came in the next day and he had awful scratches on his face and he was limpin'. He's dead now. As I said it's been awhile, and I'm still making sausage."

The place looked like a western stagecoach stop. It had pine poles and rafters.

Velma sat me down and piled food on my plate. I did not dare tell her what my marks on the questionnaire meant. The brisket had a 5/16-inch pink ribbon. The aroma pleased. It took two slices with my fork to part the meat. It had superior flavor. I gave it an 8. A pork rib had honey on it. "I don't always do the ribs the same way," was her interjection. It had almost no fat, good tenderness, and superior flavor. I rated it an 8. Her homemade sausage won the day. She made it from shoulder ham. No monosodium glutamate. No preservatives. No fat to speak of. The flavor said winner. I crowned it with a 10.

She served garlic-buttered potatoes, jambalaya, pinto beans, and potato salad for side orders. Dessert was homemade dewberry cobbler and homemade ice cream.

Just a half-mile down the road is Vaughan's Blueberry Farm, a place worth visiting. The bushes are six feet tall. When the blueberries ripen in June, the cobbler at Lazy H turns blue. The middle of June would be the perfect time to get some blueberry cobbler.

Lazy H started out with an old-time smokehouse. They built a barbecue pit out of iron with sand insulation. She used nut-bearing wood, and the rest was a secret.

Besides barbecue, Lazy H has some good beef jerky.
Velma said they started in a tent. "Place grew like a dirt dauber nest."

Livingston

McKenzie's Barbeque

See Huntsville for more information (page 171).

Rating: 8

1000 Commerce Land, Livingston, Texas 77351-3920
Phone 409-327-3221
Web site
www.mckenziesbarbeque.com

Counter order, take-out, catering. No beer. Brisket plate $6.25.

Open 10:30 A.M. to 9 P.M. Closed Sunday. Accepts checks and credit cards.

Longview

Bodacious BBQ

See Tyler for more information (page 189).

Rating: 8.5

2227 S. Mobberly, Longview, Texas 75602
Phone 903-753-8409
Roland Lindsey, owner.

904 North 6th Street, Longview, Texas 75601
Phone 903-753-2714
Shannon McKenzie, owner.

1402 West Marshall Avenue, Longview, Texas 75604
Phone 903-236-3215
Jeff and Mary Scarborough, owners.

1300 NW Loop 281, Longview, Texas 75604
Phone 903-759-3914
Scott Branch, owner.

102 Jet Drive, Longview, Texas 75602
Phone 903-643-9191
Fax 903-643-7648
Gary and Janie Adams, owners.

Counter order, take-out, catering. No beer. Brisket plate $6.25.

Open 10 A.M. to 9 P.M. Accepts credit cards.

Lufkin

Stringer's Lufkin Bar-B-Que

Rating: 8

203 South Chestnut Street,
Lufkin, Texas 75901
Phone 409-634-4744
Fax 409-634-6084

Menu order, take-out, drive
thru, catering, banquet facilities. No beer. Brisket plate
$5.60.

Open 7 A.M. to 9 P.M. Monday
through Saturday. Accepts
checks and credit cards.

Lufkin is a lumber town in the middle of a vast pine forest. Trucks with stacked pine logs appear everywhere, some in the large parking lot of Stringer's Lufkin Bar-B-Que. When the front parking lot fills up, they fill up the lot across the street. Considerate diners keep a lane open for the cars that queue up at Stringer's drive-in window.

A normal restaurant exterior did not prepare me for a hunting lodge interior. Inside, everything but the floor was appropriately knotty pine—unstained and covered with a clear coat of varnish. It resulted in a bright, comfortable, and cozy ambience.

The brisket had a 3/8-inch pink ribbon. *Encouraging*. The aroma waffled. *Discouraging*. It had zero fat. It parted with one firm slice of my fork. *Encouraging*. Chewing it, I strained to find flavor, but it came through—hickory. I rated it an 8. A pork rib looked superb, although it had a little too much fat. The flavor sparkled. I gave it an 8. The sausage yielded three drops of fat from the squeeze test. It was slightly salty, but over all I thought the flavor above average. I rated it a 7. A slice of ham got a 9—9 for flavor, 9 for tenderness, and 9 for leanness. A piece of chicken had little smoke flavor and was slightly moist. It was tender and lean. I gave it an 8.

They served regular sides, but irregular was their "Fried Rolls." Deep fat fried, these rolls melted in my mouth. These are addicting rolls.

George Foreman and Farrah Fawcett ate here—at different times and not together.

In 1950 Eugene Gann opened Lufkin Bar-B-Que. Two years later he hired Queen Esther Stringer to help for a few days. She and her husband bought the place and started adding on to it. In 1960 she leased it to Gailand Jeffy Courtney for ten years. In 1970 the Stringers returned as owners and added a half-block for parking and bought a church across the street and "converted" it into a huge banquet hall. In 1983 the Stringers sold the business and property to the present owners, son Paul and his wife, Brenda.

Marshall

Bodacious BBQ

Packed with country antiques and collectibles.

See Tyler for more information (page 189).

Rating: 8.5

2100 Victory Drive. Marshall, Texas 75670. Phone 903-938-4880. Joe Eisenhood, owner.

Counter order, take-out. No beer. Brisket plate $6.95.

Open 10 A.M. to 9 P.M. Accepts checks and credit cards.

Mount Pleasant

Bodacious BBQ

See Tyler for more information (page 189).

Rating: 8.5

100 W. Ferguson Road, Mt. Pleasant, Texas 75455-4808. Phone 903-572-7860. Bob Adams, owner.

Counter order, take-out, drive thru, catering. No beer. Brisket plate $6.50.

Open 10:30 A.M. to 8 P.M. Closed Sunday. Accepts checks and credit cards.

Nacogdoches

Mike's Barbecue House

Historians claim Nacogdoches as the oldest town in Texas. It began in 1716. El Pasoans contest this, but in fact, El Paso voted to become a part of Texas in 1850. Before that, it endured under Mexican control—despite the Republic of Texas claim to the area.

La Calle del Norte (North Street) claims to be the oldest public thoroughfare in the United States, because prehistoric Indian tribes used it.

At the south end of the trail, I found Mike's Barbecue House. I don't think it is the oldest anything.

Tall pine trees shade Mike's, and tall spiraling corrugated metal columns support a canopy that provides shade for customers at the entrance.

I went through the barbecue line and took my tray to a table. The brisket wore a quarter-inch pink ribbon. *Another rotisserie.* My fork severed it after two slices. The aroma did not stir. It was very lean, and the flavor mumbled. I gave it a 7. A sparerib had a little too much fat but otherwise was flavorful and tender. I tagged it with a 7. Mike's regular sausage yielded but two drops of fat from the squeeze test, but the flavor moaned. I gave it a 6.5. A hot link had one-alarm heat and gave up three drops of fat from the squeeze test. The pepper drowned out the other seasoning. I gave it a 6.5. A piece of chicken was moist and lean. The flavor fooled around and did not show up. I gave it a 6. A slice of ham had great tenderness but too much fat and not enough flavor. I gave it a 7. A slice of turkey had superior qualities in the taste, tenderness, and leanness categories and received an 8.

Sweet coleslaw, barbecue beans, Cajun rice (this item shows up near the Louisiana border), potato salad, stuffed jalapeños, and baked "taters" stuffed with barbecue made up the sides order list.

Rating: 7

1226 South Street,
Nacogdoches, Texas 75964
Phone 409-560-1676

Cafeteria style, take-out, drive thru, catering. No beer. Brisket plate $5.00.

Opens 11 A.M. Closes 8:30 P.M. Sunday through Thursday, and 9 P.M. Friday and Saturday. Accepts checks.

The dessert of the day was cherry cobbler.

The interior motif said country western. Red brick painted walls topped raw wood wainscot. Ceiling fans spun, and farm and ranch tools and accouterments clung to the walls.

Mike McClelland, owner, works hard. He started his business in 1986 in a smaller place further out of town. He had the chance to move to this present and larger location near downtown Nacogdoches and took it. The new place featured a drive thru, which had a continuous line of customers while I visited, and a meeting room that accommodated forty guests.

Pittsburg

Blalock Bar-B-Que

A signal light flashed in John Blalock's mind—the old Louisiana and Arkansas Railroad Depot would make a great barbecue restaurant. He bought it, moved it to its present location, reconditioned it, and opened Blalock Bar-B-Que.

The huge thick planks of the station freight floor, the old ceiling with its heavy cross beams, and the raw wood walls provide a nostalgic atmosphere.

John hunts, and some of his finest trophies along with a huge longhorn steer decorate the walls.

I went to the counter, got barbecue samples, and took a seat at one of dozens of tables. The brisket lacked aroma, and when I tried to cut it with a fork, I had a tussle. It had almost no fat. The flavor chugged. I gave it a 6. A pork rib had a little too much fat, whistle-stop flavor, and tenderness. I rated it a 7. The regular sausage seeped a puddle of fat from the squeeze test. The flavor rang a bell, and I gave it a 6. A Pittsburg hot link had excessive fat, and its flavor never left the train station. I scribbled a 4. I do not recommend Pittsburg links to anyone.

A slice of turkey was very moist, had round-trip flavor, and was very tender and streamlined with almost no fat. I gave it a 9. The ham had little fat, all-aboard flavor, and tenderness, and I labeled it a 9.

Rating: 7.5

103 Greer Boulevard,
U.S. Hwy. 271, Pittsburg,
Texas 75686
Phone 903-856-2321

Cafeteria style, take-out, catering. No beer. Brisket plate $7.25.

Open 11 A.M. to 8 P.M. Monday through Saturday. Closed Sunday. Accepts checks.

Blalock served traditional pinto beans, coleslaw, and potato salad. For dessert, I had a choice between pecan pie and a peanut rounder.

John Blalock is a tall, blonde Apollo. He told me he bought a Bewley smoker (not a rotisserie). He does not use any rub or sop and smokes the brisket twelve to fourteen hours. He said his barbecue sauce had lemon, garlic, black pepper, vinegar, ketchup, and Worcestershire sauce in it.

The economy of Pittsburg, Texas, depends heavily on Pilgrim Chicken processing. But I did not see any chicken the day I visited Blalock's.

Rusk

Bodacious BBQ

A great baseball collection makes this Bodacious unique. I saw an autographed picture of Roger Clemmons; collectible photos of Babe Ruth, Ted Williams, Stan Musial, and Nolan Ryan; and a picture of the 1931 Houston Buffaloes, Texas League Champions. I looked carefully at the team photo and found Jerome "Dizzy" Dean and Joe "Ducky" Medwick. Russell and Christy Turner are the owners.

See Tyler for more information (page 189).

Rating: 8.5

Hwy. U.S. 69 South, Rt. 3 Box 237 B, Rusk, Texas 75785
Phone 903-683-2611

Counter order, take-out, catering. No beer. Brisket plate $6.00.

Open 10 A.M. to 8 P.M. Closed Sunday. Accepts checks.

San Augustine

Hilltop Bar-B-Q

I. Lester Porter is a black man of many seasons. He remembers when kerosene was 5 cents a gallon and his family had two lamps. Their total energy bill for a month ran less than 10 cents. Porter said, "When I grew up, I wondered what business I could do that the white folks wouldn't run me out of town for." He smiled. "It came to me—barbecue. And that's what I do." He worked hard and succeeded. He said, "From cotton sack in the fields to money sack in the bank, there's a story there somewhere."

Lester received national publicity when *U.S. News* included Hilltop Bar-B-Q in an April 15, 1996,

Rating: 7

At the circle, Hwy. 21 at U.S. Hwy 96, San Augustine, Texas 75972
Phone 409-275-5116

Counter order, take-out, catering. No beer. Brisket plate $5.90.

Open 10 A.M. to 8 P.M. Closed Sunday. Cash only.

article entitled, "Hot on the Trail the Barbecue Grail." His place and Country Tavern in Kilgore were the only two barbecue places listed.

The exterior looked like something out of the twenties, and the interior was not the Waldorf-Astoria—just a plain, clean, and simple café.

I ordered my plate of samplers at the counter and took a seat. The brisket had a good-sized pink ribbon. The aroma enticed me. In the shear test, the meat parted with one hard push of my fork. My bite cried, "superb." I gave it an 8. A beef rib was extremely tender and had above average flavor but had too much fat. I labeled it with a 6. A piece of Boston butt pork resisted cutting. It took three hard slices of my fork to part it. It had above average flavor and was very lean. I rated it a 6.

Lester served potato salad, pinto beans, baked beans, and fried okra for side orders. His wife, Faye, cooked all the vegetables and baked some very good corn bread and fresh pie every day. I was lucky. The day I ate, she served lemon pie.

While I ate, I noticed that a black deputy sheriff ate at one table and two white businessmen dined at another. It had a mix of customers with one thing in common—love of barbecue.

I asked Lester about his pit. He said he built it himself out of a GE transformer. *Amazing.* He said he used hickory and pecan to smoke his meat. "Hickory until the pecan trees fall. Last year, we had a storm come through, and we had a lot of pecan trees fall."

He barbecues the brisket twenty-four to thirty hours in low heat. *That's real barbecuing.*

Silsbee

West Texas Bar-B-Que

Silsbee lies west of the Big Thicket National Preserve. When locals tire of wrestling alligators, they head west to "West Texas" for some real pit barbecue.

"Country" described the place. I went to the counter to order and stared at a long row of homemade pies—lemon meringue, chocolate meringue, pecan, coconut meringue, and egg custard. A sweet voice broke my concentration. "Can I help you?" It was the owner, Mrs. Nita Nolen.

I ordered my samples and took a seat at a table

Rating: 9

Hwy. 96 North, Silsbee, Texas 77656

Phone 409-385-0957

Counter order, take-out, catering. No beer. Brisket plate $5.50.

Open 10 A.M. to 8 P.M. Closed Sunday.

with a red plastic tablecloth. A sign read, "No dancin' on tables with spurs on." The brisket had a big pink ribbon. The smoke aroma erased pie from my mind. It took one firm slice with my fork to part the meat. I saw little fat. My bite danced with flavor. I gave it a 9. A pork rib rated a 9—excellent taste, tenderness, and very lean. A slice of pork roast had great tenderness, above average flavor, and little fat. I rated it a 9.

Bo Jackson brand supplied the sausage. Richard Nolan, husband of Nita and "gopher," said, "We've been using Bo Jackson for fourteen years." I understood why when I tested it. It produced but one drop of fat from the squeeze test. It had superior flavor. I gave it an 8.5. That was a high number from me for sausage, and the sign about dancin' brought on new meaning.

The barbecue sauce was tangy. I detected some chili powder, garlic powder, plus the basic ingredients of ketchup, vinegar, and Worcestershire sauce in the barbecue sauce.

The creamy coleslaw had carrot bits. Potato salad had some pimento. The pinto beans were traditional. Being near Louisiana, jambalaya was in order and found delicious.

All this came with warm, homemade rolls.

I pigged out and devoured a piece of egg custard pie.

The pies are a big seller. The day before Christmas Eve and Thanksgiving, West Texas sells 150 to 200 of Nita's pies.

West Texas had a twelve-foot-long metal barrel pit. They used mesquite and smoked the brisket ten to twelve hours. Richard said that he drove to Flatonia to get the wood. "I pick up three cords every six weeks."

Extra effort pays off for West Texas Bar-B-Que.

Texarkana

Big Jake's Smokehouse

Buccaneer Jean Lafitte used the old smuggling trail, Trammel's Trace, to sell contraband. The trail went from Nacogdoches to Texarkana to St. Louis, a wild town that would fence anything. A rumor persisted that somewhere along the route, south of Texarkana, Lafitte buried two million dollars in Mexican silver bars.

If you get hungry looking for Lafitte's silver, why not pull into Big Jake's and eat some soul-satisfying barbecue?

Driving west on U.S. Hwy. 82, New Boston Road, I discovered Big Jake's on the right side of the road beneath some huge shade trees. The building looked like a converted Dairy Queen, and later I found out that it was. I went in and ordered samples of barbecue.

A slice of beef brisket had a little too much fat (some folks like it that way) and a pink ribbon that measured a quarter of an inch. *Another rotisserie.* The aroma was faint. It took one hard slice of my fork to part the meat. The flavor was thin but nice. *Hickory is like that.* I gave the brisket a 7. A pork rib looked inviting. It had little fat, snappy flavor, and superior tenderness. I gave it an 8. The Eckridge pork sausage yielded three drops of fat from the squeeze test. The flavor was salty, and other seasonings were mild. I rated it a 7.

Pinto beans and potato salad were the usual recipes. They added milk to thin the coleslaw base.

Big Jake's offered carrot cake, sweet potato pie, and pecan pie for dessert.

Owners Tom and Wanda Arnold did a good job of changing the Dairy Queen into a barbecue place. The motif was Western. Farm collectibles, antiques, old photographs, and framed art prints covered the walls. Large photo reproductions of John Wayne

Rating: 7.5

2610 New Boston Road, U.S. Hwy. 82, Texarkana, Texas 75501
Phone 903-793-1169

Counter order, drive thru, take-out, catering. No beer. Brisket plate $5.99.

Open 11 A.M. to 9 P.M. Daily. Accepts checks and credit cards.

added drama to the scene.

The day I visited Big Jake's, mom and dad were away and son Eric assisted me. He said they used hickory for smoke. The regular barbecue sauce was from Bodacious. The hot sauce had some powerful cayenne and hot pepper sauce in it. Big Jake's had two Southern Pride rotisserie pits, and they smoked brisket for fourteen hours at 200 degrees.

I asked Eric if anything unusual happened here. "Unusual for me. When we opened this place, I worked every day for three months. I was dragging."

That is what it takes to make a business go.

Bob's Smokehouse

Texarkana was home to Scott Joplin, the ragtime musician who won a Pulitzer prize, and the Caddo Indians. Seventy Indian ceremonial mounds dot the countryside.

Rating: 7.5

2504 Richmond Road, Texarkana, Texas 75503
Phone 903-832-3036

My interest was in a mound of barbecue.

I survey an area before I work it, and every person I asked recommended Bob's. The place did not look like a barbecue joint. It looked more like a Baskin-Robbins. The interior was what I called "bleak modern."

Cafeteria style, take-out, drive thru, catering. No beer. Brisket plate $7.99.

Open 10:15 A.M. to 9 P.M. Monday through Saturday. Accepts checks and credit cards.

I went through the cafeteria line, received my samples of barbecue, and took a seat at a wood-simulated Formica table. I looked at a nice piece of brisket. *A thing of beauty and warmth in a plastic world*. It lacked aroma. *Must be hickory smoked*. It fell apart when I touched it with my fork. It lacked fat. I stuck it in my mouth and chewed it. The brisket had hickory smoke, a light but delightful flavor. I gave the brisket an 8. A pork rib had too much fat in a diet world. The flavor sang, but the meat was not quite tender enough. I gave it a 7. Eckridge supplied the regular rope sausage. It oozed three drops of fat from the squeeze test. The flavor was superior. I gave it a 7.5. The Mexican sausage came from Colorado. It also oozed three drops of fat from the squeeze test. It had chili powder and two-alarm fire from red peppers, and I gave it a 7.5.

The potato salad was traditional. Coleslaw was

creamy. Pinto beans had onions and chunks of sausage and ham. Other sides were corn "cobettes," fried okra, and a baked potato stuffed with everything and topped with a pile of barbecue.

Walter owns Bob's. On TV he says, "My name is Walter, but you can call me Bob." Bob was the original owner, and Walter Richardson is the third owner. Walter said he used I.B.P. "119 (fat on one side)" brisket. He had a Bewley pit and smoked brisket twelve to fourteen hours at 225 degrees. He did not use a rub, but he used a barbecue sauce sop on brisket, ribs, and chicken. I asked about his sauce. "I use Cattleman's and throw in some secret additions."

David and Lefty Frizzell, Senator Phil Graham, and Joe Stampley tarried here.

Springer's Smokehouse

Springer's Smokehouse is a family run business. Dad Ron Springer runs errands back and forth between the two locations and manages the business end of things. Mom Sissy Springer runs the cash register at the Texas Boulevard location. Daughter Chrissy runs the Summerhill place, and daughter Michelle runs the Texas Boulevard location.

They started in 1989. Senator Phil Gramm, country singer Joe Stampley, and soft rock pianist Billy Joel dined with them during that time.

Two Bewley pits did the smoking at Springer's. The wrangler used hickory wood for smoke. He smoked the brisket eighteen to twenty-four hours at 175 to 180 degrees. The only rub he used was on the ribs, and the ingredients were a secret.

Springer's brisket had a 5/16-inch pink ribbon. In the shear test, it parted with one hard slice of my fork. The aroma was very good for hickory. It was very lean, and the flavor yodeled. I gave it an 8. A pork rib had superior flavor and tenderness and contained little fat. I rated it an 8. I stared at an Old Ike Hot Link sausage slice. It came from Hot Springs, Arkansas. It was red in appearance, oozed three drops of fat from the squeeze test, and screamed

Rating: 8

720 Texas Boulevard at 8th Street, Texarkana, Texas 75501-5128
Phone 903-792-4787

3505 Summerhill
Phone 903-7893-6457

Counter order, drive thru, take-out, catering. No beer. Brisket plate $5.95.

Summerhill location open 10 A.M. to 9 P.M. Monday through Saturday.

Texas Boulevard location open 10 A.M. to 7 P.M. Monday through Saturday.

Accepts checks and credit cards.

with three-alarm heat. The red peppers overpowered other seasoning. I gave it a 7. The regular pork and beef sausage yielded two drops of fat, but the garlic flavor mumbled. I gave it a 7.

The barbecue sauce had some brown sugar, a little vinegar, ketchup, onion, black pepper, and Worcestershire sauce.

Potato salad, creamy coleslaw, spicy pinto beans, corn on the cob, and baked potatoes made up the side order list. Like most places in East Texas, they offered a potato with everything plus piled on barbecue.

Don Springer said he was the first to pile on the barbecue on a stuffed potato back in 1991.

Don also had some sage advice: "Never eat barbecue in a restaurant where the chairs are metal."

I never did figure that one out.

Tyler

Bodacious BBQ

"Great balls of fire!" Snuffy Smith said. He looked at what Loweezy was cookin' and said, "Bodacious!" Next came Roland Lindsey who thought the word "bodacious" would be the perfect name for a new barbecue restaurant.

Now sixteen Bodacious restaurants dot the face of Texas. The parent company owns some of them and the others have franchise owners.

I visited the Bodacious on Troup Highway. Lee and Joan Campbell have the franchise. Lee wasn't around, but Joan accommodated me on my visit. I asked her if all the Bodacious places were alike. "The barbecue's the same, but the ambience varies," she said.

She prepared a plate of samplers for me, and I sat down at a table and commenced my tests. The brisket had a quarter-inch pink ribbon. *Another rotisserie?* The aroma said "pit." The meat had almost no fat. I took a bite, and the flavor said "bodacious." I gave it an 8. A pork rib had bodacious flavor, no fat to speak of, and superior tenderness. I gave it a 9. The sausage oozed three drops of fat and had above

Rating: 8.5

1879 Troup Highway, Green Acres Shopping Center, Tyler, Texas 75701
Phone 903-592-4148
Lee and Joan Campbell, owners.

13069 FM 14 at I-20, Tyler, Texas 75706
Phone 903-531-2306
Larry and Diane Garner, owners.

Counter order, take-out, catering, banquet facilities. No beer. Brisket plate $6.93.

Open 10 A.M. to 9 P.M. Accepts checks and credit cards.

average flavor. I gave it a 7. A slice of turkey was moist and had zero visible fat and Hootin' Holler flavor. I rated it a 9.

Bodacious bottles its barbecue sauce and packages its rub. The ingredients are on the labels. Basic ingredients for the sauce were vinegar, ketchup, Worcestershire sauce, onion, and molasses.

Side orders listed standard potato salad, pinto beans, and coleslaw. Didn't see "Sufferin' Succotash" anywhere.

Dessert listed lemon meringue pie or pecan pie.

Chad McConnell, son, took me in back and showed me their barbecue pits. I found no run-of-the-mill pits. No rotisserie. These come from A N. Bewley Mfg. in Dallas. Like a normal long pit, the one I saw had a large firebox on one end; the smoke crossed the meat on grills in the oven and exited in a pipe at the end. In addition, the pit had a thermostat that electronically controlled the damper on the firebox and kept the temperature at 200 degrees.

Chad interrupted my thinking. "We do our brisket on this one."

Another pit had the firebox below the grates in the oven. The heat and smoke from the logs came up a pipe and diffused on a concave shaped stone over the pipe end. Chad said, "This pit is perfect for ribs, chicken, turkey, and ham."

Chad said that they use I.B.P. (Iowa Beef Packers) 120 brisket. That brisket has the fat on both sides.

Most barbecue restaurants buy the 119 with fat on one side.

Bodacious rubs brisket with their special seasoning and barbecues it eighteen to twenty-six hours.

Bodacious BBQ

See Bodacious story above for more information. Owners Larry and Diane Garner.

Rating: 8.5

13069 FM 14 at Interstate 20, north of Tyler, Texas 75706
Phone 903-531-2306
Fax 903-595-0603

Counter order, take-out. No beer. Brisket plate $6.79.
Open 10 A.M. to 9 P.M. Accepts credit cards.

Hickory Fare Bar-B-Que

Rating: 7.25

2333 E Southeast Loop 323,
Tyler, Texas 75701
Phone 903-561-8881
Fax 903-509-4146

1717 W. Gentry Parkway,
Tyler, Texas 75702
Phone 903-592-6953

Cafeteria style, take-out,
drive thru, catering. No beer.
Brisket plate $6.75.

Open 10:30 A.M. to 9 P.M.
Accepts credit cards.

Victor Petrenko, Elizabeth Manly, Ben Johnson, Reba McIntyre, George Jones, Pam Tillis, Conrad Twitty, Hank Williams Jr., Don Meredith, Ralph Neely, and Von Erics patronized this famous spot on Tyler's fashionable east side. Russian skating star Petrenko ate barbecue for the first time and gobbled down three helpings.

Signed photos of the above grace Hickory Fare's walls and add glamour to its country decor.

Food at hand, I tested the elixir of the stars. The brisket had a familiar quarter-inch pink ribbon. *Another rotisserie*. It took three hard-pushed slices to cut through it. The aroma mumbled. It had little fat. I rated it a 6. *How could this be? Something else must attract the stars*. A good-looking pork chop caught my eye. It looked firm with no fat. I took a bite and found it had superior flavor and tenderness. I gave it an 8.5. *That's what brought out the stars*.

Eckridge supplied the sausage. It oozed a puddle of fat from the squeeze test and had above average flavor. I gave it a 5. The hot link had superior flavor, some fat, and one-alarm fire. I gave it a 6.5. A slice of turkey had very good flavor, was tender, and had very little fat, if any. I gave the turkey an 8. A ham stole the spotlight and the show. It had the tenderness of a Reba McIntyre love song and the flavor of luscious ice skater Elizabeth Manley and a little fat like Victor Petrenko. I gave it a 9.

I detected brown sugar, a tad of vinegar, ketchup, and Worcestershire sauce in the barbecue sauce.

The sideshow featured creamy coleslaw and potato salad. The pinto beans were traditional. Garden okra, country French fries, and hot buttered corn filled the bill.

Dessert was peach cobbler and/or soft ice cream.

Owner James Lancaster is a large, affable man. He told me how Ben Johnson would come to Hickory Fare and tell him stories about his experiences in the movie business. James was eager to know about John Wayne. Ben told him that Wayne would drink and play poker all night and then be the first actor on the scene and know all his lines, and Wayne had a generous and friendly disposition.

Another story did not involve a star, but a rancher from Montana. He came to Hickory Fare and bought $300 worth of barbecue to take home. He said that they have no hard woods where he came from and that all they can do is grill.

James confessed that he barbecued with a rotisserie and used hickory wood. He smoked brisket for eighteen hours.

James went on nonstop, telling jokes and stories. I wished I could have hung around longer.

Jeremy's Bar-B-Q and Ribs

Owner Patricia Shokrian did not know what to do with this building. She loved barbecue, so she opened Jeremy's. Her facility is bright, new, and spacious.

For a new place, it had an old look on my slice of brisket: a quarter-inch pink ribbon. *Another rotisserie.* Patricia asked me not to mention the name of the manufacturer of her rotisserie smoker. But why? Others have her brand.

The aroma of the brisket murmured. The meat had a little too much fat. In the shear test, the meat parted after the second slice of my fork. The flavor was better than most rotisserie-smoked brisket. I

Rating: 7.5

3020 SSW Loop 323, Tyler, Texas 75701
Phone 903-509-9817
Fax 903-509-9807

Cafeteria style, take-out, drive thru, catering, banquet facilities. No beer. Brisket plate $6.29.

Open 11 A.M. to 8 P.M. Monday through Saturday. Accepts checks and credit cards.

gave it my usual rotisserie 7. A pork rib had superior flavor, some fat, and above average tenderness. I dubbed it a 7. Hillshire provided sausage. It gave up three drops of fat from the squeeze test. The flavor was above average. I gave it a 7. The turkey was very lean, had superior flavor and tenderness, and I rated it an 8. The ham scored the same in every department, and I gave it an 8.

Jeremy's served two barbecue sauces. The rib sauce was sweet. It had cayenne, Worcestershire sauce, black pepper, a little ketchup, plus other secret ingredients. The regular barbecue sauce almost twinned the rib sauce but lacked the cayenne and black pepper.

The coleslaw was extraordinarily good. It had a light oil base and chopped onion tops. The pinto beans contained some chili powder, and the potato salad was traditional.

Here's Patricia Shokrian's coleslaw recipe:

cabbage	purple cabbage for color
carrots	coleslaw dressing
2 fresh lemons	mayonnaise
2 tablespoons of chives	paprika

Keep it light.

Jeremy's served peach cobbler and\or ice cream for dessert.

She confided that she smoked brisket for eighteen hours at 200 degrees, and her rub was a secret.

I asked Patricia if anything unusual happened here. She reminded me that Jeremy's is on a busy highway. She remembered how a semi lost control and crashed into the building.

Because of the large size of the dining rooms, Jeremy's does a big business in weddings, rehearsals, and graduation parties.

There's more than one way to crash.

Winnsboro

Dwain's Barbecue

Dwain's building has three parts. The middle part dates back to either an old house or the original school building of Chalybeate Springs, Texas, and could be over a hundred years old. Dwain Martin added the kitchen when he converted the building from a mom-and-pop grocery store to a barbecue

Rating: 7.5
Hwy. 11, four miles east of Winnsboro
Phone 903-365-2377

place in 1976. The place burned to the ground in December of 1996. The middle part suffered severe smoke damage, and the kitchen burned up. A year ago Bill and Annette Miller bought the place, restored the kitchen, and added a front room.

Cafeteria style, take-out, catering. No beer. Brisket plate $5.95.

Open 11 A.M. to 7 P.M. Tuesday through Saturday. Accepts checks and credit cards.

I walked up to the counter and met Bill Miller, who was carving the meat. He cut me what I needed and I took a seat. I stared at another rotisserie-smoked piece of brisket. The aroma murmured. I found very little fat. It took two tough slices with my fork to part it. My bite attested to above average flavor. I gave the brisket a 7.

A pork rib had too much fat, average flavor, and above average tenderness. I marked it a 6. A pleasant surprise was Wilson brand pork sausage. It produced only one drop of fat from the squeeze test and had superior flavor. I gave it an 8.5. Roughneck sausage had the same basic ingredients as the regular but had red pepper added. It flared one-alarm fire. I gave it an 8.5. A slice of turkey was very low on flavor, had superior tenderness, and no visible fat. I gave it a 7. The ham had superior tenderness and flavor and no visible fat. I labeled it with an 8.5.

The side orders were traditional. The potato salad had mustard, and the coleslaw was creamy. The dessert list: pecan pie, lemon icebox pie, chocolate meringue pie, coconut meringue pie, blackberry cobbler, and a fruit cup of peaches.

Mr. Miller hand built plywood booths for his new room. They looked strong and straight. "I built them so that people would be comfortable through their meal but would want to move on when they were through."

I called the decor country kitchen. The wood paneled walls and the ceiling were white. A wallpaper border of a farm scene with chickens ran along the top of the walls and added the right touch of color.

If you have a guitar, you need to check in with Bill because they have a genuine guitar-pickin' good time every month at Dwain's. Gary Don Jones, lead guitar for Ray Price, makes many of these get-togethers.

Bill Miller told me that he smoked the brisket fourteen to sixteen hours. The brisket, frozen at the start, smokes at 300 degrees for three hours and then the thawed-out meat smokes at 185 to 190 degrees the remainder of the time.

Across the highway stands a Texas Historical Marker commemorating Chalybeate Springs. Early pioneers called it Musgrove Springs, named after the first owner of the property. They changed the name to Chalybeate because of high iron content in the water (chalybeate means "tasting like iron"). A village sprang up. A school resided where Dwain's is today.

Chalybeate Springs once had churches, stores, and a post office. A two-story hotel with spa added to the town's grandeur. Then hot springs became less popular. The town declined. They razed the hotel in 1935, and the school closed in the 1950s. The steps leading from the hotel down to the railroad tracks remain.

Part Seven

Prairies and Lakes

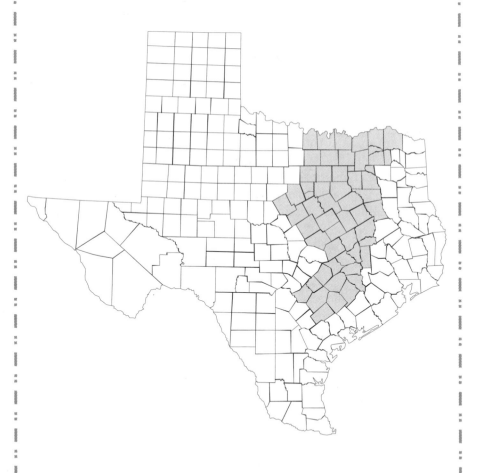

Addison

Spring Creek Barbeque

See **Richardson,** Texas, for further information (page 263).

Rating: 8

14941 Midway Road, Addison, Texas 75244
Phone 972-385-0970

Cafeteria style, take-out, catering. Beer served. Brisket plate $7.35.

Opens 11 A.M. Closes 9 P.M. Sunday through Thursday and 10 P.M. Friday and Saturday. Accepts checks and credit cards.

Arlington

Bodacious BBQ

For more information, see Tyler (page 189).

Rating: 8.5

1206 East Division, Arlington, Texas 76011-7340
Phone 817-860-4248
Mike and Fran Ruegsegger, owners.

Serves beer. Brisket plate $8.75.

Opens 11:00 A.M. Closes 3:00 P.M. Monday through Wednesday and 9:00 P.M. Thursday through Saturday. Closed Sunday. Credit cards accepted.

Colter's Bar-B-Q

See **Dallas** for more information (page 215).

Rating: 8

1322 North Collins, Arlington, Texas 76022
Phone 827-261-1444
Fax 817-274-0108

4435 Little Road, Arlington, Texas 76016
Phone 817-572-3930
Fax 817-483-7683

Serves beer. Brisket plate $7.25.

Opens 11:00 A.M. Closes 9:00 P.M. Sunday through Thursday and 10:00 P.M. Friday and Saturday. Accepts credit cards.

Gaylen Nationally Famous Barbecue

Not far from The Ballpark at Arlington, home of the Texas Rangers, sits Gaylen Nationally Famous Barbecue on North Collins Street. North Collins at I-30 is a major intersection and provides one of the best ways to reach the baseball stadium.

A "perfect" night begins with winning ribs at Gaylen and then a winning game for the Rangers.

Beware, only the ribs at Gaylen are guaranteed to win. Of course, if the Rangers lose, one out of two isn't bad.

I entered the cafeteria line and selected a small piece of each barbecued meat. I sat in a wood booth. The room had a down home mien. I looked at a beautiful 5/16-inch wide pink ribbon on my slice of brisket. *Encouraging.* It had little fat. It fell apart with a nudge of my fork. I lifted a bite to my nose and sniffed. The aroma lifted my spirits. I took a bite and enjoyed excellent smoke flavor enhanced by a secret seasoning. I rated it a 9.

A pork rib showed some fat, but beneath its hard crust was melt-in-your-mouth barbecued pork. I fully understood why Gaylen had national fame for its pork ribs. I gave them a 9. Owens supplied the sausage. It seeped three drops of fat from the squeeze test. It had a mild flavor, and I gave it a 6. A slice of ham had superior tenderness and almost no fat. The salt content mastered the smoke flavor. I tagged it with an 8. A piece of turkey had great moisture and excellent tenderness and leanness. It possessed a light flavor, a nice flavor, and I gave it a 9.

The regular barbecue sauce had a heavy tomato base, and the hot barbecue sauce had enough red pepper to ring the alarm twice.

I met Leland Hallett, co-owner with his father-in-law Norman Miller. Leland showed us his three brick pits.

"We use oak and smoke brisket twenty to twenty-four hours."

Rating: 9

826 North Collins, Arlington, Texas 76011
Phone 817-277-1945

Counter order, take-out, catering. Beer on tap. Brisket plate $8.75.

Opens 11 A.M. Closes 9 P.M. Monday through Thursday and 10 P.M. Friday and Saturday. Accepts checks and credit cards.

No wonder the barbecue tasted so good.

"We rub all our meats with our own special blend of spices. I stick it with a fork. If the fork slides out easy like, I know its ready."

"Any celebrities eat here?" I asked.

"Gary Reed, Mark Chestnut, John Elway, Dan Marino, and…"

"And?"

"Well, Mike Godfrey."

"Who's Mike Godfrey?" I said.

"He was a comic cowboy and one of the best bull riders in rodeo. Trouble is, Mike broke his neck riding a bull." He reflected on that. "Some people get down when something like that happens, but Mike comes in here regularly. He's in a wheelchair, but his mind isn't. He's an inspiration to have around."

As we shook hands, Leland said, "Be sure to tell your readers about our all-you-can-eat for $10.95."

Spring Creek Barbeque

See Richardson for further information (page 263).

Rating: 8

4200 South Cooper Street, Arlington, Texas 76015
Phone 817-465-0553

Cafeteria style, take-out, catering. Beer served. Brisket

plate $7.35.

Opens 11 A.M. Closes 9 P.M. Sunday through Thursday and 10 P.M. Friday and Saturday. Accepts checks and credit cards.

Bastrop

Cartwright's Bar-B-Q

Clyde Clardy's family owned Bastrop Bar-B-Q way back when. The state bypassed Bastrop with Hwy. 71, and Clyde sold the business. It was such a good business and had such a good reputation, seven different owners tried to make a go of it but failed. Steve Cartwright bought it in 1989. He lost $17 thousand trying to resurrect it. "The first day, my wife and I took in $80. I knew what I had to do, so we moved the business—not the building—to a lot

Rating: 8

490-A Hwy. 71 West, Bastrop, Texas 78602
Phone 512-321-7719

Cafeteria style, take-out, drive thru, catering. No beer. Brisket plate $5.50.

Opens 10:30 A.M. Closes 8 P.M. Monday through Thursday, 9 P.M. Friday and Saturday, and 6 P.M. Sunday. Accepts checks and credit cards.

in front of Wal-Mart on 71. Things are now doing great."

I asked him if he had e-mail or a web site. "I have a number two pencil, a Big Chief tablet, and I'm a millionaire." He flashed a huge grin.

Steve explained that the new building contains some of the old. It had an old window with antique glass, the sign off the old Bastrop Bar-B-Q building, and a piece of glass etched with the name of his Uncle James's restaurant, "Biggers Barbeque" from Elgin, Texas.

Surprised to find out that James Biggers was his uncle, I asked Steve if he heard that his uncle is a ghost at Meyer's Elgin Smokehouse (See Hill Country, Elgin, page 108). I told him the story, and he laughed. "I wouldn't be surprised. When my uncle died, he had fifteen cents of every quarter he ever made." He added, "My aunt tried to run things and decided to sell the business. My aunt and uncle were good friends of the Meyers and all along had sort of promised the place to them."

Earlier, I went through the cafeteria line and picked up one-bite pieces of barbecue. A slice of brisket had that familiar quarter-inch pink ribbon. *Another rotisserie.* It had a little fat, unlike other rotisserie-smoked meat, and its aroma encouraged me. It took a gentle push with my fork to part the tender meat. My bite rang out with flavor. *This cannot be rotisserie-smoked meat.* I rated it an 8.

A pork rib showed more fat than what I like to see, but it had good tenderness and excellent flavor. I gave it an 8. A piece of pork loin had a little fat and great tenderness and gangbusters flavor. I tagged it with an 8. Cartwright's secret recipe sausage gave up four drops of fat from the squeeze test. It had above average flavor with one-alarm fire. I tagged it with a 6. The best came last, turkey. My piece of turkey breast had little fat, good moisture, great tenderness, and excellent flavor. I rated it a 9.

The regular barbecue sauce had a little extra red pepper in it. The barbecue hot sauce had pickle juice and cayenne. The cayenne settled at the bottom. Steve pointed out, "The more you swirl the bottle, the more cayenne goes to the top and the hotter it gets. You can have sauce as hot a you want it."

Cartwright's served a slew of vegetables: sweet and creamy coleslaw, potato salad, green beans, corn, macaroni salad, and his wife's father's recipe for pinto beans (cumin, salt, black pepper, chili powder, and brown sugar).

Dessert: pies and cookies from the Bluebonnet Pie Company in Bastrop and Blue Bell ice cream.

The interior is warehouse country—concrete floor, corrugated metal ceiling, ceiling fans with cluster lights, a wall mural depicting a wrangler feeding hands on the range, red-and-white checkered tablecloths, and rusty metal siding for a ceiling over the cafeteria line. The place was clean as a whistle. The metal and other parts are from a 110-year-old, two-story home from Winchester, Texas.

Steve said they had a brand new Southern Pride rotisserie smoker. *Impossible. The brisket was too good.* I told him of my findings concerning rotisseries. He said, "The new ones have better heat distribution. I love it. It's cut way back on wood consumption. Our wood bill went down from six thousand a year to eight hundred. We use oak and smoke brisket sixteen hours at 200 degrees. In the morning at 7:30, we kick it up to 250 degrees. The only rub we use is salt and pepper."

A sign read, "Our beans speak for themselves."

Bedford

Spring Creek Barbeque

See Richardson for further information (page 263).

Rating: 8

1504 Airport Freeway, Bedford
Texas 76021-6626
Phone 817-545-0184

Cafeteria style, take-out, catering. Beer served. Brisket plate $7.35.

Opens 11 A.M. Closes 9 P.M. Sunday through Thursday and 10 P.M. Friday and Saturday. Accepts checks and credit cards.

Bellmead

Tom's Smokehouse

In 1998 Waco Big Brothers and Big Sisters staged a benefit with a barbecue cook-off. Every barbecue place in Waco showed up, and Tom's Smokehouse won the blue ribbon.

Tom's won me the day I visited. The joint looked like a converted mom-and-pop grocery store, and inside it looked like the locker room of the Bellmead High School Pirates. They painted most of the place Pirates blue and yellow. Along one wall stood a half-dozen video game machines that customers' children play for free (not a bad idea).

I got my order and looked at a large pink ribbon on a chunk of meat. I asked a young male employee what cut it was, and he said, "Shoulder clod." He added, "We don't serve brisket." The aroma encouraged me. The meat contained almost no fat, was very tender, and was packed with smoke flavor. I dubbed it a 9. A pork rib had superb flavor, almost zero fat, and melted in my mouth. I gave it a 9. The young man said, "You should have been here on Wednesday. That's when we serve baby-back ribs. But you better get here early, because we sell out fast."

I believed him.

A slice of Boston butt pork appeared to have no fat, was very tender, and had pirate treasure flavor. I gave it a 9. The beef sausage hailed from Brenham Wholesale. It had above average seasoning and yielded two drops of fat from the squeeze test. I gave it an 8.

If you think those ratings were high, get set for the turkey and ham show. The turkey got a perfect 10. The ham did the same. The meat was succulent, tender, flavorful and lacked fat. Dream food for any pirate.

The pinto beans had chili powder and pork end

Rating: 9

3125 Bellmead Drive,
Bellmead, Texas 76705
(2 blocks NE of Waco, Texas,
on U.S. Hwy. 84)
Phone 254-799-2345

Counter order, take-out, catering. No beer. Brisket plate $5.25.

Open 10:30 A.M. to 7 P.M. Warning: leaves early when sold out of barbecue. Closed Saturday and Sunday. Accepts checks.

cuts. The potato salad had a mustard base and possessed real mashed potatoes (a big difference). The coleslaw was sweet. It had sugar, milk, and Miracle Whip. *Not bad.*

Tom and Lori Moore own Tom's. I talked with Tom while I devoured side orders. Lori was out shopping. He said, "Lori makes all the side dishes and desserts. Makes them fresh every day."

I had to choose from peach or apple cobbler, cake, or banana pudding for dessert.

I asked Tom how he got started. He said he did barbecuing part-time and received so many compliments, he decided to go into the business. He started in 1992 with a 550-square-foot run-down shack that had six tables and a little pit. Three years later he moved to this place.

He told me he used a long pit with a firebox at one end and a smokestack at the other end. "That's the only way to barbecue." He said a salesman dropped by to sell him a rotisserie. He also said they discovered that oxygen made the pink ribbon. The more times a cook opened the lid, the more oxygen went in and made the ribbon wider. "They came up with an oxygen injector for their rotisserie smoker. He demonstrated with a portable unit and burned up the meat."

Tom said he smoked the shoulder clod from 10 P.M. to 10:30 A.M. He used pecan wood.

Lori made the barbecue sauce. I detected brown sugar, cayenne for one-alarm fire, ketchup, chili powder, and maybe a little Worcestershire sauce.

Besides helping the Bellmead Pirates from time to time, Lori and Tom opened up their restaurant for a free Thanksgiving dinner benefit. Donations went to help a high school kid who suffered a broken neck.

Great folks. Great food.

Belmont

Goss Barbecue & Station

Goldie Hawn and Bill Atherton sat in the shade of Goss Barbecue and Station. They downed soda pops and waited for the next "take" for the film *Sugarland Express*.

"They cracked jokes and laughed a lot," said barbecuer L. Fleming Goss, venerable owner of the restaurant. "They must have had a half dozen takes

Rating: 7.75

Highway 90 Alternate, just west of Highway 80, next to the post office, Belmont, Texas 78604
Phone 830-424-3560

of police cars chasing Goldie and Bill. Goldie was | Open from sunup to sun-
quite a sight with scraggly hair and old clothes. She | down. Beer. Beef plate $6 per
looked like someone on the run, and I'm glad she ran | pound.
to my place."

Counter order, take-out.

The old building serves as a country store, ser- | Checks accepted.
vice station, and barbecue place. Fleming Goss is as
colorful as his store. He's tall, stocky, has a lot of white hair, and carries a lot
of age well. The store has a timeworn barn-red false front. When you enter
you step back into antiquity. Modern products have replaced Sapolio Soap,
the licorice jar, and cracker and pickle barrels, but the rest is original stuff.
Goss's folks built the place in 1916 to house a Model T garage and black-
smith shop. Behind the garage stood their cotton gin. A freak storm blew
down the gin smokestack that measured 50 feet high and 4 feet in diameter.
Goss cut off a portion of it and made his barbecue pit. "We've had that pit for
a long time, and it doesn't show any sign of wear."

I ordered a slice of brisket at the counter, which looked more like an old
railroad ticket window than a counter for barbecue. An elderly man cut the
brisket and placed it on a piece of butcher paper. He weighed the brisket.
"$1.23. Is that all you want?"

I nodded. He pointed to the door to my right. Above it hung a sign that
read, "Belmont Social Club." Inside I found four tables, comfortable chairs,
TV soap opera in progress, air conditioning, a stuffed deer head, and collectibles. I tested the meat. The fork cut it with a nudge. The bouquet was
inviting. It tasted good but had too much fat. I gave it a 7. The pork ribs
received an 8.5. They had great flavor and less fat than most. The sausage
came from Maeker's in Shiner, Texas. It consisted of half pork and half beef. I
gave the sausage the squeeze test, and too many drops of fat fell out. The
spices gave it above average flavor. I gave it a 7.

Now get this: no side dishes. Occasionally, Goss serves potato salad, but
that is rare. He explains, "This is a barbecue place. Occasionally, we barbecue chicken, and I am sorry we didn't have any for you today."

Go back in time at Goss Barbecue & Station. Take your kids. They need
to see how it was in the good old days. The place is old, but the barbecue is
fresh everyday.

Benbrook

Riscky's Barbeque

See Fort Worth for more information (page 231).

Rating: 8

9000 Hwy. 377S, Benbrook, Texas 76126

Phone 817-249-3320

Counter order, take-out. No

beer. Brisket plate $5.93.

Open 10:30 A.M. to 8:00 P.M.

Closed Sunday. Accepts checks.

Brenham

Tex's Barbecue & Catering

The name is Tex's Barbecue, but owners Tex and Bonnie Benkoski tired of explaining the spelling of their name and had Texas Barbecue painted on their outdoor sign. Near the birthplace of Texas, Washington-on-the-Brazos, Tex's is easy to find. Simply open your car's fresh air vent and let the aroma guide you.

I went through a genuine swinging screen door into a real country restaurant.

You go to the counter to order and get in line. They sell the meat by the pound or you can order by plate or sandwich. The meat is 'cued out back in four long pits made of corrugated metal and welded rebar. Tex believes in briquettes and sop. The sop has secret mixin's and does a tasty job. Meat gets 'cued about six hours.

I ordered a little of everything. I gave the brisket a 7. It had good flavor but was hard to cut with the plastic fork. Now folks, this rating business is nit-pickin' stuff, because you might give the brisket a 10 on flavor alone. The pork ribs had better than average flavor but were slightly greasy. I gave them an 8. Then I dug into some Boston butt pork. It gave way to the fork and had a mild flavor. I rated it a 9.

Rating: 8

4807 Highway 105, three and a half miles east of Brenham, Texas 77833

Phone 409-836-5962

Counter order, take-out, catering. No beer. Brisket plate $5.

Open Wednesday through Saturday 10 to 6, Saturday 10 to 4. Closed Sunday. Checks accepted sometimes.

The sausage comes from Floyd's in Chapel Hill. It had good spices and a little heat. I gave it an 8. Chicken was tender; meat fell off the bone at the touch but was a little greasy. Rated it an 8.

Sides were good, especially the butter potatoes with parsley. The pinto beans had onion, a little pepper, and other magical ingredients. They had good flavor and no sweetener.

Tex's started out as a catering service, and because of demand they started adding tables. Eventually, the place doubled in size.

Bonnie said, "We're the little place with a big reputation."

I rated Bonnie's Barbecue Sauce a 10. Here's her no-longer-secret recipe:

> *Put into saucepan:*
> *32 oz. of ketchup*
> *1 stick of margarine*
> *1 lemon, cut off ends and halve. Squeeze juice into pan and then*
>   *drop in the whole lemon.*
> *2 onions, finely chopped in blender*
> *Add enough water to cover ingredients, then add 2 cups of*
> *Worcestershire sauce, a half box of brown sugar, and salt and*
> *pepper to taste.*
> *Stir and cook slowly for 5 minutes.*

Bonnie was pretty nice to share this with us. Enjoy.

Centerville

Country Cousins

Country Cousins barbecue is strictly take-out. The place sat to the side and behind the Texaco station, beneath a monster Texaco sign.

My car had an electronic burglar alarm system. When I parked in front of Country Cousins' small frame building, the alarm went crazy. No matter what I did to correct it, it kept either locking or unlocking my car door. I gave up. I walked up wooden steps and ambled along a wooden porch to the Country Cousins order counter.

The server gave me samples on butcher paper. On the counter ledge, I tested the brisket. It had a

Rating: 8

Interstate 45 at Hwy. 7E,
Centerville, Texas 75833
Phone 903-536-3271

Take-out, counter order,
catering. No beer. Brisket
plate $4.95 (lunch).

quarter-inch pink ribbon. _Must be the new standard for the barbecue industry_. The aroma was faint, but maybe, because I was outside, the wind had something to do with that. It took two shoves with my fork to part it. It appeared to have zero fat. My bite revealed superior flavor. I gave it an 8.

A pork rib had a very superior, smoky flavor. It had above average tenderness and some fat, and I gave it an 8. Slovacek's in Snook, Texas, supplied the pork and beef sausage. It grudgingly gave up two drops of fat from the squeeze test. The flavor mumbled and I gave it a 7.

The barbecue sauce tasted traditional—ketchup, vinegar, and Worcestershire sauce.

My plate of barbecue entitled me to two sides—the only sides. The potato salad had some sweetness. The barbecue beans tasted like Campbell's pork and beans with some chili powder thrown in.

I just missed meeting the owner, Rusty Teston. He pulled out as I pulled in. The server explained that Rusty did all the smoking at his home. So, unfortunately, I did not get to interview him, but the server said that they used a rotisserie and smoked with hickory.

Open 7:30 A.M. to 8 P.M. Monday through Thursday and Saturday, 7:30 A.M. to 10 P.M. Friday, and 9 A.M. to 8 P.M. Sunday. Accepts checks.

Mama Mike's Barbecue & Steak House

Rating: 6.5

Interstate 45 at Hwy. 7 West, Centerville, Texas 75833
Phone 903-536-6262

Menu order, take-out, catering, banquet facilities. No beer. Brisket plate $5.95. ($3.99 senior citizen).

Opens 10:30 A.M. Closes 9 P.M. Sunday through Thursday and 10 P.M. Friday and Saturday. Accepts credit cards.

Stagecoach passengers spent the night in Centerville. The trip between Dallas and Houston took two grinding days. Centerville was halfway and was a place for riders to stretch, eat, and spend the night. Today, travelers on the same route stop for lunch at Mama Mike's Barbecue.

I ordered and received my usual plate of barbecue samples. The brisket had the skinniest pink ribbon. It measured one-eighth of an inch. Some places it thinned to a sixteenth of an inch. Its scent caused appetite stimulation. Cutting the meat with a fork brought aggravation. Lack of fat educed elation. The flavor called for a celebration. An 8 I gave as designation.

A pork rib had superior tenderness, a little too much fat, and lacked in flavor. I gave it a 7. The sausage delivered four drops of fat from the squeeze test, and the flavor mumbled. I gave it a 6. The barbecue sauce had one-alarm heat from cayenne. Its base had ketchup, vinegar, and Worcestershire sauce in it.

Mama Mike's potato salad had chunks from whole potatoes—no instant spuds. The pinto beans possessed chunks of bacon.

Dessert consisted of cheesecake, homemade cobbler (mama mia!), and/or ice cream.

The motif was Western. It had wood paneled walls. Ceiling fans hovered over unfinished wood flooring. A number of fine mounted trophies hung on the wall. A beautiful wild turkey with wings spread graced the wall of a meeting room.

This is Texas A&M territory, and Bucky Richardson likes the place. A sign reads: "Welcome Aggies, Cajuns, oilfield trash, Oiler fans, cowhands, steel workers, Cowboy fans, cow traders. But we will feed T-sips, SMU Mustangs, Razorbacks, Baylor Bears, TCU Horned Frogs, Rice Owls, Houston Cougars, teachers, Texas Tech Red Raiders, bankers, lawyers, insurance salesmen, horse thieves, other assorted riffraff."

Colleyville

Railhead Smokehouse B-B-Q

See Fort Worth for more information (page 230).

See Fort Worth for more information (page 230).

Rating: 8.5

5220 Hwy. 121 South, Colleyville, Texas 76034

Phone 817-571-2525

Fax 817-571-4144

Counter order, take-out, drive thru, outside seating, catering. Full bar. Brisket plate $7.75.

Open 11 A.M. to 9 P.M. Closed Sunday. Accepts checks and credit cards.

Columbus

Jerry Mikeska's Bar-B-Q

Jerry Mikeska, owner, hunter, sportsman, designed his octagonal restaurant so he would have enough wall space to hang dozens of stuffed animal trophies. He shot many of the trophies, but friends have contributed their share including the head of an African bull with unusual horns that are large and rise at sharp angles to make a "V."

A contest to see who has the most trophies exists between him and his brother Maurice, who owns Mikeska's in El Campo. At present Maurice has more trophies, but Jerry is close behind with 170. The menagerie is worth going to see, even if you are not hungry for barbecue. Jerry knows that, so when you enter, the tantalizing barbecue smoke goes to work and appetites soar.

I went to the counter and ordered a small slice of brisket.

"Sorry. We serve sirloin tri-tip instead of brisket."

That sounded good to me. Why is it always brisket? The old-time butchers barbecued brisket because that was the best way to get rid of it. Brisket is not exactly a choice cut of meat, and barbecue is the best way to make it tender and delectable. But where is it in the rule book that says barbecued beef must be brisket?

I picked up my order of barbecue samples and took a seat. The sirloin tri-tip looked inviting, but it displayed a very thin and dark ribbon. *How am I to judge this?* It had a little fat and an enticing aroma. In the shear test, it separated after the second slice of my fork. My bite produced a combination of good steak and smoke flavors. I rated it an 8.

A pork rib had good appearance and some fat. It possessed excellent tenderness and above average flavor. I gave it an 8. The star of the show was the

Rating: 8

Interstate 10 East, P.O. Box 69, Columbus, Texas 78934

Phone 409-732-2293

Fax 409-732-5232

Toll free 1-800-524-7613

Menu order, take-out, catering. Serves beer. Sirloin tri-tip plate $5.75 (no brisket).

Opens 10 A.M. Closes 8 P.M. Monday through Saturday and 3 P.M. Sunday. Accepts checks.

sausage. Mikeska makes their own, and they make many different types of sausage. The pork and beef sausage I ate yielded but one drop of fat in the squeeze test, and the flavor was excellent. I gave it a 9. That is a very high rating from me for sausage. A piece of chicken was moist and tender and had little fat and above average flavor. I put an 8 on it.

The barbecue sauce was thick and on the sweet side. I detected ketchup, Worcestershire sauce, onion, a little vinegar, and black pepper.

Mikeska offers a variety of vegetables. I went for the creamy coleslaw, which was slightly sweet, and boiled potatoes. A baked potato with sour cream, cheese, and chopped barbecue went for $3.10.

Mikeska's offers banana pudding, pecan pie, and chocolate chip cookies for dessert.

Jerry said they put seasoning on all their meats before smoking. They had Southern Pride rotisserie pits and smoked sirloin tri-tip three to four hours at 350 degrees. "You're surprised?" Jerry said.

"Yes."

"Sirloin tri-tip is more tender and doesn't have to cook so long. I pay two and a half times more for the sirloin than brisket, and my customers appreciate it."

No argument from me.

A sign on the wall read, "People are terrific! Business is good! Life is wonderful!"

Here's a partial list of famous people who dined at Jerry Mikeska's: Nolan Ryan, Gov. Clements, Gov. George W. Bush, President Gerald Ford, Senator Kay Bailey Hutcheson, Senator Phil Gramm, Bum Phillips, Dr. Red Duke, and Astros owner Drayton McLane.

As I was leaving, Jerry gave me his regular business card and another that read,

IMPORTANT PHONE NUMBERS

Governor George W. Bush
Austin, Texas
512-463-2000

Queen Elizabeth
London, England
011-441-930-4832

Pope John Paul II
Vatican City
011-39-6-6982

Bar-B-Q King of Texas
Jerry Mikeska
Columbus, Texas
409-732-2293
 1-800-524-7613

Commerce

Buck's Barbeque Restaurant

First I asked directions and then I wandered around the streets of Commerce and then asked directions again. I repeated this pattern several times. I finally came across Buck's—quite by accident. Everyone told me it was across from the city swimming pool. The swimming pool was flat and hard to see. What someone should have said was "Buck's is near the city water tower." Then even I could have found it, and maybe you can find it.

The town has Texas A&M at Commerce, formerly East Texas State University. Collegians love Buck's. Owner Carl "Buck" Johnson told me the college crowd is a quick turnover. "Just when I think I have a steady customer, the kid graduates."

A slice of beef brisket had too much fat but above average flavor and tenderness. I gave it a 6. A pork rib had more fat than I liked, excellent flavor, and tenderness. I gave it an 8. Buck's served Bryan's sausage. It oozed three drops of fat from the squeeze test and had a salty flavor. The seasoning was weak like bologna. I gave it a 5. A slice of turkey also tasted salty. It had light smoke flavor and was fairly moist and tender. I rated it an 8.

The barbecue sauce was a little sweet and had vinegar, ketchup, and Worcestershire sauce in it.

The coleslaw was creamy. The pinto beans, macaroni salad, potato salad, fried okra, sweet corn, and turnip greens were of traditional recipes. A big seller was a stuffed baked potato with all the regular fixings plus a pile of barbecue.

I took my pick of coconut pie, chocolate pie, pecan pie, or banana pudding for dessert.

General Charles Chenault was born here. I wondered if he ever ate here. Aron Tippon, the country western star, did.

I called the décor "plain country." Wood tables

Rating: 7

1010 Maple, Commerce, Texas 75428

Phone 903-886-7880

Cafeteria style, take-out, catering. No beer. Brisket plate $7.95.

Opens 8 A.M. Closes 6 P.M. Monday, Tuesday, Thursday, and Friday; 2 P.M. Wednesday; and 4 P.M. Saturday. Closed Sunday. Accepts checks and credit cards.

and Naugahyde padded benches on a plain concrete floor. Long bare bulb fluorescent lights ran across the plain ceiling. Pictures of John Wayne made the place seem cozy.

Buck told me that he used an Oyler rotisserie smoker and that he smoked rubbed and sopped brisket overnight at 200 to 225 degrees. The recipes for the rub and the sop were a deep, dark secret.

> *There was a 'cuer whose joint was rustic.*
> *He had a secret sauce and never discussed it.*

It was a shame they dropped the name East Texas State. Buck agreed.

Cuero

Barbecue Station

Cuero is the home of the Cuero Gobblers and SMU and pro football running back Arthur Whittington. Since 1970 the Gobblers have won state championships twice in football and once in track. Ten other times they reached the quarterfinals or better in football. Could there be something in the barbecue?

Cuero means "cowhide" in Spanish. That ties in with "barbecue." But before we talk barbecue, it must be said that Cuero once claimed the title of Turkey Capital of the World and in 1873-1874 residents witnessed the Sutton-Taylor feud, the bloodiest in Texas.

Perhaps the two events had something to do with the origination of the term "turkey" for another human being.

You might surmise that the folks in Cuero are competitive. No wonder the barbecue is so good at Barbecue Station.

I found the place at the edge of downtown Cuero, near the railroad track (that ties in with "Station"). Upon entering, I found myself in a cafeteria line. The place gleamed clean as a whistle. I decided the interior had a Western look. The high topside held hanging ceiling fans, and the wood paneled walls held framed artwork. Formica-topped tables had built-on wood plank benches.

Rating: 7

114 South Esplanade, Cuero, Texas 77954-3849

Phone 512-277-3417

Cafeteria style, catering, banquets. No beer. Brisket plate $4.79.

Opens at 10 A.M. Closes 6 P.M. Monday through Friday, 3 P.M. Saturday. Closed Sunday. Checks accepted.

Not wanting to get back in the crowded line again, I ordered a sampler of everything. I took a seat and began my tests. The brisket had a narrow pink ribbon, indicating a fast smoking time. The flavor danced and twitched my nose. I had to use a knife to cut it. Chewing it, I decided that it had below average tenderness, little fat, and an above average flavor. I rated the brisket a 6.

The pork ribs had superior tenderness, some fat, and above average flavor. I gave the ribs an 8. Maeker's of Shiner, Texas, makes the sausage. It was half pork and half beef. I squeezed a piece. Fat oozed out and made a puddle. I found it to have exceptional flavor. I gave it a 7. My piece of chicken was moist and tender and had good flavor. I rated it an 8.

I ascertained that the sauce had vinegar, ketchup, Worcestershire sauce, and a touch of sugar or brown sugar. It possessed a mild flavor.

Barbecue Station does a big holiday business with honey glazed hams and smoked turkey. Unfortunately, I visited on a non-holiday.

The potato salad had better than average flavor. The pinto beans had chili powder, cumin, salt, pepper, and no bacon. Tasted great. The coleslaw had vinegar and oil, no sugar.

A large array of desserts graced the serving counter including pecan pie, banana pudding, peach cobbler, and lemon and chocolate meringue pies.

I met with Barbecue Station owner David Jones. He said the business was a family affair. His wife, Shirley, baby-sits; daughter Pam and son Bobby pitch in. He said the business began as a grocery store. He added a barbecue pit in back. Folks liked the barbecue and when mom-and-pop stores could not compete with the supermarkets, he closed the grocery store and converted the entire building into a barbecue restaurant. He took me in back and showed me his pit, a 36-inch pipe casing. He used oak charcoal, rubbed the meat with a special homemade seasoning, and smoked the brisket eight to nine hours. *I knew it! Too fast.*

I asked him if any celebrities ate here. He noted that many football coaches come around during recruiting time. *I wonder why?* "One time Tom Landry came in here." He added that George Strait ate here disguised with a baseball hat and sunglasses.

David shared some recipes; each designed to serve 150 people!

Potato Salad:

50 pounds of boiled potatoes	*2 pints pimentos*
1 gal. salad dressing	*2½ pints vinegar*
1 cup chopped bell peppers	*6 cups sugar*
1 cup chopped celery	*Salt and pepper to taste*

Coleslaw:

5 lbs. chopped cabbage	1 cup oil
2 cups vinegar	Salt and pepper to taste
2 cups sugar	

The Jones family strives to please their diners. Little wonder they succeed.

Dallas

Colter's Bar-B-Q

Luther's Barbecue began franchising restaurants in Dallas in 1964. The first store was the old Redbird store near Duncanville. Luther's experienced some difficulties, and the Dallas franchise corporation took full control of Dallas operations in 1981. The corporation selected the name Colter's because it adapted to all the signs with the least expense.

I went through the cafeteria line and picked up my usual sampler plate of barbecue and sides. I looked at a slice of brisket with a beautiful pink ribbon. I sighed. The brisket had a 5/16-inch ribbon. The brisket had very little fat, and in the shear test, it took a slight nudge with my fork to part the meat. *That's really tender.* The flavor sang "Big D, little a, double l, a, s." I put a 9 on my interview form.

I looked at a pork sparerib covered with a rub. It had too much fat to suit me. My bite revealed above average tenderness and flavor. I gave it a 7. A pork baby-back rib also had a rub on it. It had little fat, excellent tenderness, and above average flavor. I graded it with an 8. The pork and beef sausage seeped a puddle of fat from the squeeze test. It possessed superior flavor. I gave it a 7. I sampled the chicken. It was delicious. It was moist and tender. It had little fat and superior flavor. I gave it an 8. A slice of turkey had almost zero fat, superior tenderness, and above average flavor. I rated it an 8.5.

Colter's served three barbecue sauces. The regular had some sweetness, the sweet sauce had more

Rating: 8

11827 Abrams Road, Dallas, Texas 75243
Phone 972-680-1990
Fax 972-231-6069

1026 Valley View Center, Dallas, Texas 75240
Phone 972-458-9307
Fax 972-458-2408

18178 Dallas Parkway, Dallas, Texas 75287
Phone 972-713-7184
Fax 972-713-7186

3904 W. Camp Wisdom, Dallas, Texas 75237
Phone 972-298-3335
Fax 972-709-7482

Cafeteria style, take-out, caters and delivers, banquet facilities, drive thru. Some locations have beer. Brisket plate $7.25.

Open 11 A.M. to 9:30 P.M. Sunday through Thursday, 11 A.M. to 10 P.M. Friday through Saturday. Accepts credit cards.

sweetness, probably from brown sugar, and the hot sauce had a two-alarm measure of Tabasco in it. I stuffed some buttered bread in my mouth to cool down.

Later I met with Jack Clop, Colter's general manager. He showed me their pits. They had two Bewley pits with water trays that provided steam to tenderize the meat. Jack said they used hickory and smoked brisket for about twenty-three hours at 150 to 165 degrees. *Those are great numbers. No wonder the meat is so tender.*

He said, "We use a special rub with almost no brown sugar on the brisket. We use a sweeter and spicier rub on the ribs."

"All our brisket is certified Black Angus," said Jack. "That's a big reason why our meat is so tender."

I told him I was impressed with their rapid expansion.

"Believe it or not, we are going into Germany with barbecue at American bases."

Some Texas G.I.'s are going to be very happy.

Dickey's Barbecue Pit

Like Timex, Dickey's keeps on going.

Big chains get bigger because they have good food and good service.

A slice of Dickey's brisket had a quarter-inch pink ribbon. It had some fat, and the aroma was fast asleep. It took two slices with my fork to part the meat. My bite revealed light flavor. I rated it a 6.

A pork rib had too much fat, superior tenderness, and above average flavor. I gave the rib a 6. A chunk of pork shoulder fared better, but it too possessed too much fat. It had superior tenderness and flavor. I tagged it with a 7. Dickey's serves two sausages. The regular pork and beef sausage yielded three drops of fat from the squeeze test, and its flavor was above average with a little heat. I rated it a 7. A piece of hot link sausage also gave up three drops of fat from the squeeze test and had above average flavor. It had one-alarm heat, which was slow to burn, and I gave it a 7.

A piece of chicken had almost no fat and was extremely tender. I labeled it with an 8. A slice of

Rating: 6.5

Nine locations in Dallas, three at D/FW Airport, two in Grapevine, one in Richardson, one in Colleyville, three in Plano, one in Lewisville, one in Grand Prairie, one in Rowlett, one in Mesquite, and one in Rockwall area.

Other locations in Austin, Chandler AZ, Phoenix AZ, Torrance CA, San Diego CA, Walnut Creek CA, Englewood CO, Aurora CO, Denver (downtown) CO, Independence MO, Kansas City MO, and Albuquerque NM. Web site www.dickeys.com

ham had superior tenderness, a little fat, but the salt overpowered the smoke taste, and I tagged it with an 8. A slice of turkey was moist, slightly salty, had almost no fat, excellent tenderness. I graded it with a 7.

The barbecue sauce was sweet and vinegary. It had a little ketchup in it and a little Worcestershire sauce and two-alarm fire from perhaps cayenne.

Sides: potato salad had chunks of boiled potato, some mayo, and parsley. The coleslaw possessed a light dressing. The pinto beans had ketchup and a little chili powder, and they called them barbecue beans. Dickey's sprinkled parsley on hot fresh rolls. They also served black-eyed peas, corn on the cob, fried okra, green beans, jalapeño beans, cucumber salad, pasta salad, and broccoli salad.

Dessert: fruit cobbler, chocolate meringue pie, and free soft ice cream.

The décor looked Southwestern. Straight-backed wooden booths sported Indian blankets to lean against. Tables had galvanized tops. Floor had black-and-white checkered vinyl tiles. Bare air conditioning ducts and rafters hid in dark green paint. Ceiling fans lazed. Walls had pictures of ranch scenes. The sum of its parts provided a cozy, comfortable atmosphere.

Dickey's uses Bewley pits, like Bodacious. Meat sits on grills, and smoke from the firebox is diffused and spread over the meat and then out a smokestack. Dickey's uses hickory wood and smokes brisket overnight for eighteen hours.

Since another pit manufacturer found that oxygen builds the ribbon, no one opens the Bewley pit enough to add oxygen at Dickey's.

Dickey's has a rapidly building franchise program. Locations will open soon in New Jersey, Missouri, and New Mexico.

Catering, phone 213-691-1495. Fax 214-691-1496.

Cafeteria style, take-out, catering. No beer. Brisket plate $7.29.

Open 11 A.M. to 8 P.M. Accepts credit cards.

Pappas Bar-B-Q

See Houston for more information (page 62).

Rating: 7.75

2231 West NW Highway at Lombardy Lane, Dallas, Texas 75220
Phone 214-956-9038
Fax 214-956-0594

Serves beer. Brisket plate

$6.95.

Opens 11:00 A.M. Closes 10 P.M. Sunday through Thursday and 11:00 P.M. Friday and Saturday. Accepts credit cards.

Peggy Sue BBQ

Snider Plaza is a quintessential forties shopping center in the fashionable north side of town near University Park and Highland Park. It is a favorite haunt of students from nearby Southern Methodist University as it was for me in 1949. Back then Mr. Arledge had a wonderful blue plate restaurant in this strip, and my wife-to-be and I frequented his place and a barbecue restaurant called Howard's. After talking with Mike Shannon, who worked at this place years ago, I found out the place had several name changes through the years. Howard married Peggy. A divorce gave the place to Peggy. Years later, Peggy sold it. Three succeeding owners tried to make a go of the place but failed. That's when Mark Hall acquired the place. Mark, a smart fellow, added Sue to the name for his wife Susan. So today it's Peggy Sue BBQ.

Mike said, "We completely restored the place and use recipes that date back to the time you ate here."

I ordered a sampler plate and looked at a quarter-inch pink ribbon. *Rotisserie time in Texas.* It graded like ninety percent of all rotisseries. It had little fat, above average flavor, and it took two slices of the fork to part it. I gave it my rotisserie 7.

A pork rib had above average tenderness, some fat, and superior flavor; I rated it an 8. A sweet tomato-sopped baby-back rib had little fat, superior tenderness and flavor. I tagged it with an 8. A piece of pork and beef sausage yielded two drops of fat from the squeeze test and possessed superior flavor. I gave it an 8. A slice of ham was slightly salty. It had superior tenderness and almost no fat. The salt overpowered the smoke flavor, and I labeled it with another 8. A slice of turkey was almost flavorless. It had superior tenderness and nearly zero fat. I rated it a 7. A piece of chicken was moist and tender and had almost no fat and above average

Rating: 7.5

6600 Snider Plaza, Dallas, Texas 75205-1352

Phone 214-987-9188

Menu order, take-out, catering. Full bar. Brisket plate $5.95.

Opens 11 A.M. Closes 9 P.M. Sunday through Thursday and 10 P.M. Friday and Saturday. Accepts credit cards.

flavor. I gave it an 8.

The barbecue sauce ran sweet with a heavy tomato base. I detected a little Worcestershire sauce and a touch of cayenne.

The new Sue in Peggy Sue is also responsible for some delectable recipes. Fresh spinach is lightly steamed with lemon butter until smooth and silky. Squash casserole has a creamy blend of corn and cheese. The coleslaw has fat-free boiled vinegar with added bits of green pepper. The potato salad has chunks of new potatoes with skins.

If that does not make your mouth water, think of the desserts: fried pies, peach cobbler, and root beer floats.

Peggy Sue BBQ reminded me of many restaurants constructed in the forties. Walls had nostalgic pictures of that era. The booths had green Naugahyde, and the tables had red-and-white checkered tablecloths. Painted cowboy hats crossed the tops of walls and added splashes of color.

Our waitress said the ribs were hand trimmed, stripped of sinew, and dry rubbed before smoking. They did not rub brisket, had a J&R rotisserie, used oak, and smoked brisket twelve to fifteen hours at 200 degrees.

Peggy Sue BBQ—our past, our present, our future.

Red Hot & Blue Memphis Pit Bar-B-Que

The bright-colored menu reads:
It was heaven or something like it, I'm telling you,
Me and my baby went out last night, just us two
We were combing the town for some red hot and blue,
Red hot blue Memphis Pit Bar-B-Que.
Stumbled on a place called Red Hot & Blue.
We stepped inside and found us a seat,
Ordered a slab of them ribs to eat.
Let me tell you what you ought to do,
Just ease on down to Red Hot & Blue.

What's the difference between Memphis style barbecue and Texas barbecue? Memphis cooks put a sweet rub on most everything and use a lot of sugar.

What's the difference between Memphis and Kansas City barbecue? Not much.

I ordered my usual sampler of barbecue meats and looked at a slice of brisket with a 1/8-inch dark

Rating: 7

9810 North Central Expressway, Suite 600, Dallas, Texas 75231

Phone 214-378-PIGS (7447)

New location: 1600 Wilson Boulevard (across from the Ballpark), Arlington, Texas 76011

Phone 817-276-7430

Menu order, take-out, catering. Full bar. Brisket plate $7.99.

Opens 11 A.M. Closes 10 P.M. Monday through Saturday and 9 P.M. Sunday. Accepts credit cards.

red ribbon. Strange. It appeared to have little fat. In the shear test, it took two slices of my fork to part the meat. The aroma murmured, and the sweet flavor peeped. I gave it a 7. Next item was dry ribs. The juiceless appearing ribs had a seasoning dust of twenty-seven ingredients sprinkled on them.

I'm not sure it takes twenty-seven ingredients to make a dry rub, but I guess it does in Memphis. To understand the long list of ingredients is perhaps to understand the Mexican army recipe under Santa Anna. They believed the way to win was to fire more shots. The Texan army believed the way to win was to fire a shot *at* somebody.

The dry ribs had some fat, above average flavor, and superior tenderness. I rated them a 7. A chunk of pork loin had some fat, superior tenderness, and above average flavor. I tagged it with a 7. Red Hot buys Earl Campbell's sausage. My piece of sausage gave up five drops of fat from the squeeze test and had superior flavor and not red-hot heat. I labeled it a 7. A piece of chicken had a heavy coat of *apres cuisener* sauce. The sauce overrode the thin smoke flavor. It had some fat and above average tenderness. I gave it a 7.

They have two barbecue sauces. The Mojo Mild has vinegar, tomato, a little Worcestershire sauce, and two-alarm red pepper heat. The Hoochie Coochie has the same mix as the Mojo except it possesses four-alarm red pepper fire. Have plenty of bread and butter ready to put out the fire.

Red Hot & Blue presented some interesting side dishes. The potato salad was so good, I asked the manager, name of Mickey, if I could have the recipe. He obliged. The recipe:

Dice boiled new potatoes and skins, add a little onion and mayo, lightly salt, and add celery seed to taste. No mustard. The key to success is to serve it at room temperature.

Red Hot & Blue's coleslaw had a light base and some celery seed thrown in. Other interesting items were corn relish, turnip greens, fried okra, corn on the cob, Memphis fries, and baked jumbo sweet potatoes.

They bake a limited number of sweet potatoes. When they run out, they do not cook more until the next day.

Dessert: banana pudding, cobblers, key lime pie, Oreo brownie sundae, and peanut butter silk pie.

Blues music filled the room, and the place looked as southern as Memphis. Long runners of ivy gathered above ivory-colored plantation shutters and deep red wainscoting. Carpet and tablecloths were slate blue. Band instruments and photos of blues musicians and singers decorated the walls.

Interestingly, Red Hot & Blue started in Arlington, Virginia, by congressman from Tennessee Lee Atwater and Tennessee governor Don Sunquist. Their hunger for and the lack of Memphis barbecue in the D.C. area caused them to take the plunge. They bought recipes from two famous barbecue places in Memphis with the agreement that they would never operate in Tennessee. So they came to Big D (rhymes with Tennessee?).

They own Southern Pride rotisserie smokers and use hickory wood. Brisket smokes twelve to fourteen hours at 225 degrees. The usual temperature for Southern Pride rotisseries is 250. Perhaps the 25 degrees difference is the reason for more fat.

A slogan reads, "We specialize in barbecue you can't get anywhere else." *Let me tell you what you ought to do, just ease on down to Red Hot & Blue.*

Solly's Bar-B-Que Restaurant

Rating: 8

4801 Belt Line at Addison Road, Addison, Texas 75240-7540
Phone 972-387-2900

Cafeteria style, take-out, catering. Serves beer. Brisket plate $6.35.

Open 11 A.M. to 8 P.M. Monday through Saturday. Closed Sunday. Accepts credit cards.

Tucked in the middle of burgeoning commercial high-rise office buildings in North Dallas and Addison is a Texas institution, Solly's.

A man named George Salih started this business in 1945. By anglicizing his name, he made it easy for Texans to pronounce it. Also, Solly's had a catchy ring, which added to its mystique.

I had no trouble finding this place. The Dallas North Tollway, the aorta that pumps life into towns as far north of Dallas as Frisco, has a Belt Line exit that makes Solly's most convenient.

I went through the cafeteria line and picked up my usual samples of barbecue. I looked at a slice of brisket with a quarter-inch pink ribbon. *Another rotisserie.* An interesting aroma caught my nose. *Unusual for a rotisserie pit barbecue.* The brisket had a little fat, and in the shear test, it parted with one slice of the fork. The flavor was superior, and I rated it an 8.

A pork rib had good appearance and little fat. It had above average tenderness and flavor. I gave it an 8. A piece of pork sausage yielded three drops of fat from the squeeze test and had above average flavor. I graded it with a 7.5. A slice of ham was slightly salty, and its smoke flavor was so light the salt overwhelmed it. The ham had excellent tenderness and a little fat, and I gave it a 7. A slice of turkey was very moist, extremely tender, and had almost zero fat and soul-stirring flavor. I gave it a 10.

Sides: The potato salad was very creamy. Coleslaw had light dressing with a touch of vinegar. Pinto beans contained some chili powder. The French fries were crisp.

Dessert: Serve yourself free soft ice cream. What a deal.

The décor suggested a roadside café of the fifties. A tube of blue neon circumvented the restaurant near the top of the ceiling. Ceiling fans spun slowly. Booths were covered with an aqua green Naugahyde. The floor had brick pavers. An abundance of plastic flowers and a condiment bar softened the design. I felt at home.

I talked with an employee who said that they did indeed have a rotisserie pit and that Solly's used hickory wood and smoked brisket sixteen to eighteen hours.

A sign read, "All food prepared daily in our kitchen from original recipes developed by the Salih family since 1945."

Sonny Bryan's Smokehouse

Sonny Bryan left this world with a barbecue pit he built in 1958. The huge pit still chugs smoke at this Inwood location. Michael LeMaster, general manager, called the pit one of a kind. "It doesn't have a thermostat or anything electrical. No gas. It builds up heat. When it sounds like a freight train, I pour water on the fire. If that doesn't stop the rumbling, I turn on a water spigot." He went on to tell me that they smoked brisket ten hours at around 300 degrees, but he had no way of controlling the heat except to throw water on the fire. I asked him what wood he used and he said, "Oakry." He smiled. "That's half oak, half hickory, and half whatever we can find."

A lady took my order when I walked in, and now she handed the food to me. Mike went back to work, and I sat down on one of two long benches in the eating area. My place was a school armchair table. My brisket slice had a 5/16-inch dark ribbon. The aroma lagged. It had very little fat. It took one push with my fork to part it. The flavor rumbled. I gave it an 8. A pork rib had some fat, was tender, and possessed

Rating: 7.5

2202 Inwood Road at Harry Hines Boulevard, Dallas, Texas 75235
Phone 214-357-7120
Fax 214-352-2307
Catering phone
214-353-0027

Order to lady standing near front door, take-out, catering. Beer served. Brisket plate $6.89.

Opens 10 A.M. Monday through Saturday and opens 11 A.M. Sunday. Closes 4 P.M. Monday through Friday, 3 P.M. Saturday, and 2 P.M. Sunday. Accepts checks and credit cards.

superior flavor. I gave it a 7. Syracuse made the half beef, half pork sausage. Three drops of fat oozed from the squeeze test. The flavor was above average, and I rated it a 6.5. Turkey was somewhat dry, a little tough, and had little flavor and no fat. I gave it a 7. Ham was tender, had above average flavor and little fat, and I gave it an 8.

Sides were pinto beans, coleslaw, potato salad, French fries, and onion rings. Desserts were fried pies and sliced apple pie.

Suddenly, I faintly heard the rumbling of the pit. With each bite, it grew louder. *Should I stop eating?* It grew louder. *Should I run?* I looked around. No one seemed disturbed. Then came a giant hissing noise and all was quiet.

Other Sonny Bryan's in Dallas:

302 North Market Street, Dallas, Texas 75202
  Phone 214-744-1610

325 North Saint Paul Street #P5, Dallas, Texas 75201
  Phone 214-979-0102

13375 Noel Road, Dallas, Texas 75240
  Phone 972-851-5131

4701 Frankford Road #237, Dallas, Texas 75287
  Phone 972-447-0102

8080 North Central Expressway, Dallas, Texas 75206
  Phone 214-891-8844

Spring Creek Barbeque

See **Richardson** for further information (page 263).

Rating: 8

2827 West Wheatland Road, Dallas, Texas 75237
Phone 972-296-1211

14941 Midway Road, Dallas, Texas 75244
Phone 972-385-0970

Cafeteria style, take-out, catering. Beer served. Brisket plate $7.35.

Opens 11 A.M. Closes 9 P.M. Sunday through Thursday and 10 P.M. Friday and Saturday. Accepts checks and credit cards.

Denison

Jones Barbecue

Denison lies five miles from the east entrance to Lake Texoma. The town is the birthplace of our 34th President Dwight D. Eisenhower and site of the "Red River Bridge War." The Red River Bridge Co. built a toll bridge near Denison. Years later Texas built a free bridge over the Red River in 1931, a half-mile east, and agreed to compensate Red River Bridge $60,000 and other considerations for their loss of projected revenue.

When Texas opened the bridge, Red River Bridge demanded $150,000. Texas counter-offered $80,000. Oklahoma governor William H. "Alfalfa Bill" Murray ordered Oklahoma Highway Patrolmen to tear down the barricades on the Texas end of the free bridge. Traffic crossed until Texas Rangers arrived at midnight and closed it again. Red River Bridge upped its toll on their bridge to 75 cents one way and one dollar for a round trip. Gov. Murray ordered his state highway department to plow up the road at their end of the toll bridge. The Texas Legislature, after furious debate, acquiesced and voted to pay Red River Bridge its price.

Now Oklahomans can get to Jones Barbecue easily and inexpensively.

I found the place a few blocks north of downtown Denison. It looked like a building from the days of the Red River Bridge War. Inside, it reminded me of an antique store. Old items pervaded available space. I spotted a beautiful collection of miniature porcelain dogs. Walls displayed completed picture puzzles. The place looked comfy cozy. It did not take long to find out that owner James "Jim" Jones not only transforms brisket into barbecue but also turns certain customers into freaks.

James smokes brisket thirteen to fourteen hours and uses oak and pecan wood. The brisket comes

Rating: 6.5

1426 West Morton, Denison, Texas 75020
Phone 903-465-3449

Cafeteria style, take-out, catering, banquet facilities. No beer. Brisket plate $4.19 and $5.19.

Opens 10:30 A.M. Closes 8:30 P.M. Sunday through Thursday and 9 P.M. Friday and Saturday. Accepts checks.

out with a pink ribbon and almost zero fat.

Customers freak out as they gaze into an old fun house mirror and grow legs twice as long as they should be.

I almost freaked out looking at a slice of brisket with a 1/8-inch pink ribbon. *How could this be?* It had zero fat and aroma. In the shear test, it parted with one hard slice of my fork. My bite revealed very light flavor. I gave it a 6. A pork rib had superior tenderness, little if any fat, and, once again, very light flavor. I rated it a 7. The sausage oozed a puddle of fat and had above average flavor. I tagged it with a 6. Salt overpowered the smoke taste in my piece of ham. It had superior tenderness and some fat. I gave it a 6. A slice of turkey breast had superior tenderness, light flavor, and almost no fat. I labeled it with an 8.

The barbecue sauce was similar to Cattleman's.

Sides: The beans tasted like Campbell's pork and beans with pieces of bell pepper and onion added. The creamy coleslaw contained bits of pimento. Hot homemade rolls were heavenly.

Dessert: banana pudding and cherry or apple cobbler.

I took the tour and saw the pit that Jim built. Sure enough, it was a rotisserie.

An old "collectible" sign read, "One man's junk is another man's pleasure."

The way Jim barbecues may be the exact way you like it. Try it.

Denton

Colter's Bar-B-Q

See Dallas for more information (page 215).

Rating: 8

2229 I-35 E. South, Denton, Texas 76205

Phone 940-383-1577

Fax 940-898-0046

Cafeteria style, take-out, caters and delivers, banquet facilities, drive thru. Some locations have beer. Brisket plate $7.25.

Open 11 A.M. to 9:30 P.M. Sunday through Thursday, 11 A.M. to 10 P.M. Friday through Saturday. Accepts credit cards.

Fairfield

Sam's Restaurant

Sam and Doris Daniels started Sam's on old U.S. Highway 75 in 1948. The highway had two narrow lanes that went up, down, and around and connected Houston and Dallas. They called a hilly stretch between Buffalo and Centerville "Dead Man's Curve." By the time folks from Houston reached Fairfield, they settled their nerves and stomachs at Sam's. Folks from Dallas took the break, resting before the bad stretch ahead. Sam's was it. Not much else was around.

Driving along Interstate 45, I realized that Sam's had a big spread. I entered through a large gift shop. A hostess seated me. I had to choose between a buffet that looked to be at least 50 feet long or from a menu. I decided on the menu, because buffet meat is never as tender as fresh cut meat. A slice of brisket had a 1/8-inch pink ribbon. *Cooked too hot, and no one opened the lid very much*. I pressed my fork against it. It did not budge. I pressed really hard and split the slice of brisket. *Not too bad*. It looked to be very lean and had above average flavor. I gave it a 7.

A pork rib had some fat, was tender, and had above average flavor. I gave it a 6. Eckridge supplied the sausage. I squeezed it, and three drops of fat oozed out. Although the seasoning was mild, it had robust flavor. I gave it a 7.5. A slice of turkey was moist, very lean and tender, and had above average fat. I rated it an 8. Ham had good tenderness, some fat, and above average flavor. I gave it a 7.

The barbecue sauce had little or no Worcestershire sauce in it. It had ketchup, some sugar, garlic powder, a little vinegar, salt, pepper, and chili powder.

I had to choose from twelve sides. Most had traditional recipes, but the coleslaw had raisins. Tasted great.

Rating: 7

Interstate 45, Exit 197,
Fairfield, Texas 75840
Phone 903-389-SAMS
Fax 903-389-8002

Buffet or menu order, take-out, catering, banquet facilities. No beer. Brisket plate $7.29.

Open 6 A.M. to 10 P.M. Accepts checks and credit cards.

Sam's attracts dessert lovers. I had to select one of thirteen pies, peach cobbler, and\or Blue Bell ice cream.

The main dining room had huge dimensions. The buffet divided around 200 diners. The décor was country. The dark rose-colored carpet complimented the light gray walls that displayed antiques, collectibles, and replicas of old signs. A newer room addition bore the name "Fairfield Room." It had realistic murals that depicted Fairfield history and points of interest.

The cook told me they used a rotisserie smoker for their barbecue. He used hickory wood. The brisket went in around 9 P.M. and cooked at 250 degrees. In the morning, around 7 A.M., another cook took the meat out.

Business bristles at Sam's. On any given Sunday, more than 1,800 eat here. Dallasites drive eighty-plus miles just to feast.

Fort Worth

Angelo's Bar-B-Q

Rating: 10

2533 White Settlement, Fort Worth, Texas 76107

Phone 817-332-0357

Counter order, take-out, catering. Serves beer and wine. Brisket plate $6.95.

Open 11 A.M. to 10 P.M. Closed Sunday. Accepts checks.

People of Fort Worth think of themselves as West Texans and Dallasites as North Texans. This city began as a fort, and a treaty with the Comanches stipulated that Indians would stay west of a line drawn through Fort Worth. Thus the Fort Worth slogan, "Where the West begins."

The line seems to affect the barbecue as well. Fort Worth folks claim a big difference in their barbecue and the barbecue in Dallas. Angelo's barbecue had my highest rating, so I would have to agree with them.

Angelo's has a huge building that accommodates huge crowds. It looks like a gigantic saloon. Stuffed animals dot the place—buffalo, deer, reindeer, antelope, caribou, longhorns, ad infinitum. Dozens of long-stemmed ancient fans spin slowly over a concrete floor. Walls have neon beer signs and other collectibles. A long bar followed the serving counter.

Service was prompt, and the line moved quickly. I held my tray of samples and searched the sea of tables and red Naugahyde booths for a clear spot. I found one and began my tests on the fabled barbecue of Angelo's. I secretly hoped that Angelo's barbecue would not disappoint as some other highly touted places had. I received good news at the start: a 3/8-inch pink ribbon. No rotisserie. It showed very little fat, if any. In the shear test, the brisket fell apart with a little push from my fork. The aroma beckoned me. I took a bite. The flavor sang "Ela!" It had a delectable seasoning that complimented the hickory smoke flavor. I bestowed a 10 upon it.

Eagerly, I picked up the pork rib. It showed little fat, and two quick bites produced good results. It had excellent tenderness and superior flavor. I gave it a 9. The sausage brought me back down to earth. It exuded four drops of fat from the squeeze test, and the two-alarm black pepper smashed any barbecue flavor. I rated it a 6.5.

The barbecue sauce had an abundance of vinegar and was slightly on the sweet side (like all barbecue sauces in this neck of the woods).

I selected two sides. The creamy coleslaw had a touch of black pepper and a dash of vinegar. The potato salad came from a traditional recipe.

Angelo's offers some melt-in-your-mouth fried pies.

Angelo George started this business in 1958. His son, Skeet George, took over in 1997. They have two brick pits, one with three shelves and the other with four. They load them with brisket and smoke them eight to fourteen hours. Angelo's uses only hickory wood and their own secret seasoning.

I asked Skeet if anything unusual happened here. "During the Southwest Exposition Livestock Show a woman walked in with a longhorn. She stopped for a while and talked to everybody and then led the bull out the back door." "Did the bull wreck the place?"

"Didn't leave a scratch."

Maybe he should keep a shovel handy—just in case.

Colter's Bar-B-Q

See Dallas for more information (page 215).

Rating: 8

4750 S. Hulen, Fort Worth, Texas 76132

Phone 817-346-3330

Fax 817-346-2840

Cafeteria style, take-out, caters and delivers, banquet facilities, drive thru. Some locations have beer. Brisket plate $7.25.

Open 11 A.M. to 9:30 P.M. Sunday through Thursday, 11 A.M. to 10 P.M. Friday through Saturday. Accepts credit cards.

Cousin's Pit Barbecue

Five couples own Cousin's. To get ten people to agree on anything is difficult at best. Acting like good cousins, they settled on the name "Cousins."

Their restaurant does its best to look like a barbecue place in the middle of a modern shopping center. Beneath the center's sidewalk overhang, Cousin's placed raw wood picnic tables and cedar limb park benches.

Inside is a different matter. Red-and-white checkered tablecloths, lazy ceiling fans, longhorn horns, neon beer signs, raw wood paneling, and a picture of John Wayne bring you back to barbecue.

I went through the cafeteria line, picked up barbecue samples, and took a seat. I stared at a quarter-inch pink ribbon. *Another rotisserie pit.* It had a little fat. Proceeding with the shear test, I parted the meat with slight pressure from my fork. *Must not be a rotisserie. This is too tender.* A smoky zephyr passed my nose. *Great aroma.* My bite revealed big-time flavor. I rated it an 8.5. A pork rib had a rub and a sop. It showed some fat and had excellent tenderness and superior flavor. The added spices seemed a bit too strong. I gave it an 8.

If I ran the show, I think I would kill the sop and keep the rub.

The sausage yielded three drops of fat from the

Rating: 8.5

6262 McCart Avenue, south of Loop 820 South, Fort Worth, Texas 76133

Phone 817-346-2511

Fax 817-263-5414

Cafeteria style, take-out, catering. Serves beer. Brisket plate $5.95 to $7.50.

Open 11 A.M. to 9 P.M. Closed Sunday. Accepts credit cards.

squeeze test. The flavor had two-alarm heat. I tagged it with a 7. A piece of chicken showed no signs of barbecue smoke. It was on the dry side but had good seasoning on the skin. I gave it a 5. The salt in the ham overwhelmed the smoke taste. It had above average tenderness and flavor. I gave it a 7. A slice of turkey had a little fat, superior tenderness, and above average flavor. I labeled it with an 8.

Cousin's sells their barbecue sauce so no secrets exist about ingredients. The list: puree tomato, vinegar, corn sweetener, water, molasses, liquid smoke, salt, pepper, paprika, mustard, garlic, citric acid, egg yolk, and spices.

Sides: "Booties Cowboy Beans," recipe contributed by Boots (one of the owners); carrots, raisins, and pineapple; dirty rice; corn on the cob; and stuffed baked potato with chopped barbecue.

Desserts: Grandma Beverly's (not an owner, just a grandma) homemade cakes, cookies, and apple and peach cobbler.

Like half of all Texas barbecue places, Cousins catered for President George Bush (George must really like barbecue). LeAnn Rimes and Dan Quayle ate here as did three Miss Texas winners—Rhonda Morrison 1991, Carly Jarmon 1995, and Michelle Martinez 1996.

The day I visited, George Oceguera and Gus Narcy were in charge. They showed me Cousin's three Oyler rotisserie pits.

"How do you turn out such good barbecue with a rotisserie pit?" I said.

"We use oak wood," said Gus. "We smoke our brisket for twenty hours at 220 degrees."

"That's it?"

"That's it."

I left, thinking of the other rotisserie barbecue places. Most smoked brisket fourteen hours at 250 degrees. Perhaps the lower heat and longer smoking time of Cousin's provides the answer to great rotisserie pit barbecuing.

Railhead Smokehouse B-B-Q

Folks in Fort Worth still call their place "Cowtown." They should. Although Fort Worth lost its cattle trade, it has by far the best barbecue places in Texas, and in Texas barbecue means beef. A visit to Railhead Smokehouse will help convince you.

Rating: 8.5

2900 Montgomery, Fort Worth, Texas 76107
Phone 817-738-9808
Fax 817-732-4059

I ordered my usual sampler at the counter. With tray in hand, I headed for a table. A long bar filled the end of the dining hall, and the bar had more customers than dining tables had barbecue eaters. I took a seat and saw a quarter-inch pink ribbon. *Another rotisserie*. It showed a little fat, and it parted after two slices with my fork. The meat had a rub, and the rub tasted great. The smoke flavor played a minor role. The overall effect stirred my taste buds. I graded it with an 8. That's a high grade for rotisserie smoked meat.

Counter order, take-out, drive thru, outside seating, catering. Full bar. Brisket plate $7.75.

Open 11 A.M. to 9 P.M. Closed Sunday. Accepts checks and credit cards.

A pork chop had superior tenderness, almost no fat, and excellent flavor. That rub worked even better on the rib than the brisket. I gave it a 9. That score is out of sight for a rotisserie pit. The sausage oozed five drops of fat from the squeeze test, and it had above average flavor. I rated it a 5.5.

They put barbecued baloney and salami on my plate, and I thought both were bad selections compared to Railhead's superior brisket and ribs. I graciously gave each of the two processed meats a 5. The salt in a slice of ham overshadowed any smoke flavor. It had above average tenderness and good flavor if you like salty ham. I gave it a 6. A slice of turkey breast had above average tenderness, very little fat, and superb flavor. I rated it an 8.5.

The thick and lumpy barbecue sauce had lots of tomato. The difference refreshed.

Sides: creamy coleslaw with black pepper, cheddar peppers, French fries, beans, potato salad, and cheese boat.

Desserts: candy and pies.

The wrangler in charge told me they had four rotisseries, used oak, and smoked brisket fourteen hours at 250 degrees. *It seems to me I've heard that song before.* "The seasoning sets the Railhead apart from the rest of the crowd."

I could not agree more.

As the man walked away, I read the large print on the back of his shirt, "Life is too short to live in Dallas."

Riscky's Barbeque

It's not risky, it's Riscky's. Polish immigrants Mary and Joe Riscky began a northside Fort Worth grocery in 1927. Their son Pete took over the reins in 1952. When Pete told his parents he wanted to start selling barbecue, they said it would never work. Pete went ahead. When Pete's son Jim became boss, he designed and built four pits. Today, the four pits at

Rating: 8
2314 Azle Avenue, Fort Worth, Texas 76106-6794
Phone 817-624-8662
Web site www.risckys.com

the Azle location supply barbecue to all eight Riscky restaurants.

I studied a slice of Riscky brisket that had a quarter-inch dark red ribbon. *Rotisserie?* It had little fat, and it took two slices of my fork to cut through the meat. The aroma was faint. It had superior flavor. I rated it an 8.

A pork rib had very little fat, a great rub, and hardy flavor. It had above average tenderness, and I gave it an 8. The pork and beef sausage was slightly salty and gave up three drops of fat from the squeeze test. It had above average flavor, and I tagged it with a 6.5. A slice of honey-smoked ham had enough salt to overpower its smoke flavor. It had superior tenderness, almost zero fat, and negated flavor. I labeled the ham with a 7. A slice of turkey was slightly salty and had no visible fat, superior tenderness, and excellent flavor. I gave it a 9.

The barbecue sauce had some sweetness, a little vinegar, tomato, a little Worcestershire sauce, and a thin texture.

I had a choice of fresh-made salad, coleslaw, seasoned red beans, baked potato, French fries, stuffed peppers, fried corn, or onion rings for veggies. I chose coleslaw because it serves as a neutralizer between bites of meat.

For dessert, I had a choice of banana pudding or one of many delicious pies.

The Sundance Square facility looks like a typical contemporary restaurant with a Southwestern touch. The Azle location won atmosphere honors with its old-style grocery store look. It had farm and ranch collectibles and noncollectibles. The manager said customers bring things in, set them on the shelves, and leave them. They do not dare remove them. Stuffed critters overlooked the scene—hippo, moose, deer, antelope, bobcat, javelina. Neon beer signs flashed color. I talked with Danny Donohue, the wrangler in charge of the pits. As a kid he grew up in a house behind the store. He showed me their four homemade rotisserie pits.

The pits smoke 110 briskets at a time. "We use post oak wood, no gas, and smoke briskets twelve to fourteen hours at around 250 degrees."

Danny said all the meat is hand trimmed and rubbed with *Riscky Dust* before smoking.

Many celebrities patronized Riscky's—George Jones, Merle Haggard,

140 East Exchange, in the Historic Stockyards, Fort Worth, Texas 76106
Phone 817-626-7777

300 Main Street, Sundance Square, Fort Worth, Texas 76102-7407
Phone 817-877-3306

Counter order at Azle location, menu order at the others; take-out, catering. Full bar. Brisket plate $10.95.

Opens 11 A.M. Monday through Saturday and 12 noon Sunday. Closes 10 P.M. Sunday through Thursday and 12 midnight Friday and Saturday.

David and Howard Bellamy, Johnny Rodriguez, George Strait, Summer Cassidy, and three Miss Texas winners—Stephanie Samone 1986, Michelle Martinez 1996, and Tatum Hubbard 1998.

You will miss an important part of Texas if you miss Riscky's.

Robinson's Bar-B-Que

Owner J. W. Robinson once had a barbecue place in Kansas City. He knew that Kansas City barbecue differed from Texas barbecue, so he decided to move to Fort Worth and give Texans a treat.

Robinson's looks like a converted carhop hamburger drive-in from the thirties. White paint covers everything. It's clean and neat and seats about a dozen diners. Most customers use the drive thru.

I took my usual samples of barbecue meat to a table and widened my eyes on a slice of brisket with a 1/8-inch pink ribbon. *How could this be?* It possessed very little fat and even less aroma. It parted with one good slice of my fork. The spices from a delicious rub overwhelmed any smoke taste. Because it was so lean and tender, I gave it an 8.

A pork rib had Robinson's Original Seasoning. It had a little too much fat for me but had superior tenderness and excellent flavor from the instant craver-maker seasoning. I rated it an 8. Robinson's served two sausages. The regular had beef and gave up three drops of fat from the squeeze test. The flavor rapped cool, and I gave it a 7.5. A piece of hot link had beef and pork. It surrendered only two drops of fat from the squeeze test, and its flavor jumped with two-alarm heat. I tagged it with an 8. A slice of ham had little fat and superior flavor and tenderness, and I gave it an 8.

Robinson's has no secret ingredients in their barbecue sauce and seasonings. They package and sell them through grocery stores, and the labels list the ingredients. Robinson's Kansas City Barbecue Sauce contains sugar, salt, spices, artificial smoke flavor, lemon juice, and brown sugar. Robinson's

Rating: 8

1028 East Berry, west of I-35W South, Fort Worth, Texas 76110

Phone 817-924-1009

Fax 817-926-0309

Counter order, take-out, drive thru, catering. No beer. Brisket plate $5.39.

Opens 10 A.M. Closes 9 P.M. Monday through Thursday and 10 P.M. Friday and Saturday. Closed Sunday. Accepts cash.

Kansas City Style Barbecue Seasoning has spices, ground celery, salt, and sugar. Robinson's Hot and Spicy seasoning mirrors the other seasoning product but has incendiary spices.

Dallas Cowboys Larry Brown and Oliver Miller hang around this place.

Maurice, one of the wranglers, showed me his four upright pits. They put hickory wood in at the bottom. The heat and smoke rise up through the racks and out the smokestack. Maurice said, "Because ours is hotter than other pits, we can only smoke brisket eight to ten hours. Folks seem to like it, so we don't plan to change it."

I asked Maurice, "Is there something else you would like for folks to know about this place?"

"Every day," he said, "we get up with the right attitude and hope and pray the good Lord will keep us in business."

The good Lord must like them. He's been keeping them in business since 1985.

Spring Creek Barbeque

See **Richardson** for further information (page 263).

Rating: 8

8628 Hwy. 80 West, Fort Worth, Texas 76116
Phone 817-244-7460

Cafeteria style, take-out, catering. Beer served. Brisket plate $7.35.

Opens 11 A.M. Closes 9 P.M. Sunday through Thursday and 10 P.M. Friday and Saturday. Accepts checks and credit cards.

Frisco

Hutchins Bar-B-Que

When Roy Hutchins wanted to open his barbecue place in Frisco, an old trolley occupied the land he bought. When he started to build, the city fathers told him he could not move the trolley and he would have to build around it.

He did it.

Now when you enter this Old West saloon-style building, the first thing you notice—and you cannot

Rating: 8

8999 Main St., corner of Preston and Main and north of Hwy 121, Frisco, Texas, 75034
Phone 972-335-9944

Web site
www.hutchinsbbq.com
Cafeteria style take-out, catering. No beer. Brisket plate $6.75.
Open 11 A.M. Closes 9 P.M. Closed Sundays. Checks and credit cards accepted.

help but notice—is the smokers' eating area, the interior of the trolley. Its red and white walls and wood plank floor contrast with the Western decor of the rest of Hutchins Bar-B-Que.

My wife accompanied me this visit. She was pleased to receive a plate. "The best barbecue is served on plates," said Bee.

I ordered all-you-can-eat (cost $9.95), which came with all of Hutchins barbecued meats. Bee got sliced brisket. The man behind the counter did not hesitate to pile the 'cue on two plates for me. Bee's order was sliced and weighed. As we went down the cafeteria line, we served ourselves from big pans of side orders. Bee liked the corn on the cob and green beans. I selected the usual barbecue sides of potato salad, pinto beans, and coleslaw. As I paid the cashier, Bee headed for a huge wagon that held the pickles and onions and all the fixings for a baked potato or salad.

We took a table in the back dining room and sat beneath a huge set of longhorn horns.

The ribbon on the brisket measured a quarter of an inch. I put the fork to the brisket. It took a push to cut it. The aroma was good. It tasted mild. I gave the brisket a 7. Upon observation, the pork ribs looked as lean as Twiggy. My bite smacked with flavor and tenderness. I gave the ribs a 9. The server cut the sausage lengthwise and made it difficult for my squeeze test. The Polish style pork sausage lacked filler, gave up two drops of fat from the squeeze test, and had a good but light flavor. I gave it an 8.

The chicken was a little dry, had little fat, and possessed a light touch of flavor. I bestowed a 9 on the chicken. A slice of ham was fairly lean, had mild flavor, and was very tender. The finale came with a bang: sliced turkey. It was the most moist and tender turkey I had sampled, but the flavor was barely discerned. I gave in and gave it a 10.

The sides were traditional. The coleslaw was creamy.

Finished with the meat and veggies, we helped ourselves to peach cobbler and banana pudding. I went back for a second helping of dessert and found some soft ice cream, which I topped with strawberries.

Wesley Hutchins, son of Roy, told me they 'cued the brisket with pecan wood for about fourteen hours and used no rub or sop. "But we do put a Memphis-style dry rub on the ribs."

No wonder the ribs were so good.

Roy started barbecuing years ago with a little place in Princeton, Texas. He moved to Wiley but found that place too small. He set up shop in McKinney in 1978 and in Frisco in 1993.

Garland

Colter's Bar-B-Q

See **Dallas** for more information (page 215).

Rating: 8

2015 E. NW Highway, Garland, Texas 75041

Phone 972-278-2106

Fax 972-840-2073

Cafeteria style, take-out, caters and delivers, banquet facilities, drive thru. Some

locations have beer. Brisket plate $7.25.

Open 11 A.M. to 9:30 P.M. Sunday through Thursday, 11 A.M. to 10 P.M. Friday through Saturday. Accepts credit cards.

Soulman's Bar-B-Que

See **Royse** City for further information (page 265).

Rating: 6.5

3410 Broadway, Garland, Texas 75043-1618

Phone 972-271-6885

Counter order, take-out,

catering. No beer. Brisket plate $7.99.

Open 11 A.M. to 9 P.M. Accepts credit cards.

Granbury

Bodacious Bar-B-Q

The décor is country with slate blue ruffled curtains on the windows and antiques and collectibles on the walls. For more information, see Tyler (page 189).

Rating: 8.5

1470 Hwy. 377 East, Granbury, Texas 76048

Phone 817-573-3921

Cafeteria style, take-out, catering, banquet facilities. No beer. Brisket plate $6.50.

Opens 10:30 A.M. Closes 8:30 P.M. Monday through Wednesday, and 9 P.M. Thursday through Saturday. Open Sunday 10:30 A.M. to 4 P.M. except during summer when it is 10:30 A.M. to 8:30 P.M. Accepts checks and credit cards.

Greenville

Ernie's Barbecue

On May 13, 1985, a tornado put Ernie's out of business twice. The first time was around noon. The tornado struck downtown Greenville, inflicted heavy damage on some buildings, and did enough damage to ruin Ernie's. The tornado blew down lines and cut off electricity. The second time came that evening. Repairmen, thinking everything was okay, turned the town's power back on. It shorted in Ernie's and burned the building to the ground.

Ernie decided he was not going to let it happen a third time. It was time to move. In three months time, the new Ernie's opened at its present location.

I entered Ernie's, and it looked like a school classroom with a lunch counter at the end. Long benches anchored each side, and school armrests marked the spaces for diners to sit and eat. I ordered my usual samples of barbecue. I placed my tray on an armrest and slid into place. The brisket slice had a 5/16-inch pink ribbon and little aroma. *They must use hickory. It gives light aroma and light flavor.* One gentle nudge of my fork parted the meat. *That's*

Rating: 8

8707 Wesley Street, Carroll Square, Greenville, Texas 75402-3823

Phone 903-455-4730

Counter order, take-out, catering. No beer. Brisket plate $6.70 per pound.

Opens 10:30 A.M. Closes 5:30 P.M. Monday through Friday and 4 P.M. Saturday. Accepts checks and credit cards.

237

really tender. I saw almost zero fat. The flavor mumbled. *Doesn't all hickory flavor mumble?* I gave it an 8.

Ernie's did not serve ribs so I moved on to the Eckridge beef and pork sausage. It yielded one drop of fat from the squeeze test. *Amazing*. The seasoning was light, and the flavor did the mumble-mumble. I gave it a 7.5. Ham had average flavor, great tenderness, and some fat. I gave it a 7.

I detected some one-alarm cayenne fire in the barbecue sauce.

The pinto beans had chili powder, the potato salad had a little mustard added to the salad dressing, and the coleslaw was creamy and slightly sweet.

Fried pies with various fillings comprised the dessert list.

I dubbed the décor East Texas Western. My explanation: it tried to be Western but looked East Texan.

The late Ernie Carroll started the business in 1948. Harold Smith began to work for Ernie while going to high school. His job was to pick up drink bottles and clean the place. Ernie liked him so much, he sold him a one-fourth interest. Harold retired in 1996, and Ernie's wife Gladys bought his interest and now owns the business outright. Frank Routh, the brother-in-law of Gladys, manages the day-to-day affairs of the business, and Shannon, daughter of Gladys, pitches in when they have a big catering job.

Frank Routh said, "The most interesting thing that happened here was when a Russian delegation visited us."

I hope he did not give away any secret recipes.

Hallettsville

Novosad Market

All barbecuers and fiddlers head for Hallettsville the third weekend in April for the State Fiddling Championships. If you are fiddlin' around in Texas that time of the year, you can get yourself some great barbecue. If not, head on to Hallettsville and get yourself some great barbecue at Novosad's Market. The place is just off the square, a stone's throw from the county courthouse. I found it easily because pickup trucks were parked all around it. I sauntered in and got in a long line. When I finally got to the counter, because of the line, I ordered a small piece of each meat. The lady said, "We just ran out of sausage, but more is on the way."

Rating: 8

105 LaGrange St.,
Hallettsville, Texas 77964
Phone 512-798-2770

Counter order, take-out, catering. No beer. Brisket plate $5.49.

The lady served the meat on butcher paper. I sat down at a table and began my tests. Observing the meat, I did not like all the fat I saw. The pink ribbon was about an eighth of an inch. *Not very good.* I sniffed it. *Very little aroma.* I chewed a bite. It was quite tender. And the flavor was nice, but it didn't sing. I gave the brisket a 7.

Opens 8 A.M. Closes 3 P.M. Tuesday, Wednesday, and Saturday; 5 P.M. Thursday; 6 P.M. Friday. Closed Sunday and Monday. Checks accepted.

The pork rib sang. It had very little fat. I took a big bite and was delighted to find great flavor. As I ate I wondered what kind of rub they used to make this so delicious. I gave the pork rib a 9. Also on my plate was a lamb chop. It was loaded with fat and had a hard crust. I bravely took a bite and found the meat very tender beneath the crust. It had good flavor except for the crust, which had too much salt. I gave the lamb chop a 6.

Waiting for the sausage, I looked around the room. The ceiling, the walls, and the floor moaned gray. The only color came from red checkered table-cloths. People don't come here for glitter; they come for barbecue.

About that time the lady arrived with a link of sausage. She said, "Here you are, Mr. Troxell."

My gosh, how did she know my name? They must have an underground. These people know my every move.

I thanked her and cut off a two-inch piece of sausage. I examined it and saw no fillers. I squeezed it, and a great puddle of fat spilled onto my dish. I took a bite. It had great seasoning. The sausage had a little kick in it. I gave it a 7.

They served the usual side orders, and I will not go through the whole list, but I would like to comment on the pinto beans. They were made with chili powder, garlic powder, red pepper, salt, black pepper, and bits of Novosad's smoked bacon. Very delicious. Two slices of bakery fresh home-made white bread accompanied my order. That bread tasted so good I could have made a meal out of it alone.

I asked about dessert. The lady said, "If you want something sweet, you go next door to the bakery."

Later I talked with Laura and Nathan Novosad, the owners. Nathan said his grandfather started the place back in 1959. Everything he learned, he learned from his grandfather.

I asked him how he did his brisket. He said they use oak wood and smoke it five to ten hours. *That accounted for the small pink ribbon, the mild flavor, and the fat.*

I departed, thinking I needed to get back soon and eat more of those ribs.

Haslet

Lee's Bar-B-Q & Market

Haslet is a little town northwest of Fort Worth and west of Interstate 35W and the American Airlines maintenance facility. You cannot miss seeing the bright white airplane facility. It's huge and can house the largest jet aircraft. Take exit number 66 off I-35W. Turn west. You'll be on Westport. In a few miles you will find Haslet. Immediately before the railroad tracks you will spot Lee's on the left on School House Road.

Rating: 9

103 School House Road at Westport, Haslet, Texas 76052

Phone 817-439-5337

Counter order, take-out, catering. No beer. Brisket plate $6.65.

Open 11 A.M. to 8 P.M. Closed Sunday. Accepts checks.

When I pulled into the parking lot, six people stood at the door. I sashayed up to them, and they informed me that they were in line. After a twenty-minute wait and listening to past experiences of how long they had waited to get into Lee's, I made my way through the queue for the 'cue at the counter. I ordered my usual plate of barbecue meats and took a seat in a very humble, utilitarian, little town, roadside café. The only color came from red-and-white checkered tablecloths.

A slice of brisket had a beautiful half-inch pink ribbon. *Must be my lucky day.* The aroma enticed me. It appeared to have a little fat and fell apart when my fork touched it. My bite melted in my mouth. I rated it a 9. *No wonder that real estate lady said I should check out Lee's in Haslet.*

I picked up a good-looking pork rib. It had almost zero fat, which is amazing for a pork rib. I hurriedly took a bite. It had excellent tenderness and flavor. Another 9. That's two 9s. Will I get three of a kind? Smoky Denmark out of Austin supplied the hot link beef and pork sausage. It oozed three drops of fat from the squeeze test. The flavor was above average, and I gave it a 7. The regular pork and beef sausage came from Rudolph's in Dallas. It also yielded three drops of fat from the squeeze test but had better flavor. I gave it a 7.5.

Then I looked at a beautiful piece of chicken. I took a bite and found it moist and with a good smoky flavor. It had excellent tenderness and an infinitesimal amount of fat. I tagged it with a 9. *Bingo. I got my three of a kind.* The payoff was great barbecue. The trip to tiny Haslet was worth it.

With a plate order, you get to select two vegetables. I selected a very creamy coleslaw that had a dash of black pepper, and pork and beans that tasted a lot like Campbell's but had big chunks of lean pork. I ordered a separate dish of boiled cabbage, an unusual side for a barbecue place. For dessert, I had one choice, peach cobbler.

After the lunch mob left, I talked with Clarence Lee, the owner. I asked Clarence how he got into the barbecue business. He said, "My ex-wife, who is an attorney, and a lady friend of hers decided to go into the barbecue business. They found this place. And before it opened, my wife divorced me and the other lady friend walked out on the deal. And there I was—in the barbecue business." He shook his head. "I had no experience. I figured I would just have to work harder than everybody else."

I asked him about his delicious barbecue. "I had to learn by trial and error. The pit that came with this place is an Oyler that has very high heat." He opened a pit door, and I could see that the grates set well above the flaming logs. "It took a while," said Lee, "but I finally figured out how to smoke some good barbecue." He used hickory wood. He said he started the fire and put on the brisket around six in the morning, and took off the meat between six and nine o'clock at night. "I found out that large briskets worked best with this pit because of the higher heat."

I asked him how he knew when to take the brisket off. "Do you stick a fork in?"

"No. You stick a fork in, you let the juices out. I have some tongs, and I just pick it up, shake it around a little bit, and I know when it's ready."

I guess he does. He serves some very good barbecue.

Clarence acquired the business in 1987.

Hurst

Colter's Bar-B-Q

See Dallas for more information (page 215).

Rating: 8

North East Mall Food Court, Hurst, Texas 76053
Phone 817-589-9964
Fax 817-284-5890

8600 Airport Freeway, Hurst, Texas 76053
Phone 817-589-0306
Fax 817-284-5124

Cafeteria style, take-out, caters and delivers, banquet facilities, drive thru. Some locations have beer. Brisket plate $7.25.

Open 11 A.M. to 9:30 P.M. Sunday through Thursday, 11 A.M. to 10 P.M. Friday through Saturday. Accepts credit cards.

Irving

Colter's Bar-B-Q

See Dallas for more information (page 215).

Rating: 8

2605 West Airport Freeway, Irving, Texas 75062
Phone 972-258-2422
Fax 972-255-2848

Cafeteria style, take-out, caters and delivers, banquet facilities, drive thru. Some locations have beer. Brisket plate $7.25.

Open 11 A.M. to 9:30 P.M. Sunday through Thursday, 11 A.M. to 10 P.M. Friday through Saturday. Accepts credit cards.

Sonny Bryan's Smokehouse

See Dallas for more information (page 222).

Rating: 7.5

4030 North MacArthur Boulevard, Irving, Texas 75038
Phone 972-650-9564

Serves beer. Brisket plate $6.89.

Opens 11:00 A.M. Closes 9:00 P.M. Monday through Saturday and 8:00 P.M. Sunday.

Spring Creek Barbeque

See Richardson for further information (page 263).

Rating: 8

3514 West Airport Freeway, Irving, Texas 75062-5922
Phone 972-313-0987

Cafeteria style, take-out, catering. Beer served. Brisket plate $7.35.

Opens 11 A.M. Closes 9 P.M. Sunday through Thursday and 10 P.M. Friday and Saturday. Accepts checks and credit cards.

Lewisville

Spring Creek Barbeque

See Richardson for further information (page 263).

Rating: 8

571 East Round Grove Road, Lewisville, Texas 75057-8310
Phone 972-315-2755

Cafeteria style, take-out, catering. Beer served. Brisket plate $7.35.

Opens 11 A.M. Closes 9 P.M. Sunday through Thursday and 10 P.M. Friday and Saturday. Accepts checks and credit cards.

La Grange

Prause's Market

Arnold Prause began the Prause Meat Market around 1890 in Fayetteville, Texas. Steve Prause, Arnold's grandson, said the barbecuing started about then because it was a way to sell brisket and other meat that might spoil. Seeking greener pastures, Arnold moved the business to the east side of the square in La Grange in 1902. In the thirties Prause's became the first meat market in La Grange to have a refrigerated counter.

They moved to the present site in 1952.

Today, Arnold's great-grandchildren run the

Rating: 8.5

253 West Travis, on the south side of the square, La Grange, Texas 78945
Phone 409-968-3259

Counter order, take-out. No beer. Brisket plate $6.00 per pound.

business—Gary, Tommy, Mark, Brian, and Kathy. Grandsons Glen Jr., Steve (called "Moxie"), and James are semiretired and help when needed.

If you want to know something about barbecue, ask Steve, a walking barbecue encyclopedia. He said the pit they have now came with the building when they bought it. "It's a brick pit underlined with steel. There's a firebox on one end and a smokestack on the other. The fire's hottest near the firebox, and that's where we smoke brisket. We smoke sausage on the cooler end." He added, "That's real barbecue. We use wood and no coals."

> Opens 7 A.M. Monday through Friday and 5:30 A.M. Saturday. Closes 1 P.M. Thursday and Saturday and all other days 5:30 P.M. Closed Sunday. Accepts checks.

"Why don't you use coals?" I asked.

"Coals don't produce smoke. When people use coals, the fat from the meat drops on the coals and burns. That's what creates smoke—burning fat. Now, it tastes real good coming off the fire, but several hours later you'll be belching." He pointed out how the fat from his pit falls down on the metal underlining and pours out into a bucket. "Doctors will tell you that burnt tallow is not good for you."

I remembered my grandfather, who was a doctor back in the thirties, saying, "They ought to throw out every iron skillet in America."

I remember how women kept a can of lard by their stoves to use in their iron skillets, and I remember that stomach cancer was the number one cancer disease then. Crisco came in and the can of lard went away—and so did a lot of stomach cancer.

I tried out Prause's barbecued brisket. It had a 5/16-inch pink ribbon and showed very little fat. It parted with one hard slice of my fork. The aroma teased. It had *schmecken die lippe* (my German) flavor. I rated it an 8.5.

Unfortunately, the very time I visited, they were out of ribs and everything else except sausage. That's not so bad when you consider that Prause makes its own sausage. The sausage served was half pork and half beef (they make many different types of sausage). It yielded three drops of fat from the squeeze test. The flavor contained some light but good seasoning. I gave it an 8.

I detected brown sugar, maybe a little pickle juice, black pepper, and ketchup in the barbecue sauce.

They served three potato salads—mayonnaise, mustard, and a sour cream. The latter tasted like a stuffed baked potato. Their beans smacked like Campbell's pork and beans with barbecue sauce thrown in. The coleslaw had a traditional recipe.

Gary Prause told me that they smoked brisket six to eleven hours.

The man responsible for the great barbecue is Mr. Barbecue, Monroe Schubert, cook extraordinaire. A statewide publication featured Monroe's talents in a recent article.

The Market seats one hundred, and Prause sells thirty hunks of meat on a given Saturday.

Lindsay

Dieter Bros. Restaurant

Dave Melton, one of those *daring young men in their flying machines,* tried to eat barbecue at Dieter Bros. Restaurant. Attempting to fly around the world in a balloon, he bounced off the tarmac at Dieter Bros. and landed in a field nearby. John Dieter, restaurant co-owner with his brother Pat, said, "Cop cars, emergency vehicles, newsmen, and rubber-necks roared through here in hot pursuit."

The restaurant did a lot of business that day, January 9, 1998.

The place did well the day my grandson and namesake Richard and I ate there. We arrived a little after one—the lunch crowd had left—and found an empty table. While I waited for my order, I surveyed the restaurant. The place said "little town country." It was neat and clean. I asked Richard what he thought of the place. "Snazzy, Pop."

One end had a bar with an overhead TV broadcasting ESPN. We discussed the possibility of taking in a Rangers game the following night. The waitress brought our orders. Richard had a chopped barbecue beef sandwich, and I had a little of everything.

My piece of brisket had a quarter-inch pink ribbon. *Another rotisserie.* I pointed out the quarter-inch pink ribbon on my brisket to Richard. "Ninety-nine times out of a hundred, when it has a ribbon that size, it means they have a rotisserie pit."

Richard bit into his sandwich, and I tried the shear test on the brisket slice. It separated with the second slice of my fork. No aroma blossomed. It

Rating: 7

Hwy. 82, west of Gainesville and Interstate 35, Lindsay, Texas 76250

Phone 940-665-5253

Menu order, take-out, catering. Serves beer. Brisket plate $5.25 to $6.25. $2.95 senior citizen.

Opens 10:30 A.M. Closes 10 P.M. Monday through Thursday and 11 P.M. Friday and Saturday. Accepts checks and credit cards.

showed little fat. My bite produced superior flavor. *Hmm. That's better than most rotisserie-smoked meat.* I rated it a 7. A pork rib had some fat but was tender and evinced superior taste. I gave it a 7. The pork sausage oozed a puddle of fat but had above average flavor. I tagged it with a 5.5. Dieter smokes and then grills ham. My slice had superior tenderness, a little too much fat for me, and above average flavor. I gave it an 8.

I asked Richard how he liked his sandwich. "It's cool, Pop. I like the barbecue sauce."

I sampled the sauce. It had sugar or brown sugar, bits of onion, ketchup, vinegar, a little Worcestershire sauce, and some cayenne that rang the fire alarm bell one clang.

Richard had beans and corn for sides. I chose coleslaw and potato salad. I almost ordered homemade curly French fries, but a man who eats at six restaurants a day must show some restraint.

Dieter has apple or cherry cheese strudel, a number of pies, a brownie sundae, ice cream, and a root beer float for dessert.

Later John Dieter showed us his pit, a J&R rotisserie from Mesquite, Texas. *I knew it.* I elbowed Richard. He looked at me and understood. Every now and then it is a good thing for granddads to be right about something.

John said they smoked briskets fourteen to sixteen hours at 200 to 225 degrees and used only oak. He said their rub recipe came from an uncle who bought it from a black man back in the 1960s. *So that's why the flavor scored better than other rotisseries.*

Congressman Dick Armie ate here. He did not like the sales tax.

Lockhart

Black's BBQ

A **sign** reads, "Black's BBQ. Est. 1932. Texas' oldest and best major restaurant continuously owned by the same family."

Wrong? Prause's in La Grange wins the family longevity battle. But Black's did throw in the word "best." According to the courts, everybody has the right to call their whatever the best. I think Black's BBQ was thinking about Kreuz Market down the street when they had the sign painted.

My suggestion is that Black's should drop *Texas'* and insert *Lockhart's*.

Rating: 8

215 North Main, Lockhart, Texas 78644

Phone 512-398-2712

Cafeteria style, take-out, catering. Beer served. Brisket plate $7.99 per pound.

Open 10 A.M. to 8 P.M., "8 days a week." Accepts checks and credit cards.

246

I entered Black's after the big lunch crowd. I zipped right through the line, picked up my usual samples, and took a seat. Only a couple of other tables had occupants, and they stared at a sports game on the TV.

My slice of brisket had a 5/16-inch pink ribbon. *Good sign.* It took slices with my fork to separate the meat. No fat appeared. The aroma was faint, and my bite disclosed superior flavor. I rated it an 8. A pork rib had good appearance, showed little fat, and had superior tenderness and flavor. I graded it with an 8. The sausage oozed four drops of fat, and the seasoning and meat provided superior flavor. I gave it a 7.

The barbecue sauce had the basics with a mysterious something extra. Was it pickle juice?

Sides: coleslaw, creamy potato salad, and pinto beans. Dessert: peach and cherry cobbler, apple pie, pecan pie, and banana pudding.

The décor said Western. I looked at raw wood paneling, a great collection of longhorn horns, some nice mounted deer head trophies, and pictures of Lockhart High School football teams going back to 1909.

Owner Edgar Black Jr. was out, and I talked with Nat Castillo, an employee, about their brisket. He showed me their two long and open brick pits. After staring at so many rotisserie pits, these looked beautiful to me. Nat said they used post oak and smoked briskets eighteen to twenty-four hours. They did it in two steps. They put in sticks and brisket and fired up the day before. Early the next morning, they added more sticks. It was a manual operation. No gas. No electricity. No gauges. No thermometer. Barbecuing that satisfies the soul and not the machine.

He said the only rub they used was salt and pepper.

Chisholm Trail BBQ

They say three's a crowd. First came Kreuz, then Black's, and in 1978 Chisholm Trail BBQ. Get this, Rick Schmidt, who owns Kreuz, will soon be in a new building, and his sister will have the old market. *And then there were four*—in Caldwell County, a population of 31,000.

Arriving in Lockhart, I drove past Schmidt's mammoth new building, which was under construction, Kreuz Market, which had a line of patrons standing outside its door, and Black's, that had cars everywhere.

The place was full. I went through the line and

Rating: 7

1323 South Colorado Street, Lockhart, Texas 78644

Phone 512-398-6027

Cafeteria style, drive thru, take-out, catering. Serves beer. Brisket plate $4.25.

Opens 8 A.M. Closes 8 P.M. Sunday through Thursday and 9 P.M. Friday and Saturday. Accepts credit cards.

ordered my usual line-up of barbecue samples.

I looked at a piece of brisket with a familiar quarter-inch pink ribbon. I sniffed it. Aroma from the brisket was almost nonexistent. It took two slices with my fork to part the meat. My bite divulged above average flavor. I graded it with an 8. A pork rib had a hard crust but was tender on the inside. It showed more fat than I like but had superior flavor. I gave it a 7. The home-made sausage oozed a puddle of fat, and its flavor sparkled. I gave it a 6.5. A piece of chicken had little fat, very good tenderness and flavor, and I rated it a 7.5.

The barbecue sauce had a sweet, tangy flavor.

Chisholm Trail served carrots and raisins and green salad and numerous other vegetables in the cafeteria service line.

I went back in line and selected banana pudding. I turned down apple pie (a tough decision).

Floyd Wilhelm, owner, talked to me about his place. He uses a rotisserie smoker. "We also have two wood-burning brick pits. We still use the brick pits for most of our barbecuing," Floyd said. "We barbecue brisket for twelve to fourteen hours at 250 degrees." *The smoking numbers were too fast and too hot. Those were rotisserie numbers.*

The restaurant takes it name from the famous cattle trail that locals say originated near Lockhart. Some say the famous trail began further south because the Mesquite trail comes from South Texas. The fact is that Mr. Chisholm had a trail that went from Oklahoma Indian Territory to Abilene, Kansas. The trails from Texas connected with it, and cowpokes began to use the name for the entire trail.

The Civil War created impetus for the trail. After the war, Texas was broke. They tapped their best resource, cattle, to bring prosperity back. Cattle marked their trail by eating mesquite pods, digesting them, and then leaving them behind in cow patties. Mesquite pods will not grow by falling from the tree to the ground. They require digestion. New Mesquite trees grew further north along the trail. Today, from an airplane, one can see the cattle trails by following the mesquite trails. One thing for sure, Lockhart has its share of mesquite trees.

Trivia: On May 26, 1999, representative Rick Green introduced and the legislature passed a resolution to make Lockhart the Barbecue Capital of Texas.

Kreuz Market

Step back in time when you walk into Kreuz Market. Old man Kreuz said barbecue started here—in 1900 to be exact. You enter from the back and face a blazing fire of oak in a shallow pit—right at your feet. If the line of customers is long and is not moving, you might barbecue a little. The line takes you to a man who opens the huge iron lid of the pit. The pit belches mind-locking aroma and smoke.

If that does not get your attention, the menu will. They offer no sauce, no beans, no potato salad, and no banana pudding.

The cook serves the meat on butcher paper. After you receive your meat, you go to another cafeteria line and buy onions, pickles, cheese, and drinks.

After I recovered from the shock of finding no side dishes, I discovered that they do serve Blue Bell ice cream—not a bad way to finish off a great meal.

With my butcher paper full of smoked meat, Bee and I sat in a room with a very high ceiling and five very long tables with plastic chairs. I observed that Kreuz has no barbecue sauce but has bottles of Louisiana hot sauce on the tables. *Odd.*

My wife cringed when she saw the eye-ease green walls, which were unkempt and blemished with stains from yesteryears' smoke. The walls had dents, scratches, and gunk. Amazingly, some Texans think that makes the place even better.

If you don't like this room, there is another through an aged door. This room is more ancient looking than the main dining room. All wood. Continuous tables line the walls, and eaters sit on benches. I was disappointed to find that management had removed the fabled butcher knives from the chains hanging from the tables.

This time my brisket test had to be different, because I had no fork. I had to use my fingers. *No*

Rating: 8

208 South Commerce in downtown Lockhart, Texas 78644

Phone512-398-2361

Counter order, take-out. Beer served. Brisket plate $6.90 a pound.

Opens 7 A.M. Closes 6 P.M. Monday through Friday and 6:30 P.M. Saturday. Closed Sunday. Checks accepted.

utensils anywhere. I found the brisket tender, had little fat, and was full of flavor. I gave it an 8. *And they only "smoke" it for six hours!* The day I visited, they had barbecued beef shoulder, and when I touched it, it fell apart. I gave it a 9. The sausage was homemade (75% beef and 25% pork), and I rated it a 7. It gave up four drops of fat from the squeeze test and tasted pretty mild. I had a huge pork chop that was very dry, and I gave it a 5.

Kreuz started 'cuing before sauce and side orders came on the scene. Kreuz brings the "what is barbecue?" debate into focus. Kreuz doesn't put anything on its meats and lets the hot smoke do the 'cueing. Many argue that's smoking, not barbecuing, that barbecue must be made with a rub or sop.

Rick Schmidt owns the place now, and he says the menu is the same as it was the day the business began in double ought (1900). Rick said, "And if it ain't broke, don't fix it." What do you think? Guess you will have to go to Kreuz Market to find out.

Luling

City Market

When you approach Luling, you notice the water tower painted to look like a watermelon. This is the home of the Luling Watermelon Thump Festival, which occurs every year during the last weekend in June. They have the "Thump" then because Luling happens to be the place where soil and the climate cause watermelons to ripen right before the Fourth of July. You should be here to see the sparks fly as Luling farmers ship melons to all points in America for the Fourth.

Normally, the line waiting for barbecue at City Market has forty to fifty people, but during Thump weekend, the line can be a block and a half long. The last time I stood in a line that long was when I waited to see *Gone with the Wind* in 1939 at Loews Theater in Houston.

I arrived around one thirty, and the line was down to forty people. When I got to the counter, I ordered my usual sampler. They put the meat on butcher paper and that on top of a tray, charged $4.01, and

Rating: 7

633 East Davis Street, Luling, Texas 78648 (near the railroad tracks and Hwy. 80) Phone 830-875-3972 or 830-875-9019

Cafeteria style, take-out, catering, banquet facilities. Beer served. Brisket plate $6.50 per pound.

Open 7 A.M. to 6 P.M. Monday through Saturday. Checks accepted.

sent me on my way. I sat at one of dozens of tables. I observed the brisket. Ah ha! A 5/16-inch pink ribbon. I remembered when I stood in line that City Market had large brick barbecue pits using oak wood. That accounted for the 5/16-inch ribbon. I sniffed it. The aroma mumbled. That surprised me. I pushed the fork edge against the meat, and it took a good shove to separate the brisket. I ate a bite. The flavor was mild. The brisket had quite a bit of fat so I rated it a 7.

The pork ribs had a hard crust and some fat. I thought they probably cooked them too fast, and upon further examination, I noticed that they had been sopped. *The sop and high heat caused the hard crust.* I thought the ribs had above average tenderness and flavor. I gave them a 7. The sausage was homemade. It had above average flavor, but when I squeezed it too much fat came out. I gave the sausage a 7. My tests ended because they only barbecue those three meats at City Market.

I looked at the dozens of folks eating—the diners who jam this place love barbecue that is consistently above average, enjoy the atmosphere, and like to eat where everybody else does. *They sure ain't lonesome cowboys.*

The décor was contemporary country. Light stained 105 pine siding, collectibles, and lots of tables caught my eye.

A man sat down across from me and said, "I see you're writing."

"Yes. I'm writing a book on the best barbecue places in Texas."

"Oh? Sounds great."

"I wonder why so many people come here to eat this barbecue? I think the barbecue is above average, but I don't think it's the best barbecue in Texas."

"They think it is, and that's all that matters."

I think the man hit the nail right on the head. After all, all barbecue is good. Right?

I interviewed the manager, and he said they smoked the brisket six to eight hours. *That accounts for the mild flavor.* He said they sopped the brisket. *The sop accounted for the wide ribbon and, combined with the fast cooking time, accounted for the hard crust.* I asked him why they had so many customers. He said they gave good service (they do), and if I thought what I saw here today was good business, I should come back during Watermelon Thump time. He said they normally serve from 2,000 to 3,000 people a week, but they serve three to four times that during "Thump."

The Ellis family started City Market in 1954. Now grandson Buddy Ellis has the reins. Sons Lanny and Randy assist him.

Good people. Good food. Good service. You need to try some City Market barbecue.

Mesquite

Colter's Bar-B-Q

See **Dallas** for more information (page 215).

Rating: 8

1715 Town East Boulevard, Mesquite, Texas 75150
Phone 972-270-2091
Fax 972-424-0696
Fax 972-686-6254

Cafeteria style, take-out, caters and delivers, banquet facilities, drive thru. Some locations have beer. Brisket plate $7.25.

Open 11 A.M. to 9:30 P.M. Sunday through Thursday, 11 A.M. to 10 P.M. Friday through Saturday. Accepts credit cards.

Spring Creek Barbeque

See **Richardson** for further information (page 263).

Rating: 8

3939 West Emporium, Mesquite, Texas 75150-6513
Phone 972-682-3770

Cafeteria style, take-out, catering. Beer served. Brisket plate $7.35.

Opens 11 A.M. Closes 9 P.M. Sunday through Thursday and 10 P.M. Friday and Saturday. Accepts checks and credit cards.

McKinney

Hutchins Bar-B-Que

For **more** information, see Frisco, Texas (page 234).

Rating: 8

Corner of Hwy. 380 and Tennessee, McKinney, Texas 75069
Phone 972-548-2629
Web site
www.hutchinsbbq.com

Menu order, take-out, catering, banquet facilities. No beer. Brisket plate $6.75.

Open 11 A.M. to 9 P.M. Closed Sundays. Accepts checks and credit cards.

Sonny Bryan's Smokehouse

See Dallas for more information (page 222).

Rating: 7.5

318 North Central Expressway,
McKinney, Texas 75070
Phone 972-562-5484

No beer. Brisket plate $6.89.

Opens 11:00 A.M. Closes 9:00
P.M. Monday through Saturday
and 8:00 P.M. Sunday.

Murchison

Piggy's

Piggy's is a run-down shack on the side of the road. Bee, my wife, was with me on this trip and would not go in. How could I blame her? She grew up in finer surroundings.

Several people in other parts of Texas recommended this place. A home-built, smoke-puffing barrel pit resided in the front yard. *Surely, it must be good.* Fearlessly, I went in and discovered that it's not what's on the outside that counts—sometimes. This time I found a vast improvement on the inside. It was clean and neat. It had a woman's touch. Of great interest was the collection of knickknack pigs. Pigs decorated the place everywhere you looked.

The barbecue looked good too. My piece of brisket had a 5/16-inch pink ribbon. *Nothing like old-fashioned pit barbecue.* It took two hard-pressed slices of the fork to separate the meat. I saw almost no fat. The aroma beckoned. I took a bite. The flavor squealed "Sooo-eeee." I rated it an 8.

A pork rib had too much fat, but it had tenderness and excellent flavor. I gave it an 8. A chunk of barbecued Boston butt had super tenderness, little fat, but lacked the flavor of the rib. I labeled it with an 8. Eckridge suppled the pork and beef sausage. It oozed four drops of fat but had above average flavor. I gave it a 6.5. A hot link came from Bryan. It gave up

Rating: 8

Hwy. 31 East at FM 1803
South, one and a half miles
east of downtown Murchison,
Texas 75778
Phone 903-469-4006

Menu order, take-out, catering. No beer. Brisket plate
$4.95.

Opens 11 A.M. Closes 7 P.M.
Tuesday and Wednesday and
8 P.M. Thursday through Saturday. Closed Sunday.
Accepts checks.

four drops of fat but possessed superior flavor. I tagged it with a 7.

A slice of chicken breast was not very moist. It had above average flavor and little fat. I gave it an 8. A slice of ham stole the show. It burst with flavor, was very tender, and had little fat. I gave it a 9.

The barbecue sauce had good body and some Tabasco heat. It had the basic ingredients plus some sweetener, probably sugar.

This is another family business. James W. "Jim" Dozier, wife Loretta, and daughter Janie make the place hum. Loretta does the veggies and desserts. Her coleslaw was creamy and sweet. The pinto beans had ham and sausage for flavoring. The potato salad had bits of bacon.

Loretta's desserts sparkled. On the day I visited, she presented lemon meringue, banana cream meringue, caramel meringue, chocolate meringue, and pecan pies. She also made some peach cobbler. The only store bought item was Blue Bell ice cream.

George W. Bush ate here, but my wife, ensconced in the car, wasn't budging. My wife, Bee, finally came in and was very pleased with Piggy's.

By the way, Murchison got its name from the famous Murchison family. John D. Murchison's daughter Ginger is said to own half of Athens, Texas.

Navasota

Ruthie's Pit Bar-B-Q

Rating: 8

905 West Washington Avenue, Hwy. 105 West, Navasota, Texas 77868
Phone 409-825-2700

Counter order, take-out, catering. No beer. Brisket plate $4.20.

Opens 11 A.M. Closes 8 P.M. Wednesday and Thursday, 9 P.M. Friday and 10 P.M. Saturday. Closed Sunday through Tuesday.

In 1822 one of Austin's three hundred original settlers, Francis Holland, called this piece of land Hollandale. Ten years later David Arnold renamed it Cross Roads. Twenty years after that James Nolan built a log cabin stage stop near here and named it Nolanville. Four years later the post office dubbed it Navasota, after the river that flows through it. Six decades later, James and Ruthie called this same piece of land Ruthie's Pit Bar-B-Q.

A great improvement.

I arrived in the middle of the afternoon. Ruthie's looked like a roadside café from the thirties. Inside, the walls had knotty pine paneling. Slow ceiling fans stirred the aroma of barbecue.

A man stood behind the counter. "Can I help you?"

I ordered one small slice of brisket.

"One?"

"One."

He put two slices of brisket on my plate and handed it to me.

I concluded that it is almost impossible for some servers to put one of anything on a plate. I was not going to quibble. "How much?"

"Nothing. You with that magazine?"

"No."

"What do you want to drink?"

"Water."

"You sure?"

"Yes."

"Water's over there."

I took a seat and looked at a piece of brisket with a 1/8-inch pink ribbon. *Good thing I only ordered brisket. I can eat this and leave.* I did not see any fat. *Encouraging.* In the shear test, it parted with a slight nudge from my fork. *Very encouraging.* The aroma was good. *Even more encouraging.* My bite had superior flavor. I rated it an 8.

How in the world could a piece of brisket with an eighth-inch pink ribbon be so good? I bounded from my chair and ordered every meat the server had left. "How much?"

"Nothing."

He was on to me. I went back to my table and picked up a good-looking pork rib. It had excellent tenderness, little fat, and superior flavor. I gave it an 8. A piece of Boston butt pork was very tender and had little fat. The flavor mumbled. I tagged it with an 8. Southside Market in Elgin supplied the sausage. It seeped four drops of fat from the squeeze test and had above average flavor. I labeled it with a 6.

The barbecue sauce had the standard ingredients of vinegar, ketchup, Worcestershire sauce, plus some onion. It had a good tangy taste.

Ruthie's offers sweet and creamy potato salad that has chunks of boiled potato, and red beans with some chili powder.

The server came to my table and introduced himself, Louis Charles Henley, manager and son of owners James and Ruthie Henley.

I confessed the true purpose of my visit and asked him if they had any dessert. "My sister, Pam Thompson, makes pound cake sometimes. I'm sorry, but we don't have any today." He smiled. "How did you like our barbecue?"

"Great. You can read about it in my book."

I asked him to explain to me how his brisket had such good flavor and only an eighth-inch pink ribbon. I explained to him my findings. He had no answer for that. He said they barbecue with a brick pit. "We smoke brisket eight to ten hours. We use seasoned oak. Sometimes we throw in some pecan or mesquite. As for flavor, we have a homemade seasoning we put on everything. It has no *Accent* or other meat tenderizer."

I asked him if any celebrities ate here. "We've had Bum Phillips, Oiler Doug Smith, and writer Leon Hale. Another man you may have heard of, Bob Waltrip, the CEO of the big chain of funeral homes. Mr. Waltrip has a place up here. His land surrounds the prison. Also, horse farms are all around, and we have a lot of famous horse trainers and owners come in."

"How did Ruthie's start?"

"This place used to be the playhouse of attorney Roy Moore from Houston. We had a barbecue place in Anderson and decided we could do better. When this place came available, we moved in."

A sign read, "If we please you, tell others. If not, tell us."

I'm doing my best, Louis.

North Richland Hills

Riscky's Barbeque

See Fort Worth for more information (page 231).

Rating: 8

8100 Grapevine Hwy., North Richland Hills, Texas 76106
Phone 817-581-7696

Counter order, take-out. No beer. Brisket plate $5.93.

Open 10:30 A.M. to 8:00 P.M. Closed Sunday. Accepts checks.

Palestine

Shep's Bar-B-Q & Catering

East Texas has more than piney woods, it has hickory. "It's the best," said Bruce Barrett, local TV advertising star and owner of Shep's Bar-B-Q & Catering. In his TV ads and on a sign on the wall, Bruce proclaims, "You'll never leave hungry." That caused me to remember that hunger was not my problem. I tested barbecue as many as seven times a day.

I got my order and took a seat at one of a dozen tables with red checkered tablecloths. The brisket had that rotisserie quarter-inch pink ribbon. The aroma murmured. It had a little fat. My bite produced average flavor. I gave the brisket a 6.

A marinated pork rib had too much fat, average flavor, and some tenderness. I gave it a 5.5. Hillshire supplied the sausage. The regular sausage gave up two drops of fat from the squeeze test and had above average flavor. I gave it a 6. The hot sausage had one-alarm fire, good seasoning, gave up three drops of fat and received a 5.

Marinated chicken had very little smoke flavor, was tender, and had little fat. I gave it a 6. A slice of turkey had very good flavor, little fat, and superior tenderness. I gave it a 9. The ham tested out the same as the turkey with a 9. The turkey and ham had "bring-you-back" attributes, saved Shep's bacon, and got the restaurant into this book.

Shep's had the usual sides of potato salad, pinto beans, and coleslaw. All had traditional ingredients. In addition, they served French fries, fried okra, and sweet corn.

For dessert, I took my choice of pecan pie, chocolate meringue, and cobblers.

Shep's is another family affair, and that accounts for its good service and cleanliness. It had old-fashioned Naugahyde booths, and farm

Rating: 6

1013 E. Palestine Avenue, U.S. Hwy. 79, Palestine, Texas 75801

Phone 903-729-4206.

Fax 903-729-4206.

Cafeteria style, take-out, catering. No beer. Brisket plate $5.50.

Opens 11 A.M. Closes 7 P.M. Monday through Thursday and 8 P.M. Friday and Saturday. Accepts checks and credit cards.

collectibles adorned the walls.

The business started many years ago. Mr. Shepherd named it after himself and later went out of business. Bruce and the bank stepped in January 1985. From the successful look of this business, it appeared that both knew what they were doing.

Sean Connery, "Bullet Bob" Hayes, Earl Campbell, and Bum Phillips are some of the distinguished visitors to Shep's.

Paris

Hickory House

As I drove into the parking lot of the Hickory House, a man in an apron chased a chicken among the cars. When I neared the front door, he straightened up, smiled, and opened the door for me. "We serve the freshest chicken."

He followed me in and took his place as meat carver behind the serving counter. "Some farmer drove off and left a chicken. I can't catch her." I explained how you have to have a long stick with a drawstring loop on the end. After desultory conversation, I took my order of samples, and since I was the freshest customer, I reposited my frame away from the man with the carving knife.

The brisket slice had the quarter-inch rotisserie-smoked telltale pink ribbon. It had very little fat, mild aroma and flavor, and above average tenderness. I gave it a 7. A marinated pork sparerib had excessive fat, superior flavor, and borderline tenderness. I rated it a 6. Eckridge supplied the pork and beef sausage. It oozed three drops of fat from the squeeze test, and the flavor murmured. I gave it a 6. A thick slice of marinated turkey had a black pepper and garlic rub on it. The flavor was above average. It had almost no fat and was moist and tender. I dubbed it with an 8.

I detected brown sugar, chili powder, vinegar, ketchup, and Worcestershire sauce in the barbecue sauce.

Rating: 6.5

35 Graham Street, just north of downtown, Paris, Texas 75460

Phone 903-784-5432

Cafeteria style, take-out, drive thru, catering. No beer. Brisket plate $5.75.

Open 10:30 A.M. to 8 P.M. Monday through Saturday. Accepts checks.

Potato salad and pinto beans had traditional ingredients. The creamy coleslaw was a little sugary. Corn on the cob appeared fresh. The diner had a choice of home-style or made-from-frozen French fried potatoes.

Small homemade pies of apple, apricot, chocolate, and peach made up the dessert offerings.

I called the décor somewhere between El Paso and Santa Fe. Indian blankets and artifacts plus Old West art prints decorated white walls.

I talked with the meat carver, constantly smiling manager Chris Lewis (boss Jeff Fowler worked at another job during the day). He said they had two Oyler rotisserie smokers, and they smoked brisket fourteen to eighteen hours at 180 degrees. "Maybe. The thermostat's been broken for five years." He said Hickory House started thirty years ago. His boss bought it in 1997. He excused himself to take care of a lady at the counter.

After greetings, he asked her what she wanted, and she did not know. "Anything, I guess." He announced to all, "That's a good woman. She likes barbecue and doesn't care what kind it is."

He came back to my table and talked some more about the live chicken out front. Then he said, "We bought the Grand Champion steer at the Junior Livestock Show and changed the marquee to read, 'We sell only the freshest beef.'"

Mike's Bar-B-Que

Rating: 8

1910 South Church Street,
Paris, Texas 75460
Phone 903-785-1134

Outside counter order, take-out. No beer. Brisket plate $7.75 per pound.

Open 10 A.M. to 6 P.M. Monday through Saturday. Cash only.

It was April in Paris, and I wanted to dine at a sidewalk café on the Champs-Elysees. I settled for a picnic table on South Church Street across from the cemetery. This was not Paris, France, but the weather was nice, and it was the right Paris for good barbecue.

Mike's Bar-B-Que had a kitchen with an outside order window. A long metal barbecue pit with a firebox at one end and a smokestack at the other end sat beneath a shed in back. I walked up to the window, and Mike took my order. He passed me samples through a sliding screen pass-through. The brisket had a 5/16-inch pink ribbon, a refreshing sight in this part of Texas where so many rotisseries exist. The aroma from the brisket stirred my senses. It had very little fat. The fork parted it with one firm slice. The bite had blue ribbon flavor, and I gave it an 8.

Mike did not serve pork ribs. He served ham instead. The ham had superior flavor and some fat and was very tender. I gave it an 8. A Longhorn hot link oozed a Red River of fat when I squeezed it. It had four-alarm red pepper in it. Flavor was above average, and I gave it a 6.

Mike said he smoked the brisket twelve hours at 280 degrees and used no rub or sop. The barbecue sauce was standard. He served potato salad and pinto beans with bacon and onion. No dessert.

Mike comes from Hope, Arkansas, and never knew Bill Clinton. *Who does?* He said a black man taught him how to barbecue.

If you want to eat at his place, Mike has one outdoor picnic bench, but Mike's is mostly for take-outs.

I found the best barbecue in Northeast Texas at Mike's.

Rocking W Bar-B-Q

"The last time I saw Paris" I stopped at a huge log cabin restaurant on the right bank of the Red River. I parked beneath a spreading oak tree and promenaded along a quaint long wooden front porch to the door. Entering, I made my way in a cafeteria line and said. "Je voudrais du barbecue, madam. S'il vous plait."

"Wha-a-at?" she replied.

I was back in Texas. I ordered my usual sampler of barbecue.

The brisket slice had that common quarter-inch pink ribbon that hinted, "Another rotisserie smoker." *C'est la vie*. The slice showed zero fat. *C'est bon*. It took two hard slices of my fork to part it. *C'est mauvais*. The aroma and flavor mumbled. I gave it a 7.

Rating: 7.5

3820 Lamar Avenue, Paris, Texas 75462

Phone 903-784-2239

Fax 903-737-2946

Cafeteria style, take-out, catering. No beer. Brisket plate $6.50.

Open 11 A.M. to 8 P.M. Monday through Saturday. Accepts credit cards.

A pork rib had too much fat, was very tender, and possessed excellent flavor. I gave it a 7. Rudolph's of Dallas supplied the regular and hot link sausage. One drop fell from the squeeze tests from each sausage. *Incredulite*. The regular sausage had superior flavor, and the hot link fired three-alarm heat that drowned out other seasonings. I gave both an 8. The turkey had superior flavor, tenderness, and a little fat. It was moist, and I rated it an 8. The ham was very tender, had superior flavor and some fat. I gave it an 8.5.

Sides were in abundance. I chose from creamy and sweet coleslaw, mustard and salad dressing based potato salad, fried okra, corn on the cob, red style beans with brown sugar and a nip of vinegar, and baked potato stuffed with all the regular fixings plus your choice of barbecue.

For dessert I had a choice of peach cobbler or blackberry cobbler. "Tomorrow, we may have apple or cherry," said the lady behind the counter. "Help yourself to some soft ice cream from the machine."

As I savored my cobbler, I observed the décor. I thought of it as country mishmash. Raw wood paneling displayed country collectibles, replicas of old signs, and advertisements. Fans spun beneath a corrugated metal ceiling. Booths contained long wooden tables with red checkered tablecloths. Wooden benches had padded Naugahyde backs.

Ed and Alice Atkins own the Rocking W. Alice showed me some framed certificates on the wall that cited the Rocking W for having the Best Boss, Best Cook (Dee Lloyd), Best Caterer, Best Ribs, Best Friendly Service in all of Paris.

"No matter how they change her, I'll remember her that way."

Plano

Colter's Bar-B-Q

See **Dallas** for more information (page 215).

Rating: 8

921 N. Central Expressway, Plano, Texas 75075

Phone 972-424-0696

Fax 972-424-6776

Cafeteria style, take-out, caters and delivers, banquet facilities, drive thru. Some locations have beer. Brisket plate $7.25.

Open 11 A.M. to 9:30 P.M. Sunday through Thursday, 11 A.M. to 10 P.M. Friday through Saturday. Accepts credit cards.

Dickey's Barbecue

See Dallas for more information (page 216).

Rating: 6.5

1211 14th Street, Plano, Texas 75074
Phone 972-423-9960

1441 Coit Road, Plano, Texas 75075
Phone 972-867-2901

Catering, phone 213-691-1495

Fax 214-691-1496
Cafeteria style, take-out, catering. No beer. Brisket plate $7.29.
Open 11 A.M. to 8 P.M. Accepts credit cards.

Reno

Tommy's Bar-B-Que

Rating: 7

6819 Lamar Road, U.S. Hwy 82 East of Paris, Texas 75462
Phone 903-785-2808

Counter order, take-out, drive thru, catering. No beer. Brisket plate $5 all you can eat.

Open 9 A.M. to 6 P.M. Tuesday through Saturday. Accepts checks.

Tommy was in the meat business in Oklahoma City for thirty-one years. He tired of that. His brother talked him into going into the furniture business in Reno, Texas. He did not like to dicker, so in 1989 he made a tasteful choice. He went into a business he liked. He opened Tommy's Bar-B-Que in Reno, just east of Paris, Texas. His love for barbecue and his sunny disposition made the right mix for a successful business.

The place had a genuine screen door with a

cowbell. Inside, the walls and ceiling had lightly stained particle board. Farm collectibles filled walls and shelves. Of interest were framed archival newspaper clippings and photographs. One photograph showed downtown Paris, Texas, before the "Great Fire" in 1916. Another pictured the same setting after the fire.

Tommy Scroggins had a limited menu the day I visited. A slice of brisket had a small pink ribbon and good aroma. It took two tough slices with my fork to cut the meat. The brisket had too much fat, and I gave it a 7. A pork rib had too much fat, was a little of the tough side, but had excellent flavor. I gave it a 7. Pork sausage hailed from Farmland out of Kansas. It had a salty but interesting flavor and oozed two drops of fat from the squeeze test. I gave it a 7.

Tommy's served baked beans and potato salad for side orders.

His better half, Lila, made the peach cobbler. One had a choice of ice cream on the cobbler or not. A lady in the neighborhood by the name of Ann Mann supplied apricot, apple, peach, and chocolate fried pies. They went for a dollar apiece, and they went fast.

He wound up his repartee by saying country western stars Johnny Paycheck, Gene Walson, and Reba McIntyre visited here. I noticed a plaque on the wall about the Scroggins Band. I asked him about it. "Yes, that was my band. I like music so much I built a bandstand next door, and about once a month I sponsor a country western or gospel band music night."

And that's the gospel truth.

Richardson

Spring Creek Barbeque

Big cities attract big barbecue restaurants. As a city grows so do the better barbecue places. Pure logic. The barbecue place that makes money has an abundance of customers, because their barbecue is better than the other guy's.

Sure you find the maverick owner who does quite well with one place. Chances are he will only have one place the day he dies. The owner may be high minded. He probably owns a brick pit and knows that if he expands, he will not be able to do all the barbecuing. He will not trust employees to mess up a good brisket and will never lower his standards. So he is content.

Rating: 8

270 North Central Expressway, Richardson, Texas 75080

Phone 972-669-0505

Cafeteria style, take-out, catering. Beer served. Brisket plate $7.35.

Barbecue chains buy automatic smokers, hoping that their employees will not be able to mess up the meat. Spring Creek uses Southern Pride rotisserie smokers. Rotisseries turn out above average barbecue. Rotisserie smokers—the way they make them today—will never produce outstanding brisket barbecue. Rotisserie smoked brisket is always on the tough side, very lean, and short on flavor. It will always be above average and will make it into this barbecue book.

Opens 11 A.M. Closes 9 P.M. Sunday through Thursday and 10 P.M. Friday and Saturday. Accepts checks and credit cards.

Spring Creek does a better job with their rotisseries than most. The brisket they served me parted with one hard slice of my fork. As with other rotisserie smoked brisket, it had almost zero fat. The aroma was light, and I found the brisket to have superior flavor. I rated it an 8. A pork rib contained a little too much fat but had fall-off-the-bone tenderness and superior flavor. I gave it an 8. Pork Polish sausage oozed three drops of fat from the squeeze test and had a light but pleasant seasoned flavor. I tagged it with a 7. Barbecued turkey and ham stole the show. I rated each a 9. Both were tender, packed with flavor, and showed little fat.

The barbecue sauce held no secrets. Spring Creek sells it and lists the ingredients on the label.

The potato salad tasted normal. The pinto beans had some chili powder, ketchup, and a sweetener, probably sugar, and the slaw had a creamy base.

A bakery department employee constantly offered melt-in-your-mouth homemade bread. I suspected some diners ate nothing but the bread.

Dessert: cobbler with Blue Bell ice cream.

Although Spring Creek Barbeque restaurants are large and modern, this one had a country touch. Tiffany styled lamps quietly glowed and ceiling fans slowly stirred.

Chris Carroll owns Spring Creek. He said they smoked brisket ten to twelve hours.

"How do you get it so tender?" I asked.

"We buy choice brisket from Monfort Beef out of Colorado."

Hmmm.

Royse City

Soulman's Bar-B-Que

When **I** went inside Soulman's Bar-B-Que, a big sign greeted me. It read, "We're not stingy with our meat." I found myself in a cafeteria line, and I could see other trays with plates piled deep with meat. And I wanted one bite portions of each meat. The server could not believe I wanted so little, but he gave in and granted me my request. The brisket had a familiar quarter-inch pink ribbon. *Another rotisserie smoker.* No aroma attracted me. The meat parted with a gentle shove from my fork, and a bite left me with a flat impression. It had some fat, and I gave it a 6.

Rating: 6.5

Exit 77B on I-30 east of Royse City, Texas 78189

Phone 972-636-0000

Catering phone 972-326-1745

Cafeteria style, take-out, catering. No beer. Brisket plate $7.99.

Open 6 A.M. to 9 P.M. Accepts credit cards.

A pork rib had some fat, a lot of meat, slightly above average flavor, tenderness, and I gave it a 6.5. Regular sausage yielded one drop of fat. *Very lean.* The flavor was above average, and I gave it a 7.5. A hot link yielded two drops of fat, had enough red pepper to ring a two-alarm bell, and was very lean. I gave it an 8. Ham was tender with little fat and superior flavor. I gave it an 8.5.

Side orders listed creamy and slightly sweet coleslaw, barbecue beans with pieces of sausage and chunks of onions, pinto beans, mustard potato salad, and a big seller is a "Double-barrel Baked Potato" stuffed with barbecue. One can select from many other vegetables like French fries, fried okra, corn on the cob, and green beans—just like any other cafeteria.

For dessert, I had to choose between fried pies of various flavors and a slice of chocolate meringue or sweet potato pie.

I called the décor roadhouse antique. The interior had an exposed beamed ceiling. They painted the beams and roof underlining fire engine red. Flat black painted air conditioning ducts zigzagged in geometric patterns beneath the beams. Booths had dark green Naugahyde padded seats. Wood tables had ladder-back chairs. Farm implements decorated the walls. Ceiling fans spun above tulip shaped lamps.

The manager informed me that their smoker was an A-1 Stainless rotisserie. He smoked the brisket fourteen to sixteen hours at 250 to 300 degrees.

When you eat there, be sure to get some Texas toast.

Salado

Lucye's Place

Camera in hand, I asked my wife Bee to pull over and stop so I could take a picture of Lucye's Place. As I exited our car, an older lady came out of her house and announced that we were parked in a no parking zone. Sensing hostility on her part, I said, "The car's motor is running. I'm just going to take a photo and be on my way." Her glare led me to believe that she did not approve of my action. I said, "How about posing for a picture for me?" She did a curtsy, and I feigned a picture and then turned around and took a shot of Lucye's. Returning to my car, I noticed that she appeared to be writing down our license number. We parked at Lucye's, and the lady went back inside.

Not certain that the police would not come after us, Bee and I went inside Lucye's. The place looked cozy country. Corrugated metal walls contrasted with wide plank pine floors. We took a table, and I ordered my usual sampler of small portions of barbecue. The brisket had a 3/8-inch pink ribbon. *No rotisserie*. The aroma teased me. I gave a gentle shove with my fork, and the brisket fell apart. *Fantastic*. It appeared to have almost no fat. I took a bite. The flavor sang, "Beautiful, beautiful Texas." I gave it a 9.

A slice of sirloin tri-tip also had great flavor and little fat, but it almost failed the fork test. I gave it an 8. A pork rib had great appearance, some fat,

Rating: 8.75

301 Thomas Arnold Street, Interstate 35, Exit 284, one block west of the freeway, Salado, Texas 76571

Phone 254-947-4663

Menu order, take-out, catering, banquet facilities (seat 100). No beer. Brisket plate $7.40.

Open 11 A.M. to 9 P.M. Accepts credit cards.

excellent flavor, and superior tenderness. I gave it a 9. A piece of pork loin possessed superior flavor, little fat, and superior tenderness. I rated it a 9. An undisclosed sausage maker in Belton supplied the sausage according to Lucye's recipe. It had excellent flavor and produced two drops of fat from the squeeze test. I gave it an 8. A slice of turkey had mind-gobbling flavor, was very tender and fairly moist. I gave it a 9.

I detected onions, cayenne or paprika, a little vinegar, ketchup, and Worcestershire sauce in Lucye's barbecue sauce.

The serving counter presented a number of side offerings: barbecue beans, potato salad made with new potatoes and their skins, buttered new potatoes, coleslaw, corn on the cob, fried okra, and stuffed baked potato with customer's choice of barbecue piled on top.

Lucye was the mother of Sonny Berry. Sonny married Deanna, and they own and run Lucye's. Part of his mother's old house became part of the restaurant.

Sonny surprised me when he showed me his one-year-old Southern Pride rotisserie pit. I told him my rotisserie findings. We concluded that Southern Pride makes a better rotisserie now. He said they smoked brisket about thirteen hours. But before that, they massaged the meat, stabbed it with a set of small sharp knives, and rubbed their secret spices into it.

Back in the restaurant, I read a sign, "Life is uncertain. Eat dessert first." I wished I had seen it earlier. Deanna made the desserts, and the one I chose did not disappoint. I selected a fudge brownie sundae. Other desserts were cream cheese crepes, homemade pies, and peach cobbler.

Smithville

Zimmerhanzel's Bar-B-Que

Get here before noon or you might miss some of the finest barbecued pork ribs in this neck of the woods. Folks jam this place early, and when they sell out of their last piece of barbecue, they close it down. That might be before 4 o'clock.

I got my sampler of meats and sat down amidst a bunch of fun-loving Smithvillers. The brisket earned an 8—fork cutable, an inch of deep pink, good flavor. The cook rubbed it with salt, pepper, red pepper, and garlic.

Then my taste buds received an awakening:

Rating: 7

307 Royston (Highway 71 N, Business Route), Smithville, Texas 78957

Phone 512-237-4244

Menu order, take-out, catering. Brisket plate $4.34.

delicious pork ribs. They were tender, full of flavor but had a little too much fat. Everybody wolfed them down. To make sure I didn't get into an argument, I hid my rating pronouncement with a piece of paper. I gave the ribs an 8. The sausage tasted good, but oozed a little too much fat from the squeeze test. I gave it a 7.

> Opens 8:30 A.M. for sausage, other meats ready by 9:30 A.M. Closes 5 P.M. weekdays and 4 P.M. Saturday. Closed Sunday. Checks accepted.

The coleslaw was sweet and fresh, and the mustard-based potato salad was fresh. The pinto beans were good.

If for some hunger crazing reason you are driving through Smithville, you will not miss Zimmerhanzel's Bar-B-Que. Take the business route of Texas Highway 71. The bright orange metal building with white trim, next to Brookshire Bros., will catch your eye.

Smithvillers descend from steel driving men of the Katy railroad. After you eat, you can visit the Jim Long Railroad Park and Museum at First and Main and reminisce about the good old days when Smithville was a Division Point for MKT and when a roundhouse serviced steam locomotives.

The Zimmerhanzel wrangler starts cooking very early in the morning; the doors open at 8:30 for sausage, and you have to wait until 9:30 for brisket, ribs, and chicken. These old railroad men have driving appetites and the ribs usually sell out in two hours!

You don't have to worry about remembering this place, who could forget "Zimmerhanzel"?

Sulphur Springs

Bodacious BBQ

See Tyler for more information. (page 189)

Rating: 8.5

1316 South Broadway, Sulphur Springs, Texas 75482
Phone 903-885-6456
Galen and Daria Adams, owners.

Counter order, take-out, drive thru. No beer. Brisket plate $7.50.
Open 10:00 A.M. to 9:00 P.M. Closed Sunday. Accepts credit cards.

Temple

Clem Mikeska's Bar-B-Q

Rating: 7.5

1217 South 57th Street, Exit 300, Temple, Texas 76504 Phone 254-778-5481 or toll free 1-800-344-4699

Cafeteria style, drive thru, take-out, catering, banquet facilities. Serves beer. Brisket plate $5.50.

Open 9 A.M. to 9 P.M. daily. Accepts checks and credit cards.

The only thing that prevents Clem Mikeska from putting up more stuffed hunting trophies is space. His brother Maurice of Mikeska's in El Campo has more room. His brother Jerry of Mikeska's in Columbus has more trophies. At one time, seven Mikeska brothers had seven barbecue restaurants in Texas. A nephew has one in Taylor, making only four now.

I went through the cafeteria line and ordered my usual sampler of barbecue meats, took a seat, and dug in. I stared at a piece of meat that did not look like brisket. I asked an employee what it was, and he said it was sirloin tri-tip. *My lucky day*. I pressed my fork against it, and it took two hard slices to part the meat. *A disappointment*. The aroma was faint. It had very little fat, and the flavor was good. I gave it a 7.

A pork sparerib had a dry seasoning rub, good appearance, some fat, was tender, and I gave it an 8. Clem made the sausage in back. He had what one employee called a consistent formula. "The weather may change, the season may change, but Clem Mikeska sausage always stays the same." The sausage possessed 90% pork and 10% beef and yielded but one drop of fat from the squeeze test. The flavor said soooo-eeeee. I gave it an 8. A slice of turkey was a little dry, had superior flavor and tenderness, and I gave it an 8.

I tried to figure out the barbecue sauce, but it remained a deep, dark secret. It had a light brown color, which indicated it had very little ketchup in it—unless he used yellow tomatoes. I detected some lemon and Worcestershire sauce. I kept making guesses, and Clem kept smiling and shaking his head.

I tagged the décor "chuck wagon." The walls said "hunting lodge." A bare wall was hard to find. Stuffed animal heads hung everywhere. Only his brother Jerry had more trophies per square inch. The big trophies were elk and an African Watusi steer, which had unusual, large upright horns.

Clem Mikeska's potato salad and pinto beans were from traditional recipes, and the coleslaw was slightly sweet. Other sides were a pea salad and hot buttered potatoes, which had small chunks of fresh potato. Tasted great.

Clem invented talk. I stayed two hours listening. He showed me his entire operation. He owned three barbecue pits. Two had red brick construction with merry-go-round grills. He designed and built them himself. All the grease fell down into a conical funnel at the bottom and then flowed into an awaiting pan. The fire came up from below and the grease catcher dispersed the smoke. The motion of the grills also stirred the smoke. The exhaust orifice was about three inches above the bottom of the conical grease catcher, so the smoke had to go back down over all the meat to get out the smokestack. Very clever. Then came the shocker. He smoked the sirloin tri-tip three hours at 275 to 300 degrees. That accounted for the fat and the toughness of the meat.

Clem's is a family operation. His wife Anna Jo and offspring Angela, Anna, and Stephen pitch in. A future helper is Garrett Joseph Conlon, Clem's grandson.

Clem, a charmer, said, "We may not be the best, but if we aren't the best, whoever it is, we have him mighty nervous."

Past presidents Gerald Ford and George Bush ate here as did Senator Phil Gramm, Dr. Red Duke, Tom Landry, and singer Vince Gill.

Tioga

Clark's Outpost

Experts warned Warren Clark not to own a restaurant in a small town. He and his wife Nancy Ann did it anyway. One critic was famed barbecue entrepreneur Sonny Bryan, who later wrote a letter to the Clarks congratulating them for succeeding in a small town and proving him wrong.

"Outpost" is a good word for this place. It's north of Denton and south of Whitesboro, and the amount of drop-in trade they receive is minuscule.

Before I toured a part of the state, I canvassed an area and asked, "Where's the best barbecue place in your neck of the woods?"

I never called anyone in Tioga or Whitesboro. I called Dallas, Fort Worth, Arlington, Denton, Sherman, Denison—the big towns. Clark's received recommendations from them all.

People drive long distances to eat here.

Knowing all this, I had a bad case of the "craves" pulling into Clark's Outpost parking lot. I looked at the street sign. It read, "Gene Autry Drive."

Born in Tioga, Autry grew up and became a cowboy here. After he acquired fame, he tried to get the town to change the name to Gene Autry, Texas, but the town folks wouldn't do it. Miffed, Autry went north and started Gene Autry Springs, Oklahoma.

The Clark's barbecue building came together one section at a time. Outside, it looks like an old saloon. Inside, it looks like a roadhouse out West. The original restaurant is now the reception area. While I waited to be seated, I noticed framed reprints on the walls of newspapers and magazine feature stories about Clark's Outpost, and dozens of photos of friends and celebrities. I recognized pictures of Mickey Mantle, Billy Martin, and Byron Nelson.

Dominating the display is a commemorative oil

Rating: 8.5

101 Hwy. 377 at Gene Autry Drive, Tioga, Texas 76271
Phone 940-437-2414
Fax 940-437-5529

Menu order, take-out. Full bar. Brisket plate $7.15 to $9.60.

Opens 11 A.M. Closes 9 P.M. Monday through Thursday, 9:30 P.M. Friday and Saturday and 8:30 P.M. Sunday. Accepts credit cards.

painting of Warren Clark, founder of Clark's Outpost.

The waitress brought me my usual plate of barbecue samples, and I dug in. The brisket slice had a small and very dark ribbon. *How could this be? Surely, it's not from a rotisserie.* The aroma twitched my nose. The meat fell apart with slight pressure from my fork. Little fat showed. My bite sang "Back in the Saddle Again." I rated it a 9.

A pork rib had a nice appearance but showed too much fat. It had superior tenderness and very good taste. I gave it a 7. Rudolph's supplied the all pork sausage. It yielded two drops of fat from the squeeze test and had above average flavor. I gave it an 8. The ham was excellent. The smoke overpowered the salt. *Nice switch.* It had zero fat and excellent tenderness. The flavor was better than a Gene Autry song. I gave it a 10. A slice of turkey had good tenderness, little if any fat, but the flavor warbled. I gave it a 7.

The barbecue sauce had brown sugar, a touch of mustard, some liquid smoke, vinegar, a little Worcestershire sauce, and fresh tomato. Fresh tomato made it outstanding.

Clark's provided tasty vegetables—fried potato skins, batter-fried zucchini served with horseradish sauce, smoked barbecue beans, jalapeño black-eyed peas, old-fashioned red beans, fried okra, green salad, creamy coleslaw, baked potato, French fries, and corn on the cob.

I picked homemade bread pudding with warm rum sauce for dessert. I passed on Dutch apple pie, chocolate meringue pie, coconut cream pie, and ice cream.

Widow Nancy Ann Clark, a svelte lady with a million-dollar smile, runs the show. The service is sharp, and the business is growing.

She took me out back and showed me her custom-made metal pits. They had gigantic proportions and looked more like smokehouses than pits. The wrangler in charge said they used green hickory and pecan and smoked the brisket from two days to four days.

"Did you say 'days'?"

"Yes, because of the size of the pit."

"Why are some smoked two days and others four?"

"Hot spots. Some places on the grates barbecue faster than others."

Nancy Ann said, "But the average is fifty-two hours."

Mind-boggling numbers. I explained to them the findings of a pit manufacturer who found that oxygen created the pink ribbon. "You must not open your doors very much."

"That's true, but when we do open the doors and when you consider the size of the pit, not that much oxygen gets in."

Nancy Ann took me back inside and showed me some of her notable keepsakes. She had artist R. L. Duwe do pastel portraits of ranchers up and down Hwy. 377 and hung them on the walls of a second dining room. Then she took me to a cabinet and showed me a brick. "If you read the inscription, you will find that this is the sixth brick from Southfork."

"J. R.'s home in *Dallas*?"

"Yes. When they tore down the original set, they brought this brick to me."

Gene Autry, J. R., and Nancy Ann. Three of a kind.

Waco

Michna's BBQ Inc.

Michna's uses a big gun to get business.

Uncle Tom Motyka liked to build things big out of metal. He built the ten-foot-high revolver barbecue pit that stands in front of Michna's on Franklin Avenue. He also constructed two oversized rotisserie pits behind Michna's.

These pits can produce over a 1,000 pounds of barbecue a day.

The revolver's grip has a firebox. Brisket and wood go into the chamber. The barrel is the smokestack.

The gun was too high for me to measure, so I guessed that it extended ten feet into the air.

I ambled along a zigzag walkway among ornamental plants into a building that looked like a barbecue place.

Immediately, I noticed a large buffet and seized the opportunity to serve myself. I took a seat and looked at another quarter-inch pink ribbon on the... on the... "Hey, Miss. What part of the steer is this?"

"Sirloin tri-tip."

She went about her business and I continued mine. *Sirloin. Great idea.* The pink ribbon looked like another rotisserie job. My mind drifted to thoughts of other quarter-inch pink ribbons. An inviting aroma brought my senses back to the task at

Rating: 7.75

2803 Franklin Avenue, Waco, Texas 76710
Phone 254-752-3650
Fax 254-753-0558

Cafeteria style or buffet, drive thru, take-out, catering, banquet facilities. No beer. Brisket plate $5.25.

Open 9:30 A.M. to 7 P.M. Monday through Wednesday; 9:30 A.M. to 8 P.M. Thursday; 9 A.M. to 9 P.M. Friday and Saturday. Accepts checks and credit cards.

hand. I observed little fat, and it took a hard slice with my fork to part the sirloin. Bull's-eye flavor hit my tongue. I gave it an 8.

A beef rib had less fat than most, missed-the-bull's-eye on flavor and tenderness, and I gave it a 7. A pork rib had a little too much fat but on-target flavor and tenderness. I gave it an 8. A pork loin slice had deep pink, on-target flavor and tenderness, and I rated it an 8. A slice of pork loin also showed deep pink, target-accurate flavor and tenderness, and I gave it an 8. A commercial meat company made the all-beef sausage from Michna's recipe. The squeeze test produced two drops of fat, the flavor was on target, and I gave it an 8.5. *A high mark for sausage from me.*

Chicken was very tender and had deadeye flavor. I gave it a 7. A slice of ham had superior tenderness, zero fat, and calibrated flavor, and I put an 8 on it. A slice of turkey-roll was fantastic. It was extremely tender, had very little fat and center-of-the-bull's-eye flavor, and I gave it a 9.5. A piece of turkey breast was also extremely tender, had fine caliber flavor and almost zero fat, and I gave it a 9.

Side orders included pinto beans with chili powder, coleslaw that was slightly sweet, and salad dressing potato salad and mustard based potato salad that had fresh ingredients and no overcooked spuds. I tried a small sample of beef stew with cooked-just-right vegetables. Also available were green beans, butter beans, macaroni and cheese, garden salad, hot buttered potatoes, and corn on the cob.

Peach, cherry, and apple cobbler, banana pudding, pecan pie, and German chocolate cake made up the dessert list.

I waved to Olympic champion Carl Lewis, but he did not wave back. I guess he didn't see me.

Michna's is a family affair. Bob and Sandra own it, and sons Bobby and Billy, daughter Tammy, and son-in-law Gregg pitch in.

Sandra was most helpful throughout my visit. She took me out back and showed me the two giant rotisseries that her brother-in-law Uncle Tom had fabricated out of iron. They had tremendous ovens and oversized trays.

I asked about her barbecue sauce. She said it had onions, black pepper, cayenne for one-alarm heat, vinegar, and Worcestershire sauce. Talking about the barbecuing, she said, "Because the sirloin tips were smaller than brisket, we smoked them for only fourteen hours." *Mikeska smoked his three hours.* They used a special secret seasoning for a rub.

This family business has been humming since 1989, and I suspect the young Michnas will keep it running throughout the twenty-first century.

Besides Carl Lewis, Michael Johnson, country western star Mark Chestnut, and rock star Ted Nugent ate here.

Uncle Dan's Rib House B-B-Q and Catering

Uncle Dan's on Lake Air Drive stood where a nightclub once rocked. Many of Waco's most prominent citizens consummated their relationships here, according to Uncle Dan's owner, Dan Henderson.

The old building had a makeover with professional landscaping and modern furniture and fixtures.

I looked at my cafeteria tray with a plate full of samples and saw an old friend, a quarter-inch pink ribbon. *Another rotisserie*. The rotisserie smoked brisket, as usual, had above average flavor, left little fat, and kept me chewing for a while. I gave most rotisserie-smoked brisket a 7 and this was no exception—another 7.

A pork rib had some fat, above average flavor, and tenderness. I gave it a 6.5. Eckridge, maybe the best large commercial meat company, supplied the pork and beef sausage. It discharged three drops of fat from the squeeze test and had superior seasoning. I gave it a 7. A slice of turkey was extremely tender, had sparkling flavor and almost no fat. I gave it a 9.5.

The pinto beans were normal. Uncle Dan's served two potato salads—one with mustard and one with salad dressing. They chopped up the potato salad ingredients into fine pieces, but otherwise the recipes were traditional. Chili beans tasted great. The show of the sideshow was a "Texas Style" baked potato with butter, sour cream, cheese, and choice of chopped brisket, ham, or chili with beans.

Every time I see a stuffed baked potato I think of Ernie Coker, who claimed it as his invention back in the 1930s.

Uncle Dan's offered fabulous dessert specials as well as a long list of pies, cobblers, and banana pudding.

The decor looked 1930s with its twenty-seven Naugahyde padded booths. Each table had, instead of a jukebox selector, a miniature barbecue pit that

Rating: 6.75

231 North Hewitt, Waco, Texas 76712-6421
Phone 254-666-3839
Fax 254-666-4497

1010 Lake Air Drive, Waco, Texas 76710-4551
Phone 254-772-3532 or fax 254-776-7206

Cafeteria style, take-out, drive thru, catering, banquet facilities at Lake Air Drive location. Serves beer. Brisket plate $5.15.

Opens 11 A.M. Closes 8:30 P.M. Monday through Thursday and 9 P.M. Friday and Saturday. Accepts checks and credit cards.

held salt, pepper, napkins, and sauces.

I talked shop with Dan. He proudly confessed that he had an Oyler rotisserie. He smoked the brisket twelve to fourteen hours (depending on the size of the brisket) and did not use a rub or sop. His sauce had one-alarm heat from cayenne and lots of ketchup and some Worcestershire sauce.

An invitation to a Fourth of July celebration sent to Dan and his wife from the U.S. Ambassador to Sweden and his wife, Mrs. Lyndon L. Olson Jr., hangs on the entry wall. The embassy staged the event on the third because the fourth fell on a Saturday, and Swedes will not attend anything on a weekend (weekends were meant for goofing off).

I asked him if Dan's had any entertainment. He said that the use of Dan's wit runs rampant during the lunch hour.

Uncle Dan's parting words, "We're the place to go in Waco."

Weatherford

Colter's Bar-B-Q

See Dallas for more information (page 215).

Rating: 8

1921 S. Main, Weatherford, Texas 76086

Phone 817-341-RIBS (7427)

Cafeteria style, take-out, caters and delivers, banquet facilities, drive thru. Some locations have beer. Brisket plate $7.25.

Open 11 A.M. to 9:30 P.M. Sunday through Thursday, 11 A.M. to 10 P.M. Friday through Saturday. Accepts credit cards.

Part Eight

South Texas Plains

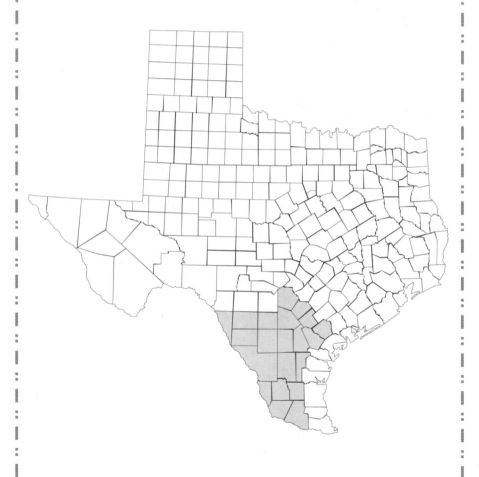

Alice

Crossroads Bar-B-Que

Rating: 7.5

406 North Johnson, U.S. Hwy. 281, Alice, Texas 78332

Phone 512-664-1157

Menu orders, take-out, catering. Serves beer. Brisket plate $6.39.

Open 11 A.M. to 9 P.M. Monday through Saturday. Closed Sunday. Accepts checks and credit cards.

First they called it Bandana, then Kleberg, and finally Alice after the daughter of Richard King of King Ranch fame. The town business went from cattle to melons and fruit to oil. The Beefmaster brand of cattle originated here, fitting for a town also known for good barbecue.

The best way to find good barbecue begins with looking for a railroad crossing sign where no railroad tracks exist on U.S. 281. The lettering on the sign says: Crossroads Bar-B-Q.

I saw it and headed in. The interior looked Tex-Mex, tablecloths red, chairs yellow, and red painted concrete floor. Western collectibles dotted the walls including a big picture of John Wayne. I ordered my usual and began the tests. It took an extra hard push to cut the brisket with my fork. It had little fat and excellent flavor. I gave the brisket a 7.

The pork rib scored well. It had great flavor, little fat, and above average tenderness. I rated it an 8. V & V supplied the sausage. I scrunched two drops of fat from the squeeze test. It had good seasonings. I gave it an 8. The sauce lacked ketchup and possessed garlic, black pepper, Worcestershire sauce, honey, liquid hickory smoke, mustard, and other secret seasonings. I liked it.

Crossroads makes its own dressing for their potato salad. They add a little mustard and pickle relish to not-overcooked potatoes. A winner. The pinto beans have onion, bell pepper, garlic, coarse ground black pepper, and salt. A real treat is the corn bread. The soft, sweet pone melted in my mouth.

They make cobblers here with crumbly crusts, the way I like them best (I never ate a cobbler I didn't like).

Like so many barbecue place owners, Frank Torres started barbecuing as a hobby. He did car bodywork but came down with spinal scoliosis. The doctors said he had to do lighter work. Friends liked his barbecuing and encouraged him to go into the business. So Frank and his charming wife, Sylvia, started selling barbecue.

He showed me his big barrel pit. Mesquite flamed in its firebox. The smoke teased my nose. He said he smoked brisket for thirteen hours, used no rub, and applied a sop. He cooks the meat for nine hours in foil, then smokes it for four hours. *Huh?* "When the fat comes to the top, it's cooked." He smiled confidently. "Less smoking time eliminates heartburn." *Huh?*

According to the "nutritional experts," heartburn comes from grilling. The fat drops on the coals, and the burnt tallow smoke clings to the meat and when digested, causes heartburn.

Beeville

Mr. Q's Bar-B-Q

Irish families settled this area in 1834. It became Beeville in honor of Col. Bernard E. Bee, secretary of war under Texas president Houston and secretary of state under President Mirabeau B. Lamar. For a few years the town switched the name to Marysville after Mary Hefferman, the only survivor of a family wiped out by Indians. But the state made them switch it back to Beeville because the legislature

Rating: 7

911 South Washington,
Beeville, Texas 78102
Phone 512-358-9477
Fax 512-358-7977
E-mail PANTRY@fhbnet.net

had designated that the county seat of Bee County had to be Beeville.

Almost one hundred fifty years later, I arrived to find the best barbecue. Agents of a real estate office agreed that Mr. Q's Bar-B-Q was the best.

I found it. Normally, you don't expect a barbecue

Menu order, take-out. No beer. Brisket plate $4.99. Open 11 A.M. to 4 P.M. (if they don't sell out). Accepts checks and credit cards.

place to be a part of a service station (or is it vice versa?). But, if it's good barbecue, you don't care where it is. Beeville folks have a good reason to be happy about Mr. Q's Bar-B-Q.

People wanting gasoline at lunchtime might want to look elsewhere because this parking lot gets jammed with cars. I had to do some creative parking behind the building. And I was lucky because I was late. The place began clearing out as I walked in. *Hmmm.*

I had to wait while they cleared a table. Seated, I ordered a small slice of brisket with barbecue sauce on the side. "Wouldn't you like something else?" said the waitress. I shook my head. Later, she plopped a plate down in front of me that had a sample of everything. "Here you are, Mr. Troxell. Enjoy. If you need anything else, please let me know." *They have my number. I don't fool anyone!*

I observed the quarter-inch pink ribbon on the edge of the brisket that marks the work of a rotisserie. *Another rating of 7. But then again, I must be fair. I must give an unbiased test.* The meat appeared to be lacking in the fat department. I pressed my fork against the meat. It resisted. I pushed harder, and it severed. I sniffed it. Little aroma. I chewed it up. A little above average in flavor. I gave it a 7.

The pork rib had too much fat, was tender, and had above average flavor. I gave it a 7. At this point, I concluded that they used a rotisserie. I squeezed the sausage, and a few drops seeped out. The flavor was mild. I gave it a 7. The chicken was somewhat moist, had a little fat and above average flavor. I rated it with an 8.

Seven, seven, seven, eight. Above average numbers. I don't blame owners for using rotisseries.

The sauce had a ketchup and Worcestershire sauce blend. It was normal, the way most like it.

Before eating the side orders, I looked around. The décor said country. I saw old barn siding and farm implements and collectibles all around me.

The potato salad had a mustard/mayo base with pickle and pimento. The pinto beans were average. A rice dish with chili powder and cumin had a Tex-Mex zing to it.

280

Floresville

Cow Camp Bar-B-Q

Canary Islanders settled Floresville, the same islanders who helped propagate San Antonio in its early years. Those pioneers found rich, black soil here for farming and ranching and good rainfall. Today, Floresville is an agricultural and ranching hub.

Millions of people visit San Antonio, a few miles northwest of here. But did you know that many San Antonians drive to Floresville just to eat barbecue at Cow Camp Bar-B-Q?

I spotted the ranch-style building ahead with a parking lot full of pickup trucks and sport utility vehicles. I walked into the place behind a rancher with a ten-gallon hat and polished boots.

I had luck on my side. Because I arrived late, I found an empty seat in back.

I cased the joint. It was ranch to the longhorn bone. Walls had old barn planks and corrugated metal. A señorita waited on me. Trying my Spanish, I said, "Me gusto mucho una poquito muestra de todos carne."

"I don't think my boss would allow me to bring all our meat out here. Just what is it that you want?" She froze a placating smile. I told her. She brought the food back. "If you need anything else, please ask." She took a few steps and turned around. "And ask in English, por favor?"

I laughed. Then I sobered and began yet another great test. The brisket had a 3/16-inch pink ribbon. The aroma mumbled. I had to push with my fork to cut the brisket. It was lean. I chewed a bite. *They used a sop.* It was different. I rated it an 8.

The pork ribs stole the show. They had flavor and tenderness beyond belief. Cooked longer with lower heat, they would have less fat. I gave them a 9 anyway. I looked around, more than half the customers

Rating: 8.5

Hwy. 181 (929 Tenth Street), Floresville, Texas 78114

Phone 210-393-3636

Menu order, take-out, catering. No beer. Brisket plate $5.25.

Opens 10 A.M. Closes 8 P.M. Monday, Tuesday, and Thursday and 9 P.M. Friday and Saturday. Closed Sunday and Wednesday. Accepts checks.

were eating ribs. *No wonder they drive from San Antonio.* The sausage had half pork and half beef. The flavor sang, but it oozed too much fat from the squeeze test. I rated the sausage a 7. The chicken was sweet and dry. The flavor chirped. I gave it an 8.

The sweet barbecue sauce had brown sugar, Worcestershire sauce, ketchup, onions, and other seasonings.

The potato salad was creamy. The pinto beans had some chili flavoring. The coleslaw contained lots of fine chopped carrot.

Nestor and Linda Palacios bought the business from a friend. Good old-fashioned hard work paid off. "We like to do things right," Linda said. "Our customers come from everywhere and keep coming back."

I told her I really loved the pork ribs. She said, "We won 'Taste of the Town' with our ribs."

Get there early. The ribs sell out fast.

Karnes City

Market Bar-B-Que & Fresh Meats (formerly Smolik's)

No rating

208 East Calvert, Karnes City, Texas 78118
Phone 830-780-3841

Menu order, counter order, take-out, catering. No beer. Brisket plate $6.25 per pound.

Opens 8 A.M. Closes 1:30 P.M. Monday through Thursday, 3 P.M. Wednesday through Saturday. Accepts checks.

The first Polish immigrants to Texas settled near Karnes City. They discovered rich land for farming and ranching. A century and a half later, Mr. Veladi reaped a whirlwind from selling beefsteak through his Veladi Restaurants, and built "Southwinds," a pristine ranch with a two-story antebellum plantation-style home. In 1998 Mr. Kerns (of nursing home fame) bought Southwinds at an auction for ten million dollars.

While the financiers worried about Southwinds, I headed for Smolik's Bar-B-Que. A geologist told me it was some of the finest barbecue in the state. A city manager said he used to drive from Beaumont to Fort Worth's Angelos for barbecue, but Smolik's was better.

This I had to see. According to my findings, Angelo's rated a 10.

I took Hwy. 181 Business Route to reach downtown Karnes City. Smolik's nestles between the Karnes City Chamber of Commerce and a beer joint.

I entered through genuine, antique screen doors. The whole place looked antique. A meat market counter faced me, but no one tended the meat. Through another door, I saw folks talking, laughing, and eating. I went on back and found the barbecue. A big sign read, "As of Jan. 1, 1999, the official name is Market Bar-B-Que & Fresh Meats." Okay. That's fine, but the sign outside says Smolik's.

I went to the counter and ordered a small piece of everything. Partner Lupe Valdez said, "I'm sorry, but all I have left is sausage."

"My gosh. It's lunchtime," I replied.

"Just had a lot of hungry people through here. It happens."

I took a couple pieces of sausage on butcher paper back to a table.

I looked around. Nothing fancy. Walls and ceiling were painted a light lime color. Seven long tables with long benches. Drinks iced down in an old-fashioned soda pop cooler. The menu was on a small sign. No sides. Meat by the pound. Soft drinks only. *Simple. The old-fashioned way.*

I squeezed the sausage. Not one drop of fat. I saw no filler—just hunks of meat. I tasted it. It had sound barrier breaking flavor. I gave the sausage a 10. I asked Lupe about his sausage. He said he made it; it was all beef and had his secret seasoning. *No wonder it was so good.*

Lupe and his wife, Marie, bought the place from Mr. George Smolik in 1992. George had the place thirty-three years, and his father had it thirty to thirty-five years before that.

"Same building?" I asked.

"Same building."

"It was built in the twenties?"

"That's about it."

Before I left, I told Lupe I would try to get back another time and test his brisket and ribs.

An elderly lady overheard our conversation. "You don't have to. Lupe has the best barbecue in the world."

I ran out of time due to my deadline for copy, so I never returned. The sausage was so good I knew I had to put The Market Bar-B-Que & Fresh Meats in my book, even though I did not test brisket and ribs, the favorites of Texas barbecue eaters.

Laredo

Cotulla Style Pit Bar-B-Q

You don't have to go across the Rio Grande to discover new foods and recipes. All you have to do is dine at Cotulla's. How about eating Barbacoa de Cabeza? For folks north of Austin, that translates into barbecue of head (the head of a cow). You don't eat the whole head. You don't even see the head. You see thin strings of barbecued meat that are appetizing in appearance, tender, and flavorful.

The Sanchez family owns the place. The grandfather started the business in the little town of Cotulla. He had a food store and gave credit to migrant workers. When the workers finished harvests in the north, they would return and pay their bill to Mr. Sanchez. One day, the migrant workers stayed up north, never to return. Grandfather shut down the store and headed for the big town of Laredo. On May 8, 1967, he opened this barbecue restaurant and named it after the town that gave him his start. The day I visited, his grandson Manuel managed the business.

Before meeting Manuel, I, for the first time, did not order everything. The menu shocked me. Would you order Barbacoa de Cachete (cheek)? Lengua (tongue)? Cesos (brains)? Ojos (eyes)?

Eyes! Remember the Indiana Jones movie? Would you order Barbacoa Ojos? No way, Jose. I ordered only the standard BBQ, beef brisket and sausage.

A señorita brought me my order, served on a plate with silverware. *Whatever happened to plastic forks and butcher paper?* I had to nudge the brisket to part it. The lean slice had good flavor and a quarter-inch pink ribbon. I gave it an 8. The Polish sausage came from a supplier. I know they 'cue it, because I saw the sausage in the pit. But for some reason, they also grilled it. The sausage reminded

Rating: 8

4502 McPherson Rd., Laredo, Texas, 78041

I-35 exit U.S. 59, left on McPherson Rd.

Phone 956-724-5747

Menu order, take-out, catering. Serves beer. Brisket plate $5.59.

Opens 6:30 A.M. Closes 5:45 P.M. Monday through Saturday and 2:30 P.M. Sunday. Accepts credit cards.

me of fried bologna. Good, but different. I rated it a 5. If you order a brisket plate, you also get shredded—not chopped—brisket. It has a delicious flavor. I tried a specialty: barbecued fajitas. Fantastic.

The sauce has mostly vinegar and tomato, a good tang and a thick texture.

Cotulla's caters to all tastes. It does so to stay in business. Folks from south of the border and "Winter Texans" do not cotton to Texas barbecue right off. So Mr. Sanchez also serves Mexican food and seafood and wins them over to barbecue.

"Mariaches" outsell everything. They're large homemade tortillas stuffed with whatever you want—brisket, sausage, ojos, etc. On a weekend, Cotulla's sells around 4,000 mariaches.

Standard potato salad and pinto beans head a list of mostly Mexican side orders. The menu itemized domestic beers but no desserts.

After the meal, Manuel showed me his huge brick barbecue pits out back and in another building. They used mesquite and 'cued the meat for twenty-four hours. No rub. No sop.

Cotulla's interior design captured a blend of Texas and Mexico. Stuffed deer heads abounded. Manuel said hundreds of hunters eat here. "They pay up to $3,500 for a weekend to hunt deer in LaSalle County. Then they come here and get some good barbecue for $5.95."

If you have an ojo for good food, try Cotulla's.

South Texas Smokehouse

Rating: 8

7200½ Santa Maria St., Laredo, Texas 78041
From I-35 take Del Mar exit, one block west, look to far right for bright red building with Lone Star Texas flag. Phone 956-712-0227.

Counter order, take-out, catering. Beer served. Brisket plate $5.25.

Open daily from 11 A.M. to 10 P.M. Accepts checks and credit cards.

Other parts of the state declare that Texas served under six flags, French, Spanish, Mexican, Texan,

Confederate, and U.S. However, in Laredo, they added a seventh, the Green Flag of the Republic of the Rio Grande, which, according to historian Jerry Thompson, lasted 283 violent, tumultuous days in 1840. Laredo was its capital. The fledgling republic invaded Mexico and captured Victoria. They were driven back, Texas would not help them, and the government collapsed. In 1841 the Texas Rangers, led by John Coffee "Jack" Hays, took Laredo for the Republic of Texas.

It seemed that everybody wanted Laredo. Can you blame them?

Today, Laredo is one of America's fastest growing cities and home of South Texas Smokehouse.

You cannot miss this place. It looks like Judge Roy Bean's except it has bright red paint. The interior has a contemporary country look. White walls have bright red wood trellises. A large TV entertains.

I stepped up to the counter and ordered one small slice of beef with sauce on the side. I sat down and observed a half-inch pink ribbon on my slice of brisket. I gave it the fork test. The meat parted with one slice of my fork. It had great aroma and a little fat. I chewed it gently. The flavor sang "Deep in the Heart of Texas." I gave it an 8. I went back to the counter and ordered the works.

A tender beef rib had excellent taste and, like the brisket, had little fat. I rated it an 8. The pork rib had a little too much fat, above average tenderness, and light flavor. I rated it a 9. The Polish sausage came from Sam's. South Texas did a good job of smoking it. It oozed three drops of fat from the squeeze test. I gave it a 7. The chicken was tender, moist, and flavorful. I tagged it with a 9.

The barbecue sauce had ketchup, vinegar, brown sugar, liquid smoke, Worcestershire sauce, black pepper, cayenne, mustard, cumin, and Louisiana Hot Sauce.

The sides shined. The potatoes in the potato salad were not overcooked. It had sweet flavor. I was keen on the beans.

South Texas serves a 16-oz baked potato that outsells the other sides. The cook piles chopped brisket, sausage, onions, cheese, mushrooms, and hot butter on the potato. It sells for $3.95.

After the meal, I talked with Tony Gonzales, the owner. Tony worked for twenty years for Schlumberger, an oil field supply manufacturer and service company. He started 'cueing for Schlumberger customers as a way of entertaining them. The demand for his cooking increased, so he started South Texas Smokehouse.

He gave me his secret for good barbecuing. He puts the meat in a brine solution and sets it in a refrigerator for eight to twelve hours. The salt "opens" the meat and makes it more tender. Then he smokes it for eighteen hours.

When I left, I went around back and saw his barrel pit and plenty of mesquite.

Leon Springs

Rudy's "Country Store" and Bar-B-Q

Rating: 8

24152 Interstate 10 West,
Leon Springs, Texas 78257
Phone 210-698-2141
Fax 210-698-0547
Web site www.rudysbbq.com

Cafeteria style, dine in or out, take-out, catering. Serves beer and wine. Brisket plate $7.95 per pound.

Opens 10 A.M. Closes 10 P.M. Sunday through Thursday and 11 P.M. Friday and Saturday. Accepts checks and credit cards.

Just north of San Antonio on 1-10, you will see Rudy's Country Store and a sign that says, "The Worst Bar-B-Q in Texas." Do not believe it. Owners Rick Luders and Doc Holiday have hungry 'cue eaters standing in a long line. Doc does the 'cueing. He uses oak wood in German-style pits and 'cues brisket up to ten hours. Doc rubs the meat with secret stuff and never sops it. Doc is so good at 'cueing that he has 'cued for the Los Angeles Lakers, the San Antonio Spurs, the Dallas Cowboys, and recently for Bill Parcels and the CBS Sports crew.

I entered a rustic building with signs everywhere, walked beside a long tank trough packed with bottled drinks and ice (it's amazing how much more appealing bottled drinks are in ice). I selected a drink from sodas, teas, or beers. I ordered sides from a man behind the counter and then ordered meat from a carver. The cashier carefully weighed the meat and hollered out what I owed. I treated three others and my bill was under fifteen dollars. *Not bad*.

The brisket received a 6 because it had to be cut with a knife. The flavor delighted all. The pink ribbon on the brisket edge measured about a quarter of an inch. My grandson, RKT3, had a chopped brisket sandwich, and he said it was the best he had ever eaten. I tasted it and agreed with him. Pork ribs, a little on the greasy side, received a 7. But the pork loin was fantastic, tender, succulent, and full of flavor. I honored it with a 9.

Rudy's barbecues Opa's sausage from Fredericksburg, Texas. It had a mild flavor but gave up four drops of fat from the squeeze test. I gave it a 7. Then came a real treat: Rudy's turkey. Tender (fork cutable), moist, and flavorful. *Ummm*. I gave it a 9.

The mild barbecue sauce (sause as spelled here) tastes great. It is in such great demand, Rudy's sells it in bottles.

Sides were beans (a good pepper flavor), mustard based potato salad, coleslaw, and creamed corn (excellent). They loaded our food onto red plastic Coca-Cola bottle crates. We ate off paper on red-and-white checkered tablecloths.

Rudy's has another location at Sea World in San Antonio. Two franchises have sprung up, Austin and—would you believe it? Albuquerque, New Mexico.

Enjoy.

Rudy's Sause

Ingredients: water, high fructose corn syrup, tomato paste, vinegar, spice blend (corn solids, sugar, citric acid, modified food starch, salt, garlic, onion, dextrose, vinegar powder, paprika, spice, beef powder, caramel color, oleoresin paprika, and spice extractive); sauce mix (spices, onion, garlic, and silicon dioxide to prevent caking), Worcestershire concentrate (vinegar, water, molasses, corn syrup, salt, caramel color, garlic, spices, anchovies, tamarind, and natural flavors), salt, molasses, lemon juice concentrate, and sodium benzoate (less than 1/10 of 1% as a preservative).

Pearsall

Cowpokes Bar-B-Q

Rating: 7

Interstate 35 North at FM 140, exit #101, Pearsall, Texas 78061

Phone 830-334-8000

Menu order, take-out, phone orders and catering. Brisket plate $5.99.

Open 8:30 A.M. to 8:30 P.M. Sunday through Thursday; 8:30 A.M. to 9:30 P.M. Friday and Saturday. Disc, Amex, Visa, MC, and Diners.

During the 1870s, travelers between Frio and Pleasanton stopped here to fetch water from a sheep ranch well. They called it Waggoner's Well. The water must have been good and plentiful because in 1882 the International-Great Northern Railroad bought 2,000 acres around the well and started the town of Pearsall. Today, the surrounding area has oil production, ranching, farming, and some prime hunting. Every year Pearsall has wild game festivities and a wild game dinner. You'll probably miss the wild dinner, but you won't be disappointed because Cowpokes Bar-B-Q has two large concrete brick pits smoking up good barbecue all year round.

Headed south on I-35, Cowpokes' big red barn-shaped restaurant is hard to miss.

I arrived early—ahead of the crowd. The place seated at least a hundred. A worker said, "Folks pack this place by noon." I took a seat and after looking around, deemed the inside décor to be ranch modern. Everything was clean and neat, and everything was in its place. It was so nice I had a negative thought. *A place this nice couldn't have good barbecue.*

The brisket looked appealing. It had a half-inch pink ribbon. *Pretty good.* It resisted fork cutting, so I had to use a knife. *Tough. I knew it!* I sniffed it. *Not bad.* I chewed it. *Excellent flavor.* What did they do to make it taste so good? I found out later. Cowpokes rubs the brisket with a secret seasoning, and when it's done, they sop it to get the salt and pepper off. *That's a switch.* Moreover—get this—they 'cued it twenty-four to twenty-six hours. The brisket comes from Iowa Beef Packers, blue grade. It cut like a 5 but tasted like a 9. I gave the brisket a 7.

The star of the show was pork ribs. I gave them a 9. Tender. Very little fat. Superb flavor. *Would give Wright's in Vidor a run for the money.* I tasted two sausages. Both hailed from Opa's in Fredericksburg. The jalapeño sausage was three-alarm hot and contained too much fat. I gave it a 6. The regular sausage had a mild flavor and too much fat. *I'm getting awfully fussy in my old age.* I gave it a 6.

Then I dug into what looked like shredded beef. Juicy and a little chewy, I liked it. It was perfect for making a tortilla wrap, an item they have on the menu for $1.75. The moist chicken had tenderness and good flavor. I gave it a 9. The sliced turkey had good flavor and, like most turkey, was a little on the dry side. I gave it an 8.

The barbecue sauce was sweet and vinegary.

The potato salad came from the missus's recipe. The potatoes were firm and superb flavor came from a blend of salt, black pepper, mustard, and relish. The coleslaw was very good—slightly sweet and not too vinegary.

If you miss the wild game dinner, you might also miss George Strait and his mom and dad. They like it here.

I asked Cowpokes owner Sam Hotchkiss why his barbecue had such fine flavor. He said, "We use mesquite. It has good flavor and isn't as hot as oak." He smiled and divulged a barbecue secret: "And I sear 'em real good on one side."

Okay. There you have it. You too can have great barbecue. Just do like the master.

San Antonio

Bill Miller Bar-B-Q

This barbecue chain became a giant because they sell delicious, genuine barbecue at a very reasonable price. No rotisserie. No coals. No gas. No electricity. Twelve all-brick open pits burn green live oak from the Hill Country. Briskets smoke eighteen hours. A half-inch or more of pink ribbon appears on the edge of the meat.

Balous Miller, son of deceased Bill Miller, said, "The *San Antonio Express News* held a 'Blind taste test' and rated Bill Miller Bar-B-Q the best. Our iced tea is famous. Lipton Tea told us that we sell more iced tea than any institution in the United States of America."

I visited a Bill Miller at Anderson Loop 1604 and U.S. Hwy 281. It had all the standard Bill Miller features: light brown glazed tile walls, red quarry tile floor, ceiling fans, and ranch paraphernalia. The interior seemed cold and sterile, as you might find in some government institution. The only color is the serving counter. I went through the cafeteria line and ordered a sampler. After paying the cashier, I helped myself at a condiment bar.

Seated, I began my tests. The brisket yielded to slight pressure from the fork edge. The aroma sang. I gobbled it up. Great flavor. I gave it an 8. The pork ribs were tender and flavorful and had little fat. I gave them an 8. The homemade sausage oozed a couple of drops of fat from the squeeze test. The sausage had a peppery flavor. I gave it an 8. The chicken had good flavor but was a little dry. I gave it a 9. The ham was tender and a little short on flavor. I rated it an 8. The sauce was normal.

Going through the cafeteria line, you can pick from many different side dishes.

The end of the cafeteria line had brownies and pies. I thought the sugar-free lemon pie with cool

Rating: 8

46 locations in San Antonio, three in Austin, and five in Corpus Christi.

Phone 210-225-4461

E-mail

rozhubbard@aol.com

Web site

www.billmillerbbq.com

Menu order, take-out, drive thru. No beer. Brisket plate $3.50.

Open 7 A.M. to 10 P.M. Accepts credit cards.

whip topping was fantastic.

I asked Balous if anything exciting happened here. He said a man died at one of his restaurants. "He was trying to rob us. His son held a gun on everyone while his dad tried to undo the safe. The father got his finger stuck in the safe and couldn't get it out. He died of a heart attack. The son cried out for someone to call an ambulance as he ran out the door."

We talked shop. "Dad started the business in 1952. Today, sons John, Doug, and I along with brother-in-law Louis run the business. We strive to please our customers. We give good service. Our motto is CARE, Customers Are Really Everything. We thank all of them."

The County Line

Rating: 9

10111 I-10 West, San Antonio, Texas 78230
Phone 210-641-1998

Opens 11 A.M. Closes 10 P.M. Sunday through Thursday and 11 P.M. Friday and Saturday.

606 West Afton Oaks Boulevard at FM 1604 (Anderson Loop), San Antonio, Texas 78232-1236
Phone 210-496-0011

Open Monday through Thursday 5:30 P.M. to 9:30 P.M., Friday and Saturday 5 P.M. to 10 P.M., and Sunday 11:30 A.M. to 2:30 P.M. and 5 P.M. to 10 P.M.

Riverwalk, 111 West Crockett Street #104, San Antonio, Texas 78205-2549. Phone 210-229-1941. Open 11 A.M. to 10:30 P.M. daily.

The County Line has locations in Austin, Lubbock, San Antonio, Houston, and El Paso. As Texas's barbecue ambassador, they also have locations in Denver, Colorado City, Albuquerque, and Oklahoma City.

I visited the Interstate 10 location in San Antonio and left sated and elated. Arriving, I recognized a quality Texas atmosphere. The decor fulfills a lonesome cowhand's fondest dream. I called it country slick. Inside, chandeliers of cattle horns and of wagon wheels shed light on dozens of tables and booths.

If the weather is right, you can feast outdoors.

The County Line touts their steaks, ribs, and

chops but does not overlook the rest.

Bee, my wife, accompanied me on this outing. She ordered a platter of ribs, and I opted for a sampler platter.

When the pretty waitress plunked that huge plate of meat in front of me, my mouth watered. *But what was this? Sauce poured all over the meat? Zounds. How will I do my tests?* I quickly searched to find meat without sauce. I did...about two inches of brisket, about an inch or two of each rib, and four bites of the peppered turkey. The brisket had almost zero fat, magnificent flavor, and it parted with little effort when I cut it with the fork edge. I gave it a 9.

I gave the pork ribs a 9. They had little fat and good flavor, and the meat almost fell off the bone. The beef rib proved to be tough. I gave it a 7. An outside meat processor makes the sausage according to County Line's recipe. It gave up three drops of fat from the squeeze test. It was short on spice. I rated it a 7. Then came a real treat: peppered turkey. The meat had superior flavor but needed more moisture. I gave it a 9.

The barbecue sauce smacked with a twang of orange. Bee loved it. "You should rate it a 10."

Delicious homemade bread that tasted like honey cake accompanied my order. County Line also offers homemade ice cream. They have three flavors, and I dined on vanilla bean. Delicious.

The boss man said they 'cued meat eighteen to twenty hours.

When I thought it was all over, they furnished hot finger towels. A nice touch to an unforgettable BBQ experience.

> Menu order, dine in and out, take-out, catering, banquet facilities. Full bar. Brisket plate $10.95. Accepts credit cards.

Tom's Ribs

Tom's Ribs are making their mark all over Texas—for a good reason: people like to eat lip-smackin' good ribs.

Tom's outdoor sign has a big pig on it, but no fear, beef's inside. The decor says gothic western. Collectibles cling to the walls. License plates hang from the ceiling rafters and in between collectibles.

Service was snappy. The waitress took my order. I ordered from the lunch menu the "Big 4"—ribs, brisket, sausage, and chicken—which cost me $11.99. My ribs were "Tom's Famous Baby Back Pork Ribs." Cooked with barbecue sauce, the ribs

Rating: 8.5
2535 N. W. Loop 410, San Antonio, Texas 78230
Phone 210-344-7427
Fax 210-344-7497

13323 Nacogdoches Road, San Antonio, Texas 78217
Phone 210-654-7427

had good flavor and little fat but were a tad short on tenderness. I rated them a 9.

Next, I tried the brisket. It had a 5/16-inch pink ribbon. I pressed hard with a metal fork to cut it. It had good flavor and little fat. They smoked it eighteen to nineteen hours. I gave it an 8. The sausage was from a supplier, had good spices, and leaned to the lean side. I gave it a 7. I rated the chicken a 7.

Whiskey River Baked Beans headed up a long list of sides. The Whiskey beans were more akin to Boston baked beans than regular barbecue pinto beans. Baked potatoes came with all the fixings. Also on the menu were French fries, corn on the cob, green beans with new potatoes, hot buttered carrots, and the regulars, coleslaw and potato salad.

If you have room, try the homemade desserts.

Menu order, take-out, banquet facilities and catering. Full bar. Beef plate $5.99. Opens 11 A.M. Monday through Saturday and 11:30 Sunday. Closes 10 P.M. Sunday through Thursday and 11 P.M. Friday and Saturday. Accepts credit cards.

Index

Index

Other books from Republic of Texas Press

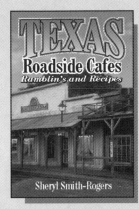

1-55622-733-7 • $18.95

1-55622-737-X • $24.95

1-55622-694-2 • $18.95

1-55622-685-3 • $18.95

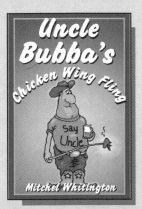

1-55622-695-0 • $16.95

1-55622-624-1 • $18.95

1-55622-652-7 • $18.95

1-55622-651-9 • $18.95

1-55622-649-7 • $18.95

Other books from Republic of Texas Press

Mysteries and Ghost Stories
Best Tales of Texas Ghosts
Ghosts Along the Texas Coast
Phantoms of the Plains: Tales of West
   Texas Ghosts
Spirits of San Antonio and South Texas
Spirits of the Alamo
Unsolved Texas Mysteries
Unsolved Mysteries of the Old West
When Darkness Falls: Tales of San
   Antonio Ghosts and Hauntings

Humor and Trivia
A Treasury of Texas Humor
A Treasury of Texas Trivia
A Treasury of Texas Trivia II
Born Again Texan!
Bubba Speak: Texas Folk Sayings
First in the Lone Star State: A Texas
   Brag Book
Fixin' to be Texan
The Funny Side of Texas
Puncher Pie and Cowboy Lies
Rainy Days in Texas Funbook
Texas Wit and Wisdom
Texas Highway Humor
That Cat Won't Flush
This Dog'll Really Hunt: An Entertaining
   and Informative Texas Dictionary

History
A Cowboy of the Pecos
After the Alamo
Alamo Movies
The Alamo Story: From Early History to
   Current Conflicts
Battlefields of Texas
Browser's Book of Texas History
Daughter of Fortune: The Bettie Brown
   Story
Death of a Legend: The Myth & Mystery
   Surrounding the Death of Davy
   Crockett

History (cont.)
Exploring the Alamo Legends
Eyewitness to the Alamo
The King Ranch Story: Truth and Myth
Last of the Old-Time Cowboys
Lawmen of the Old West: The Good Guys
Mythic Texas
Red River Women
Tales of the Guadalupe Mountains
Texas Indian Myths and Legends
Texas Tales Your Teacher Never Told You
Texas Ranger Tales: Stories That Need
   Telling
Texas Ranger Tales II
Volunteers in the Texas Revolution:
   The New Orleans Greys

Recreation/Field Guides
A Trail Rider's Guide To Texas
Horses and Horse Sense
Lone Star Menagerie: True Tales of Texas
   Wildlife
The Texas Golf Guide
The Texas Golf Guide (2nd Ed.)
They Don't Have to Die: Home and
   Classroom Care for Small Animals

Travel
Dallas Uncovered (2nd Ed.)
Exploring Branson: A Family Guide
Exploring Dallas with Children: A Guide
   for Family Activities
Exploring Fort Worth with Children
Exploring New Orleans: A Family Guide
Exploring San Antonio with Children:
   A Guide for Family Activities
Exploring Texas Skies with Children
Los Angeles Uncovered
Seattle Uncovered
Salt Lake City Uncovered
San Francisco Uncovered
Tuscon Uncovered
Twin Cities Uncovered